Soft Systems Methodology

Soft Systems Methodology

Conceptual Model Building and its Contribution

Brian Wilson

BWA (consultants) Ltd.

JOHN WILEY & SONS, LTD
Chichester • New York • Weinheim • Brisbane • Singapore • Toronto

Copyright © 2001 by   John Wiley & Sons Ltd,
Baffins Lane, Chichester,
West Sussex PO19 1UD, UK

National   01243 779777
International   (+44) 1243 779777
e-mail (for orders and customer service enquiries): cs-books@wiley.co.uk
Visit our Home Page on http://www.wiley.co.uk
or http://www.wiley.com

Other Wiley Editorial Offices

John Wiley & Sons, Inc., 605 Third Avenue,
New York, NY 10158-0012, USA

Wiley-VCH Verlag GmbH, Pappelallee 3,
D-69469 Weinheim, Germany

John Wiley & Sons (Australia) Ltd, 33 Park Road, Milton,
Queensland 4064, Australia

John Wiley & Sons (Asia) Pte Ltd, 2 Clementi Loop #02-01,
Jin Xing Distripark, Singapore 129809

John Wiley & Sons (Canada) Ltd, 22 Worcester Road,
Rexdale, Ontario M9W 1L1, Canada

British Library Cataloguing in Publication Data
A catalogue record for this book is available from the British Library

ISBN 0-471-89489-3

Typeset in 10/12pt Bembo by C.K.M. Typesetting, Salisbury, Wiltshire
Printed and bound in Great Britain by Antony Rowe Ltd, Chippenham, Wiltshire
This book is printed on acid-free paper responsibly manufactured from sustainable forestry, in which at least
two trees are planted for each one used for paper production.

To Sylvia

Contents

Foreword

Senior executives in most organisations nowadays spend much of their time working up mission statements, strategic objectives and annual business plans which are then cascaded down through their organisations. However, these same executives then spend little, if any, time trying to work out, in a consensual way with their staffs, just what 'joined-up' activities need to be undertaken at all levels within that enterprise in order to achieve those plans. Often, they simply copy what is decreed by business gurus as current 'best practice' without giving serious thought as to whether this will fit their organisation which will have its own unique history and culture. Consequently, it is little wonder that strategic planning has gained something of a bad name over the years.

Business process re-engineering, another management tool – indeed, some would say fad – has moved in and out of fashion over the years and was meant to provide some linkage between an organisation's intentions and its activities. However, most business process re-engineering is based on a bottom-up approach which means, almost inevitably, that it will be non-strategic in nature and will run the risk of simply building on the mistakes as well as the successes of today without distinguishing between them. Furthermore, the tools used by many organisations and their consultants or advisers are often incoherent and are based on nothing more than convention sets and 'common sense', whatever that much-abused term might mean. What is lacking is any methodology, defined by the *Oxford English Dictionary* as an '*orderly arrangement of ideas*'.

Several years ago, my organisation – an e-business consultancy, already involved in advising clients what technology to invest in – became increasingly involved in advising clients on how that technology could be most effectively used within their organisation by its most valuable resource – its people. This meant getting much more involved in organisational analysis and adopting a more holistic approach that took account of the softer issues that people bring in to any problem situation. Given the failings of much strategic planning and business process re-engineering, we began to look for an analytical technique that was:

- strategic in its approach, i.e. top-down and forward looking
- rule-based and intellectually rigorous but, at the same time, flexible enough to apply to all types and size of organisation
- defensible so that conclusions could be confidently justified to our clients in a way anyone in their organisation could understand
- consensus building so as to achieve that essential ingredient – 'buy-in'.

It was our good fortune that, at about that time, a colleague introduced me to SSM and to Dr Brian Wilson. Since then, SSM has proved its worth repeatedly in a number of assignments undertaken or supported by The Smith Group, often in association with Dr Brian Wilson. Some of this work now features in case studies for this book.

SSM does not lay any claim to be the only club required in the organisational analyst's 'golf-bag' as most business-improvement projects ultimately require the formulation of harder process models which more closely articulate the activities, procedures, resources and controls relevant in the real world. However, we have found the great strength of SSM is that it can provide the consultant with a coherent and logically defensible insight which then enables an informed analysis, untainted by the emotional baggage of the organisation in the problem situation as it currently exists.

In essence, SSM supports the derivation of a roadmap from the 'what is' to the 'what might be' by engaging the organisation in a structured and logical debate about itself and what it should be doing. It is therefore 'non-threatening' in the sense that it does not seek to impose the analyst's 'solutions', which are often clouded by experiences of other organisations. The premise that all organisations are unique leads to the conclusion that the imposition of such solutions is not a defensible approach and, in any case, often will not lead to the essential organisational 'buy-in' that makes the difference between success and failure in any change management activity. SSM, on the other hand, can be thought of as offering a logically defensible baseline from which informed deviation can be made in the case of those desirable changes which, nevertheless, may not always be feasible for cultural, political or personal reasons.

Brian Wilson has over 30 years' experience in the application and development of SSM. He continues to develop novel ideas on model building, particularly the concept of assembling the Enterprise Model which he introduces in Chapter Seven. This we have found to be particularly valuable where the full richness and complexity of the area under study cannot be captured by other methods. Our experience has shown that the resulting two-dimensional models, which may easily run to over one hundred or more activities, offer a complete and clear view of the problem area. This aids understanding as interactions can easily be traced and analysis shared more readily with the problem owner.

Indeed, these qualities of completeness and clarity, inherent to SSM, were major features of the Single Army Activity Model (Appendix 3) that Smith helped to produce in conjunction with Brian Wilson. These qualities were crucial given that the model: contains over 1500 activities; maps them to organisational structures; captures all of their multiple information inputs and outputs and, in turn, can be used to map these information flows to discrete information systems. What is, in effect, a logically linked hierarchy (i.e. business model, information model and system model) has proved invaluable in making defensible business cases for capital investment in technology.

Brian Wilson's last book has become a well-thumbed feature on my office bookshelf - except when other colleagues keep borrowing it! I have no doubt that this book will also become essential reading for those wishing to exploit a straightforward yet powerful approach to grappling with the analysis of complexity within organisations or answering the question 'how do I think about what I should be doing?' It is my experience, and that of my colleagues, that SSM offers an elegantly simple approach that is both powerful yet non-threatening and one that forces organisations to confront questions essential to their very survival such as 'are we doing the right thing?'

Mike Duffy, MSc, MBA, MIEE, CEng
Operations Director
Information Security Division
The Smith Group

Preface

The production of a new book or publication must be justified on the basis that it contains a message not replicated elsewhere. It may build upon previous work or react to other publications but, above all, the message should make a significant contribution to a particular area of endeavour.

The area relevant to this publication is that known as Soft Systems Methodology (SSM) which first emerged into the public domain in 1981 through the book *Systems Thinking, Systems Practice* by Peter Checkland. This was followed in 1984 by my book *Systems: Concepts, Methodologies and Applications* (appearing as a second edition in 1990).

The essential difference between these two texts was that Peter described SSM within the context of the history of rational thought, i.e. what the subject of SSM was. Mine was an attempt to describe 'how to do it' within the context of problem solving in general.

Thus SSM is a relatively young discipline and, prior to these publications and since, we have both had some thirty years of experience of trying to teach the subject and a similar period in applying and developing the ideas through consultancy. There has also been a significant amount of academic research but the strong tradition behind the development of the subject has always been 'action research'. It is this that is concerned with learning from the relationship between theory and practice and which leads to that learning that can be applied. This is important to me as an engineer and influences what I accept as a legitimate interpretation of the ideas and what I also observe as defensible practices.

Over the last 25 years or so, publications have appeared which purport to describe, develop and give practical guidance on SSM that unfortunately are based upon significant misinterpretations of the basic concepts.

The aim of an engineer is to ensure that what is constructed actually works and that structures put in place do not fall down. I believe that this aim also applies to intellectual structures and intellectual constructions. The engineer ensures this, in relation to physical artefacts, by using design rules that are derived from theory arising from the observed regularities of the natural world together with pragmatic heuristics that come from observing practical and transferable effects.

For an intellectual discipline to aspire to the same aim, similar rules must be developed and applied. It is the case that the discipline of calculus cannot be said to be applied if the rules for formulating differential equations are not followed. Similarly, SSM cannot be said to be applied if its basic rules are not adhered to.

Thus, as well as describing recent action research and the resultant developments related to model building in particular, this books aims to clarify the underlying conditions which need to be met if the basic building block of SSM – the Root Definition and conceptual model – is a well-formulated and defensible intellectual construct.

The motivation for this text is to try to overcome some of the misinterpretations and malpractice referred to above. I hope that this work adds to the understanding of the basic ideas and enables powerful and defensible application.

I first started to think about 'systems' as a serious intellectual construct (rather than the all-embracing label, casually attached to most parts of the real world) when I worked for the UK Atomic Energy Authority on the safety and dynamics of gas-cooled nuclear power stations. Thus I had to consider not only the nuclear end of the business but also its interaction with the steam-raising plant. This assembly represented 'the system', though my interest in it was as a control engineer. At this stage I was what we now term, a 'hard' systems thinker.

A major transition in my life occurred when, in 1966, I was appointed to a new department at the University of Lancaster by the late Professor Gwilym Jenkins. I was the first appointee to the Department of Systems Engineering and I am now the last surviving 'Founder Member'. I will always be grateful to Gwilym for providing this opportunity. A second transition in my thinking, which was a gradual transition, came from the many years of collaboration that I enjoyed with Professor Peter Checkland. We worked together in both the teaching and the practice and I am grateful to Peter for the many hours of discussion and debate about these ideas, which so transformed the concepts that I now use. The shift from multi-dimensional calculus (as a modelling language) to verbs in the imperative is no mean feat for a control engineer.

I am also indebted to the many students and organisations with whom I have worked over the past 34 years together with the past and present members of staff within the university, who have been both friends and colleagues.

I would like to acknowledge the following organisations who have given their permission for the inclusion within the book of project references and descriptions though, in particular, I would like to thank The Smith Group and Hi-Q Systems with whom I have had a long association and with whom I have worked on some of the projects mentioned. The organisations are: Askam Ltd, The Army, The CEGB (SW region), The Dukes Theatre, The Meteorological Office, Morecambe Bay NHS Trust, The Royal Navy, TSB Homeloans and the West Yorkshire Police.

I would like to thank Lieutenant-Colonel Hunt and Major Galvin for their permission to include in Appendix 3 their paper describing the application of the Single Army Activity Model and I would like to acknowledge the following contributions: my brother, Roy, for the production of Figure 1.1, Lindsay Cundall and Joan Haworth for their help with typing and finally, I would like to thank my wife, Sylvia, who did most of the conversion of my thoughts and script into legible typescript and coped admirably with the frustrations of working with both me and the technology.

Wherever possible actual working diagrams and models have been illustrated. However because of the size restrictions of the book the details (particularly of the larger models) may not be clear. They are included for completeness and to give the reader some idea of the scale of models sometimes required. The detail can be obtained by accessing the following ftp site: ftp://ftp.wiley.co.uk/pub/books/wilson/

Preamble

ORGANISATIONAL ANALYSIS

Organisational analysis is here interpreted as an attempt to resolve problems and concerns related to situations which are organisation based. There will be many such concerns related to social, inter–personal and cultural facets of organisation-based life and these cannot be ignored if the organisa-tional analysis is to make contact with the people involved. However, this is not the emphasis of this particular book. There are many concerns which require a description relevant to an organisation in terms of the business processes that are or might be undertaken, and it is on these that this particular work is focused.

The essence of this focus is illustrated by Figure 1. Each of the concerns illustrated requires an answer to the question: 'what do we take the organisation unit to be or to be doing?' This may be what do we take it to be now, in the future or, more generally, what could it be? The use of the term

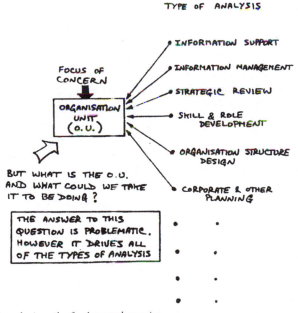

Figure 1. *Organisational analysis – the fundamental question*

'organisation unit' is meant to be completely general and independent of scale. Thus an organisation unit could be a multinational enterprise, a single company, a function, a department or even an individual. What follows within the remainder of this book is also independent of scale and is generally applicable.

We are *not* seeking to describe the organisation (or organisation unit) as part of the real world. Such an attempted description would have to be in terms of 'how' the organisation unit is doing 'what' it is doing.

What we *are* trying to do, however, is to build a concept which will map onto the organisation unit. The concept will be in the language of 'what' and not 'how'. If the mapping is deemed to be adequate we will have a description of *what we are taking the organisation unit to be doing* and it will be of adequate scope to progress the particular analysis being considered.

If the organisation unit is something specific and well defined such as a chemical process or a power-generating plant, the question 'what are we taking the organisation unit to be?' can be answered by using the language of one of the branches of mathematics – differential calculus, statistical simulation, etc. The question is said to be answered when the model so constructed replicates the behaviour of the particular organisation unit over the required domain of interest.

If the 'organisation unit' is less well defined, as is the case when it contains people, the above use of mathematics-based tools of analysis cannot be applied and 'replicated behaviour' cannot be used as the criterion for the acceptability of the resultant answer to the question 'what do we take the organisation unit to be?'

An organisation unit containing people represents a much more complex situation than one which does not. This is one of the features that gives rise to the distinction between 'hard' and 'soft'. The above example of a chemical process represents a well-defined organisation unit, which can therefore be described as 'hard'. Our concern here is with those situations (organisation units) which can be said to be 'soft', i.e. ill defined.

As a way of thinking about this complexity consider a spectrum which extends from commonality to uniqueness. A description of an organisation unit that makes use of a functional breakdown is towards the 'commonality' end of this spectrum. Thus for a production-oriented organisation (A) one would expect to have functions representing research and development, production, marketing, finance, etc. Such a description, however, is equally applicable to another production-oriented organisation (B) but, in reality, they are very different organisations. What makes them different is that they are at the stage they are now because they have different histories, they contain different people, they are culturally different and their organisation is the result of the application of different values. Thus, in order to differentiate between A and B, the organisations need to be described in a way that places them at the other end of the spectrum, i.e. by recognising that they are unique.

Another feature of this complexity is that the people who are incumbents of the many roles within the organisation have their own interpretations of what the role is and what it is they are trying to achieve. They will have their own interpretation of the relationship of their role to the organisation mission and they will have their own interpretation of the organisation mission itself. It is this aspect that makes the answer to the question 'what do we take the organisation to be?' so problematic.

The situation is additionally complicated by the fact that an organisation unit is never static. All organisation units operate in environments that are continually changing and the organisation units themselves are in a state of continual adaptation.

Figure 2 illustrates a concept for an organisation in this transitional state. What the 'organisation unit' is now is problematic given the above reasons concerning its complexity. What the 'organisation unit' will be in the future is even more problematic since the responses to the pressures for

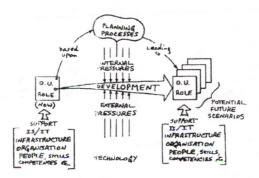

Figure 2. *An organisation unit (OU) in transition*

change will be completely unknown. The best that can be defined will be potential future scenarios. Thus, it will be the case that the answer to the question of what the organisation unit is taken to be will have time-dependence as one of the components of this complexity. Unlike a chemical process or a power-generating unit, in which time-dependent processes are governed by repeatable phenomena, there is no such repeatability about the processes that determine the future state and role of an organisation unit.

This book describes ways of thinking about the complexity described above and develops a language through which that thinking can be articulated. It represents an alternative to mathematically based languages and a defensible way of exploring (and defining) the answer to the question: 'what do we take the organisation (organisation unit) to be?' so that we can then develop an appropriate and relevant concept for it.

THE SCOPE

The coverage of this book is limited. It aims not to represent SSM in totality but to concentrate on that aspect of the subject that can be taken to be logic-based. Figure 3, taken from the book *Soft Systems Methodology in Action* (Checkland and Scholes 1990), illustrates a simplified view of the process of SSM. Here two streams of analysis are shown; one which is culturally based and the other which is logic based. They must exist together if the resultant analysis is to make progress towards change in the situation of interest. Part of the commitment to change comes from the assembly of convincing argument arising from the defensible logic pursued via the right-hand stream of analysis in Figure 3. It has been my experience of observing this activity over a number of years that defensibility has been eroded through inappropriate practices.

The book is concerned not with the totality of the logic stream but with the formulation of defensible intellectual constructs to be used within it. Some application is included, but only where it is felt to be useful to extend a particular story.

The basic 'building block' of those intellectual constructs to be used within an analysis that can be said to be SSM is the Root Definition/Conceptual Model assembly. Figure 4 illustrates a simplified view of this process. The Root Definition (RD) captures the purpose, taken to be relevant, and the Conceptual Model (CM) represents those structured activities that must take place if the purpose is to be achieved. Thus the RD defines what the *system is* and the CM describes what the *system must do* to be the one defined. Unlike an analysis that can be said to be 'hard', the intellectual constructs used

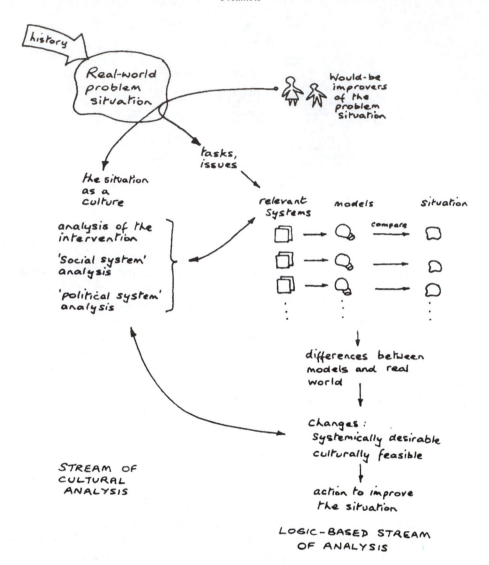

Figure 3. *The process of SSM (from: Checkland and Scholes 1990)*

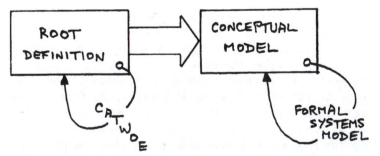

Figure 4. *The logic-based process*

within SSM cannot be 'validated' by reference to the part of the real world to which they are relevant. Thus, for defensibility, they must be 'validated' against something, otherwise they lead to nothing more valuable than opinion. Within SSM the 'validation' is still within the intellectual domain. The purpose of CATWOE (in Figure 4) is to ensure that the RD is well formulated and the purpose of the Formal Systems Model (FSM) is to ensure that the CM produced *is* a defensible model of a human activity system (or holon, if that language is preferred). Once sufficient experience of the process, illustrated by Figure 4, has been accumulated both CATWOE and the FSM may well be internalised by the analyst, but he or she must always be prepared to make the 'validation' explicit.

This then is the focus of this book. This process has already been described (Checkland 1981; Wilson 1984, 1990; Checkland and Scholes 1990), but the practice and the secondary literature suggest that the messages were not adequately conveyed. Hopefully this book will help.

REFERENCES

It is unusual for a text aimed at an academic and practitioner audience not to contain an extensive list of references. That is, however, the case here. References to the subject of SSM are contained in the three publications given above and for a wide appreciation of the field the reader is directed to those texts. The motivation to produce this particular book came from a specific paper (Checkland and Tsouvalis 1996). This seeks to undermine the logic-based stream of systems thinking that emerged from the 'action research' programme that gave rise to SSM. It is *not* action research that has led to the arguments for 'renouncing rationality in its singular or universal form', but improper use of the basic concepts. The reader is directed to this reference if they wish to appreciate the need for the emphasis on the principles and rules of construction contained in Chapter Two. Apart from the above reference and those related to the subject generally, the major source of reference for *this* publication is practice. The practice is mine, supported by my observations on the practice of others, as they have been learning to make their thinking processes explicit through the application of these particular concepts. Most of this is unpublished.

Chapter One

Models and Methodology

MODELLING

We always make use of models whenever we reach value judgements about a particular situation though frequently they are implicit and unquestioned. If they remain so then the value judgements reached cannot be defended; they merely become matters of opinion.

Take the rather trivial example illustrated by Figure 1.1. Two people have watched a particular programme on television; a not-uncommon activity in most households. They have both seen exactly the same display on the screen and yet they reach totally different conclusions about whether it was a good or a poor programme. They then argue about who is right; again not an uncommon activity. There is no point in having this argument since *they are actually both right*. The value judgements about the quality of the programme will be based upon different concepts in the heads of the two observers as to what constitutes a good television programme. The concept in the head of observer A emphasises visual impact, which was apparently not observed, whereas the concept in the head of observer B reflects intellectual stimulation which appears to have been the nature of the programme.

If these concepts could be made explicit instead of implicit, as models representing a television programme, they could then be compared against the observed happenings on the television screen and each observer's judgement defended. They may still disagree over the relative merits of the two models but, at least, the argument can be carried out on a more defensible and rational basis instead of at the level of unsubstantiated opinion.

In the more significant area of organisation-based activity the situation surrounding organisational problems and issues is highly complex and the need for defensible argument is that much more important. Such situations are characterised by complex operations and management processes that may have grown over time, unclear and/or multiple objectives, changing environments and people with different attitudes, histories and agendas.

The definition of 'what is right' in relation to some issue or problem is unlikely to be achievable and therefore *defensibility* becomes the criterion to be used in assembling arguments to support the judgements reached or recommendation made in response to the issues or problems.

Similarly the concept of 'optimisation', prevalent in Operational Research studies, is difficult to defend in such messy situations as it is unlikely that there would be agreement as to what constitutes an optimum.

Thus, in business analysis generally it is *defensible argument* to support business change (not optimisation or the right answer) that is sought. For the argument to be defensible an explicit 'audit trail' is required which itself will be based upon some kind of model to represent the situation.

Figure 1.2 illustrates the process of a strategic review. A reviewer (or review team) is investigating the overall performance of some organisation unit. The process is not scale dependent and thus the organisation unit could be a complete company, a department, a division, a function or even

Figure 1.1   *The impact of mental models*

an individual. The questions that the reviewer is seeking to answer are related to effectiveness (is it doing the right sort of things?), efficiency (is it doing them with minimum use of resources?) and efficacy (does it work?). The result of answering those questions will be the production of recommendations for change as indicated.

An additional question worth asking about this process is: How does the reviewer reach the recommendations from observing and questioning the organisation unit?

In Figure 1.3 three possible answers are added to the process. Using intuition and/or experience are very common, but there are two major drawbacks. First, the intuition or experience cannot be accessed, and second, the value judgements of the *reviewer* (based upon the intuition and/or experience) are *unlikely* to be the same as the value judgements of the *reviewed*. These drawbacks may have a significant impact on the acceptability of the recommendations to the personnel within the organisation unit. This was the problem of the observers of the television programme depicted in Figure 1.1.

It is *explicit analysis*, utilising a specific 'standard', that stands the best chance of leading to recommendations which are acceptable as long as some way of accommodating the value judgements of the personnel within the organisation unit can be incorporated. Here 'standard' is used in its general sense of beng something against which a comparison is made. It is not an absolute or a

Figure 1.2   *The process of a strategic review*

mandatory statement with which something should comply. The 'standard' used for comparison, as well as being coherent, needs also to be relevant to the particular group of organisational personnel to whom the review is relevant.

The derivation of this 'standard' is therefore crucial to the success, or otherwise, of the review process. It is also the subject of most of this book and will be covered in detail later. In essence, this 'standard' is the organisational equivalent of the model of the concept of a television programme in the heads of the two observers represented by Figure 1.1.

It must be apparent that deriving a model to represent an organisation unit (of whatever scale) will be significantly more complex than this rather trivial example if it is to accommodate the multiple concepts in the heads of those people concerned with the strategic review.

Although the problem of multiple concepts has been introduced through the notion of a strategic review it is a general problem associated with modelling business processes for whatever purpose. To produce a model as a representative description of an organisation unit it is necessary to describe its basic purpose, i.e. what it is trying to achieve and also what it must be doing (in terms of its business processes) to be successful in realising that purpose. Given the range of concepts referred to above there will be multiple views about basic purpose and hence about the necessary business processes.

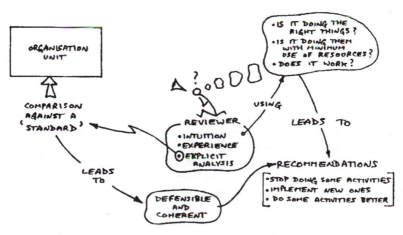

Figure 1.3   *A defensible and explicit process*

Suppose that the organisation unit is a police force. It might be argued that its basic purpose is any one or any combination of the following:

- to apprehend those violating the law
- to maintain security of people and property
- to control situations likely to lead to a breach of the peace
- to maintain community well–being
- to facilitate the transfer of goods and people through and within a defined conurbation
- to respond to incidents

Depending upon what is taken to be a statement of basic purpose a particular set of business processes will be determined. A different set will be obtained for a different choice of purpose

It is fairly apparent that an actual police force is not described by any one purpose extracted from the above list. Its purpose will be some mixture of those listed plus others. However, different individuals (members of the Home Office, of the community and of the force itself) will subscribe to different mixtures. While accepting that the police respond to incidents and have some interest in traffic a member of the community may emphasise 'the maintenance of security of people and property' as what they think a police force is for. On the other hand, a member of the CID may well emphasise 'the apprehension of those violating the law'. Thus there will be no *one* answer to the question: what is a police force for?

Although this is an example in which a fairly obvious range of potential definitions of purpose can be derived in which the differences are clear, it is a problem common to all organisations. In some cases the range may be more limited, though equally clear. However, in some situations the differences may be more subtle and difficult to define, but they are equally significant.

The foregoing leads to the realisation that when concerned with describing the real world of human activity, unique, valid and non-contentions descriptions **of** *reality are not possible.*

To make progress in analysis of this kind it is necessary to make *and to maintain* a distinction between 'the real world', which is complex, messy and contains people, and the intellectual process of 'thinking about the real world', which can be simple, precise and defensible.

Making this distinction helps in understanding the status of models; models in general not relevant only to human activity. Figure 1.4 captures this idea.

Models (of any kind) are *not* descriptions of the real world they *are* descriptions of ways of thinking about the real world

We are led into confusion surrounding this distinction by the process of model building when making a 'hard' interpretation of a situation. For example, if a simulation model of a production process is produced on the basis of a mathematically oriented modelling language, it can be validated by comparing the output of the model derived from some input demand with the output of the actual process when responding to the same demand. In this case there is taken to be no disagreement over the objectives or purpose of the production process and the existence of a 'validated' model leads to the belief that it *is* a model of the real world. It is not. It is still a model of a way of thinking about the real world whose input and output map onto reality.

It may seem to be pedantic to insist on this distinction when concerned with a 'hard' situation, but if the example has aided the understanding of the distinction then it has served its purpose. It is not pedantic to insist on maintaining the distinction between reality and the intellectual process in relation to soft interpretations. Unless this distinction is maintained, the subsequent analysis will be flawed and may descend into debate about opinion.

Figure 1.5 is a useful way of thinking about the distinction emphasised here. At the top of the figure is a representation of a process of analysis regarding some part of the real world. The analyst will make sense of what is being observed by using a set of concepts or intellectual constructs.

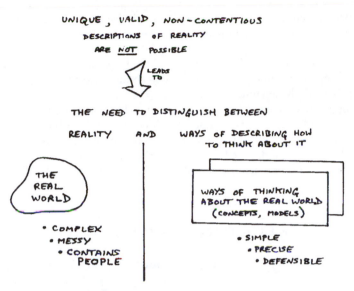

Figure 1.4 *A necessary distinction for the analysis of organisational problems*

Dependent upon the nature of the real-world situation a selection of concepts will be made. The remainder of Figure 1.5 gives a few examples.

The choice of the concept on the right will lead to a defensible statement about some concern related to the particular area of real-world activity given on the left. If the choice of concept is relevant to the kind of analysis being undertaken, then the conclusions reached will not only be defensible they will also be appropriate.

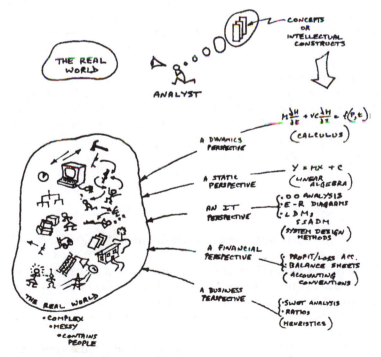

Figure 1.5 *Ways of thinking about the real world*

It is the case that, given a particular situation, one choice of concept will lead to one set of defensible conclusions, whereas an alternative choice may lead to other (but equally defensible) conclusions.

Acceptability of one or other set of conclusions will be determined by the appropriateness of the concepts chosen. 'Appropriateness' may well be determined indirectly by the recipient of the conclusion rather than by the analyst.

It is not sufficient just to derive the appropriate concepts. How they are to be used in the proposed analysis must also be made explicit. This means deciding on and describing the intellectual process that makes use of the concepts. Both the concepts and the intellectual process may change as the analysis proceeds, but if it is not declared at the outset the changes may occur unconsciously and so remove the audit trail and subsequent defensibility. What is being described is methodology.

METHODOLOGY—WHAT IS IT?

Introduction

The purpose of this section is to answer the above question and to discuss methodology in terms of its relation to the analysis of business problems in general. It is a bit of a buzzword and every analyst will claim that they have one or several (including me), but do they all mean the same thing and does it matter? To go back to its origins and to say that it is the 'logos' (study) of method isn't very helpful so here, at least, is a useful interpretation.

It is probably easier to describe what methodology is by first illustrating what it is *not*. It is frequently confused with method or technique, but it is much less prescriptive than either of them. Both of these approaches to problem solving may best be described by the 'cookbook' analogy. Their characteristic is that they provide precise definitions of 'what to do' and, if followed, will produce a defined outcome. Methodology, on the other hand, will not guarantee a solution. The nearest equivalent phrase is 'a structured approach'. However, it is an approach which requires judgement; in terms of both its application and the structure itself. A particular methodology is a set of guidelines which stimulate the intellectual process of analysis.

To appreciate this last statement and to understand fully what methodology is it is necessary to return to the distinction between 'the real world', i.e. the source of the problem or problems to which the methodology is to be applied and the process of *thinking about* the real world.

It is in the latter domain that methodology resides. Technique, method and methodology are all ways of thinking about problems and hence represent structured ways of undertaking the intellectual processes involved in analysis. It is only the degree of prescription that differentiates between them and because methodology is the study of methods, any methodology may contain methods and/or techniques.

Methodology and Problem Solving

The degree of variety in real-world problems is enormous, but it is useful to see them as lying within a spectrum which extends from 'hard' to 'soft'. There are a number of ways in which 'hard' and 'soft' can be defined but the definition I wish to take is in terms of *the degree of agreement about what the problem is* among the particular population of individuals to whom 'the problem' is of concern.

Thus, the design of a piece of software to meet a given specification is a hard problem (as long as the specification is 'a given') whereas the specification of information requirements to meet business needs is a soft problem particularly if the needs as specified by potential users are at odds with those required to support the business, or if indeed the business requirements themselves are problematical.

At the hard end of the problem spectrum Systems Engineering (SE) methodology is applicable and essentially consists of the following stages.

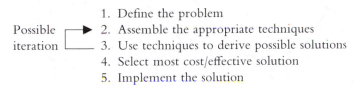

1. Define the problem
2. Assemble the appropriate techniques
3. Use techniques to derive possible solutions
4. Select most cost/effective solution
5. Implement the solution

At the soft end of the problem spectrum the first of the above stages 'Define the problem' is itself problematic since it usually depends upon *who* defines it. Given that there will usually be a number of people concerned with or involved in 'the problem' there will be a number of legitimate definitions. Thus SSM has to start by defining, not a problem but a *situation* that is problematic.

Thus at an equally broad level SSM could be characterised by the following stages:

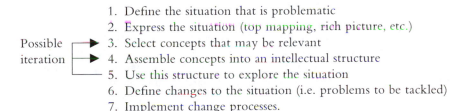

1. Define the situation that is problematic
2. Express the situation (top mapping, rich picture, etc.)
3. Select concepts that may be relevant
4. Assemble concepts into an intellectual structure
5. Use this structure to explore the situation
6. Define changes to the situation (i.e. problems to be tackled)
7. Implement change processes.

In SE the techniques contain both the concepts and the structure and are well defined. In SSM the concepts and the structure are independent and need to be specified separately. This may involve greater iteration around the stages indicated as progress is made in learning about the situation. Two examples of SSM relative to two general types of problem are illustrated by Figures 1.6 and 1.7 using the concepts of human activity systems (see Chapter Two).

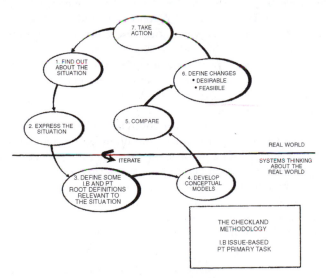

Figure 1.6   *The Checkland methodology (following Checkland 1981)*

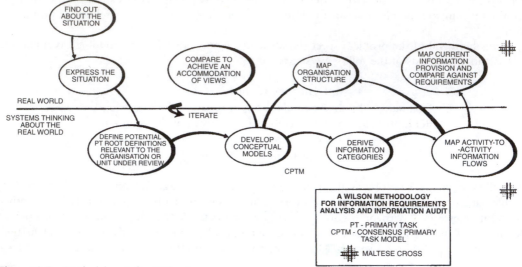

Figure 1.7 *Methodology (after Wilson)*

At the hard end of the problem spectrum the methodology (or perhaps method) is being used essentially to answer a 'how' type of question. 'What' is required is not problematical, it is only 'how' to achieve it that is the problem. At the soft end 'what to do' is problematical as well as 'how to do it'. Once stage 7 is reached in Checkland's SSM 'hard' methodology may be used though it is usually the case that managing the change process is also taken to be soft.

Intellectual Planning

As stated in the introduction, methodology is a description of *how to think about* the process of analysis prior to doing it. Hence the intellectual process of choosing concepts and deciding how they might be structured in a methodology is really concerned with *thinking about how to think*; an unusual process. It has the advantage, however, that the resultant methodology is tailored to fit the particular situation, and the analysts know *why* they are doing what they are doing and *how* and *what* they are doing relates to what they will be doing next. Given the great variety of organisational problems, considerable flexibility must exist in the concepts and structures available to the analysts. Unless the particular methodology is assembled as a conscious part of the analysis it is unlikely that the changes and/or solutions identified will represent an effective output of the analysis. Additionally, the specific methodology needs to be explicit in order to provide a defensible audit trail from recommendations back to initial assumptions and judgements.

Thinking about how to think about a problematic situation can produce the most powerful and defensible application of the range of intellectual tools available to an analyst, yet there are still managers around to whom intellectual activity is anathema. It is seen to be 'academic', not practical. 'Don't sit there doing nothing, get on with the job' is still a prevalent attitude. Let me conclude this section by borrowing a quotation about planning by Sir John Harvey-Jones and rewriting it in terms of thinking. Thinking about how to think *is* about planning the intellectual process:

> Thinking about how to think is an unnatural process and nobody knows that you are doing it. It is much more fun to get on with *doing* something and, besides, you can be observed doing it. The nice thing

about not thinking is that the eventual disaster comes as a complete surprise rather than being preceded by a period of worry and depression.

It is not uncommon for some analysts to start to tackle the apparent problem without doing this intellectual planning. Thus the first activity is 'undertake interviews' or 'collect data'. It is then experience and/or intuition that is brought to bear on the data assembled from this first activity. This means that the analysis is driven by the data collected and hence receives an emphasis based on what emerged during the interviews or the analyst's interpretation of the data presented in documents.

Undertaking interviews and/or reading documents is still the means of assembling data but this activity needs to be preceded by the intellectual planning referred to above. Thus when a question is asked during interview the analyst already knows what to do with the answer. Similarly, data collected from documents will have meaning with respect to the analysis being undertaken. It is not unreasonable to interview and/or collect data merely to assemble background understanding but in general, when pursuing the actual analysis, *don't ask a question unless you know what you will do with the answer*.

THE CONCEPT—HUMAN ACTIVITY SYSTEM

Returning to Figure 1.4 but expressing it in the context of a range of organisations, (i.e. Figure 1.8) indicates that the characteristics of such organisations are equivalent to the characteristics of the real world as illustrated in Figure 1.4.

However, to these I have added the characteristic of 'uniqueness'. This means that no two organisations can be identical. Even two companies in the same line of business and of a similar size will be different. This is because the people who make up the company will be unique to that company, there will have been different generations of them, different behaviour histories and resultant cultures. These features are unlikely to be replicated elsewhere.

Thus, in relation to general problem solving a solution that is found to be appropriate in Company A is unlikely to be appropriate in Company B. It is unfortunate that a number of managers ignore these cultural characteristics when wishing to improve the performance of their own organisations. It is not uncommon to make visits to see how the other company undertakes its business processes and then to attempt to introduce such new practices at the home base. It is not too long ago that attempts were made by a number of British companies to introduce Japanese methods; without significant success. In this example there were national cultural differences but the differences are still there within a single nationality. 'Benchmarking' is a modern tendency to define 'best practice' and companies seek to introduce it without questioning what 'best' means for their particular organisation.

If each company or organisation is unique, what do they have in common? The assumption upon which SSM is based is that: *Whatever the nature of the organisation, assume that the individuals within it are pursuing purposeful activity.* They may well be pursuing different purposes but they are not acting randomly.

Purposeful activity therefore represents a common feature of all organisations. The set of possible purposes stated earlier for a police force could all be legitimate definitions of purpose and therefore each could be the source of a business model.

If we can define purpose then we could derive a description of what the organisation must do to achieve that purpose. However, these single statements of purpose are not a description of the real-world organisation but describe a particular perception of it. It is therefore better to see the definitions and the resulting model as a *concept relevant to the organisation* which can be used in thinking about the organisation. Within SSM these concepts are called Human Activity Systems (HAS).

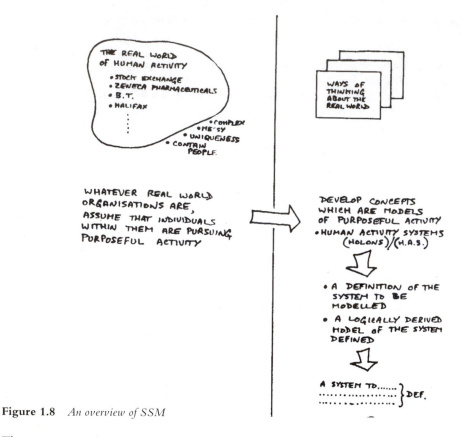

Figure 1.8   *An overview of SSM*

They are systems because they represent a set of purposeful activities together with the relationships (logical) between them. The activities, in principle, could be undertaken by human resources if the system were to map onto reality. Checkland now calls these constructs 'holons'. This conveys no meaning and therefore I will retain the terminology of a HAS. However, it does not matter which label is used as long as the underlying concept is understood.

An everyday definition of the systemic paradigm is that the whole is more than the sum of its parts. If the concept was merely a set of purposeful activities it would be an aggregate since the whole would equal the sum of its parts. The set becomes a system by the inclusion of the relationship between the parts. The set plus the relationships produce what is known as an *emergent property*, (see Checkland 1981; Wilson 1990). Thus a system may be defined by its emergent property. In relation to a hard system the emergent property becomes its specification of purpose or design specification.

A system whose specification of purpose is to have the capability of transporting passengers over intercontinental routes at speeds greater than that of sound can be represented by the real-world manifestation of that system (i.g. Concorde). This purpose would not be achieved by its component parts alone, they would not achieve anything. Each part must have its appropriate relationship to the other parts (i.e. the assembled Concorde) in order to achieve its designed purpose.

The emergent property in relation to a HAS will also be its definition of purpose. Thus for the police example given earlier six potential emergent properties have been identified which would lead to six different models relevant to a police force.

The notion of emergent property for a HAS is captured in the technical term—Root Definition. The formulation of Root Definitions and their relationship to HAS models are discussed in detail in Chapter Two.

Chapter Two

Basic Principles of HAS Modelling

INTRODUCTION

The core content of this chapter has appeared previously in Checkland (1980) and Wilson (1984, 1990) but I now believe that the treatment in those books was too superficial and totally inadequate. There has been so much misinterpretation, misunderstanding and actual distortion of the basic ideas in both the practice and writing associated with SSM that I feel that the ideas need restating and the basic rules clarified. Without some formality in the construction of conceptual models and the maintenance of discipline in their formulation (and that of the Root Definitions that drive them) the process becomes woolly, less defensible and without the rigour associated with other well-developed intellectual processes.

The use of calculus becomes flawed if the basic rules for the formulation of differential equations are not properly applied. Matrix algebra, non-linear optimisation and other approaches to the intellectual manipulation of concepts related to 'hard' problems become confused without the application of the appropriate rules and discipline associated with the construction of the respective concepts.

Just because we are trying to use ideas and concepts to analyse highly complex, messy and confused areas of real-world activity rather than specific, well-defined problems associated with 'hard' interpretations, we should not allow those concepts and ideas to become equally confused and messy. *It is as important to seek whatever rigour we can in the development and formulation of concepts for application to 'soft' areas.* An important recent publication (Checkland and Tsouvalis 1996) seems to be arguing for less precision, rather than more, in the interpretation of the basic ideas. It is also being argued here, with support from other referenced works that because the practice of the last 25 years suggests that would-be practitioners have found the ideas difficult, the ideas should be changed. It is the practice that needs to be rethought and reinforced. Difficulty in application is not a sustainable argument for the demolition of the concepts upon which SSM was originally based.

Apart from the desire to present the outcome of further action research, it is the above argument that is largely the motivation underlying this present work.

The content of this chapter therefore is a reiteration of the basic concepts within SSM. It is not new but I hope that the treatment is more useful and more digestible than that which has appeared previously.

In Chapter One the argument was put forward that because we can consider that all individuals within organised groups are acting to try to achieve some purpose (though not necessarily the same purpose) we can usefully derive models that are models of purposeful activity. The argument was also mounted that the models thus derived are not intended descriptions of reality but are descriptions of *ways of thinking* about reality.

Thus what we are doing when constructing a model is actually deriving a concept or an intellectual construct. Since we are making the distinction between this and reality we would expect the language used within the model to be different from the language of the real world.

For example, if we are taking a 'hard' interpretation of reality and are wishing to investigate the dynamics of a heat exchanger, we would represent the concept in terms of equations such as

$$M \frac{\partial h}{\partial t} + VC \frac{\partial h}{\partial z} = f(P, t)$$

This is the language of multi-dimensional calculus whereas the associated real-world language might be in terms of tube temperature, flow rates, etc.

The language of calculus does not exist in the real world; only within the intellectual process of investigating the real world. Even a simple equation like

$$P = Y - C$$

is an intellectual construct to represent profit (P) in terms of income (Y) and cost of generating the income (C).

Profit, income and cost are probably the kind of language used in relation to some real-world transactions. However, P, Y and C are the algebraic equivalents used within the intellectual processes concerned with calculating profit.

If we are to develop models related to purposeful activity we also need a modelling language. Over many years of application it has been shown that a useful language is:

Verbs expressed in the imperative

There are many verbs in the English language so it is a very rich and sophisticated modelling language. The use of the imperative is appropriate to achieving a purpose because it is the form of an instruction to do something, i.e. *construct, develop, distribute, etc.* Therefore the models represent a description of what has to be done (as a set of interlinked instructions) to achieve some prescribed purpose.

The all-important first stage therefore is to define the purpose to be achieved by the activities within the model. This is what was described in Chapter One as the emergent property.

ROOT DEFINITIONS: CONCEPTUAL MODELS

To aid the maintenance of the distinction between the real world and the intellectual process, we need a name for the definition which is not recognisable as a real-world term. The name chosen was Root Definition (RD) as a way of trying to capture the essence (root) of the purpose to be served.

Like differential equations, RDs don't exist in reality. The equivalent in real-world terminology might be business objectives, mission statements, specification and so on.

The models developed from RDs will contain not only the activities expressed through verbs in the imperative but also the logical dependencies between the activities. They therefore have the characteristics of systems and, as stated in Chapter One, are termed Human Activity Systems (HAS).

This label is useful because it describes what the model is. It is a system of activities that *could* be undertaken by human operators. As stated in Chapter One, some authors (Checkland *et al.*) use the term 'holon'. This is an invented word and has no meaning as a descriptor. 'Holo' as a precursor indicates wholeness but otherwise adds nothing to the label.

In practice however, it does not matter which label is used as long as the underlying concept is understood. Human Activity System is the label used here.

TRANSFORMATION PROCESS

Constructing a definition of purpose, which is what the RD is seeking to do, requires a particular structure. At its core, a RD describes a transformation process. Thus, by the way of example, if the purpose to be defined is to invest spare cash the transformation process is:

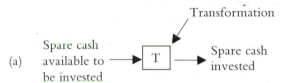

(a)

The purpose will have been achieved when the input is transformed into the output. An alternative to the input–output representations which tends to have more general usage is to describe T as 'a system to invest spare cash'. Here it is the process itself that is being described rather than the input and output. Both descriptions are consistent and hence either can be used.

As in all processes of analysis, rules are required to ensure that the processes are properly formed and applied. Thus there are rules for formulating algebraic and differential equations, for manipulating matrices, etc. They are necessary if the resulting processes are to have some degree of rigour and are to be defensible. The same applies here.

The first rule is that for a transformation process to be properly formulated its input and output must be of the same kind, i.e. either physical or abstract. Thus in the above example both the input and the output are in terms of cash. What is changed by the transformation is its state, i.e. from 'available to be invested' to 'invested'. Other examples might be

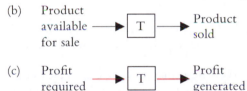

The first of these (b) has physical inputs and outputs; the second (c) has abstract inputs and outputs. What would *not* be legitimate would be the following transformation.

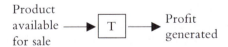

A physical input cannot be transformed into an abstract output.

This may, at first sight, appear to be a significant limitation, as you might argue that this is precisely what all commercial enterprises seek to do. However, here we are not trying to describe reality but to develop a concept relevant to reality. I would therefore argue that in developing an intellectual construct which follows this rule and is also relevant to a commercial enterprise example (c) may be taken. In describing the transformation process (T) we might say it is a system to generate profit, through the sale of products. Here 'the products' are the resources used by the transformation process in converting the input (profit required) into the output (profit generated). It is frequently the case that the input and the output are confused with the resources used to bring t the transformation. In a physical transformation the input and the output may well be identified as a resource. Thus cash and product can both be seen as resources of an organisation, *but we are not describing the organisation*. For our concept the transformation, described as a 'system to obtain cash through the sale of products', is legitimate whereas 'a system to transform products and the need for cash into cash obtained' is not.

These examples are only a few of the many transformation processes that could be taken to be relevant to a commercial enterprise. Thus, whatever the transformation process is taken to be, the above basic rule applies to its input and its output.

As the transformation process is the core of a RD, as a simple example we could take it to be the actual RD. You don't need to know how much cash is available, the preferences of the investor or who the investor is to be able to produce the activity model. Thus if we take the RD to be;

A system to invest spare cash

we can model it by relying on logic only and in so doing we need to answer the following questions:

(a) What has to be done to acquire the input?
(b) What must then be done to reach the output?
(c) What must then be done to make the output available?

(Remember that the answers for these questions are derived from logic not from the real world.) The answers are given below.

(a) • Determine how much cash is available to be invested
    • Obtain cash
(b) • Identify ways of investing cash
    • Assess the relative feasibility in terms of the cash available
    • Define the criteria to select one or more of the investment options
    • Select option(s)
(c) • Implement the selected option(s)

Although the above list describes the activities to be done, the model must also include the logical relationships that need to be present. The model is given in Figure 2.1. This is termed 'a conceptual model' since it is only a model of *a concept*.

In determining the logical dependencies it is necessary to argue that the activity on the head of an arrow is dependent upon the activity on the tail. Thus the activity 'Assess the relative feasibility in terms of cash available' cannot be done unless the amount of cash available is known, i.e. the result of doing the activity 'determine how much cash is available to be invested' and also what the various ways of investing are, which is the result of doing the activity 'Identifying ways of investing cash'. Similarly, the option(s) to be implemented cannot be determined without knowing what the options are and the basis (criteria) for selecting one or more of the options.

Each full arrow therefore represents a logical dependency.

Within Figure 2.1(a) (which is the complete model) there are also two other kinds of arrow associated with an additional pair of activities that are different in kind from the others. These activities are not included in the above list ((a)–(c)) but they are nevertheless necessary within a complete model of a HAS. (See the 'Formal Systems Model', Figure 2.2, and respective discussion.)

For the model to be coherent and to guarantee the achievement of the purpose defined by the RD, each of the activities (a) to (c) in the above list (which may be termed 'operational activities') needs to be monitored to determine if each activity is being done well and then control action taken on any activity which falls short of the desired performance. Thus a control subsystem must be included in each HAS model in order to guarantee the achievement of the defined purpose.

The control sub-system must *at least* contain an activity which monitors the performance of each activity and another activity which acts on the assembled performance information (i.e. a control

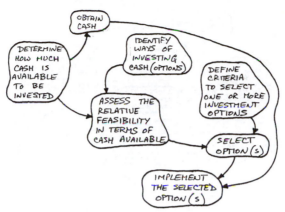

Figure 2.1   *An investment model*

activity). Two different kinds of arrow are included within this subsystem. The broad arrow into the 'monitor' activity represents performance information from each of the operational activities. Thus the monitor activity is logically dependent upon each of the operational activities, but instead of including a full arrow from each activity (which would make the model overcomplex), these arrows are summed into the one broad arrow with a label so that the content of the arrow is known (the connections are illustrated by the dashed arrows).

The second arrow, which is different from the remainder, is the *crooked* arrow indicating control action from the activity 'Take control action to . . .'. This represents a transient or temporary logical dependency which can be aimed at any of the operational activities. If the operational activities were to be done in reality and if, for example, the activity 'Define criteria to select one or more invest-ment options' is not done well enough, then control action would be taken to ensure that its performance improved. This could apply to any or all of the operational activities.

The control subsystem ensures that if this set of activities actually existed in the real world, then they would work together to achieve the defined purpose.

Figure 2.1(b) is an alternative model format favoured by Checkland. It is essentially representing the same concept though in my view it has several drawbacks. First, in order to understand the two control systems it is necessary to understand the distinction between the performance measures relevant to the two 'monitor' activities. Measures of performance are defined through what are known as the three 'Es', i.e. E_1, E_2, and E_3. E_1 is the measure of *efficacy* (i.e. does the activity actually work?); E_2 is the measure of *efficiency* (i.e. what resources does the activity consume?) and E_3 (i.e. is the activity the right thing to be doing?); this is the measure of *effectiveness*. These measures are discussed in more detail later since they are more concerned with the information needed to support the concept rather than the derivation of the concept itself. However, in Figure 2.1(b) the monitor activity within the inner boundary is concerned with the 'operational' activities and hence addresses E_1 and E_2. The monitor activity within the outer boundary is concerned with E_3.

E_3 is unnecessary in relation to the example given here. The activities have been derived using logic and hence for the RD chosen they must be the right things to be doing. The control system within the inner boundary thus corresponds to the control system in Figure 2.1(a); the monitor activity being concerned with measuring E_1 and E_2 for each of the operational activities.

The second problem associated with this format is that the control activity is represented only by the single word 'control'. Thus it gives no indication as to 'why' control action would be taken (what the actual control action would be cannot be defined). The control system must be there to ensure that the purpose defined by the RD is achieved. In relation to this simple example this does not appear to be a problem. However, in a more complex example, where this systems model was one 'subsystem' among others there would be multiple controllers (with different why's') and their

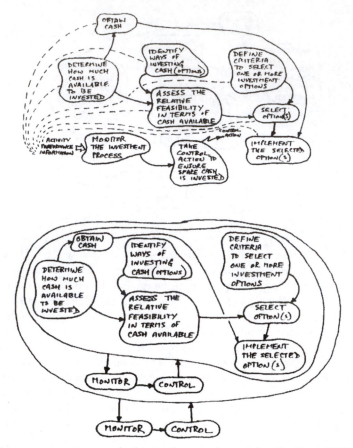

Figure 2.1 *(a) A system to invest spare cash. (b) An alternative format (after Checkland 1981)*

specific purpose would need to be stated within the 'control' activity in order to differentiate between them. There will be more discussion of this feature later when addressing subsystem decomposition of a model.

A further drawback is related to the meaning attributed to the arrows. It is a general requirement of diagram construction that when a chosen symbol or arrow is replicated within a diagram, the meaning associated with it must be consistent. A diagram becomes incoherent if symbols and arrows which *look the same* do not mean the same.

In a conceptual model the full arrows represent *logical dependencies* where an activity on the head of the arrow is logically dependent upon the activity or activities on the tail. In Figure 2.1(a), since the input to the monitor activity is specifically information flow, a different kind of arrow is used and it is labelled as such. In Figure 2.1(b) this is *not* the case.

Referring to the relationship of the arrow linking 'the control' activity to the remainder of the model, Figure 2.1(b) indicates that every activity within the inner boundary (the operational activities) is logically dependent upon the control activity. This may be the case but it is more likely that only a selection of the operational activities will be subject to control action and that action will only be temporary. This again is a different kind of dependency. It is of the nature of 'action' and is selective and temporary. It is worth making this difference of meaning explicit by choosing a different kind of arrow. Figure 2.1(a) illustrates this; the label 'control action' being added to the 'crooked' arrow in order to be specific about what the arrow means.

Finally the use of boundaries within the one model can become confusing and inconvenient when assembling models to form a 'consensus primary task model' and performing 'organisation mapping'. This feature will also be discussed in detail later.

It is therefore the format of Figure 2.1(a) that will be used throughout this book. This model represents a concept, the manifestation of which in the real world would work. It is therefore a useful device to compare against, and ask questions about, some real-world investment process which may not be working well, in order to find out why.

Figure 2.1(a) is a very simple model, but it has served the purpose of defining the modelling language (verbs in the imperative), illustrating the kind of structure in the model (logical dependencies) and the form and notation of a control subsystem. The RD and the resultant model *together* represent the concept (or the intellectual construct).

DEFENSIBLE LOGIC

At this point it is worth elaborating on the form of logic employed. It is not the highly precise form of logic practised by mathematicians but a defensible logic based upon a generic real-world rationale. Thus before the activity 'Identify ways of investing cash' can be represented in a model it must be known that there is not only one way of doing it.

Similarly, the fact that some of these investment options may not be feasible relies on some accumulated real-world knowledge that some forms of investment are more cash consuming than others. Thus if the spare cash to be invested is a few pounds then the option of investing in fine art is not feasible, whereas a bank account, stamp collection, premium bonds, etc. are feasible options.

This required knowledge is essentially factual and results from generally acquired experience of living on this planet. The essential restriction is that the knowledge used is *not* acquired from the *specific* situation for which the analysis is being undertaken and for which the concept is being developed. Thus it can be argued that *without knowing the specific situation* the model of Figure 2.1 is a *defensible* model of a system to invest spare cash. It is also the case that similar knowledge is being used in producing the RD. It must be known that spare cash can be invested. The first important step in developing a concept of a HAS therefore is to select some purposes that are believed to be relevant to the real-world situation under investigation.

Returning to the police force example in Chapter One, a number of potential purposes were listed. Thus if we choose 'A system to apprehend those individuals who violate the law' we are making the judgement that it would be useful to develop the model of what *the system* would have to do to be the one described by that RD. We are not saying that this is what a police force is, but that is what we are taking it to be. Thus the choice of this system represents *an assumption* that it would be useful to view a police force as such. We can also view it as 'a system to protect people and property', and so on.

Thus whereas in analysing a 'hard' interpretation of a situation we would seek to develop a single 'validated' model, soft systems analysis requires the development of a number of models. Thus:

- Each model is relevant to the situation.
- None of them is a representation of it.

Since none of them is a representation it is no longer possible to 'validate' the model by testing it against the real world. We can only determine if the model is well enough structured to be a model of a HAS.

MODEL TESTING

It is in this testing process that we make use of the Formal Systems Model (FSM). This has been described earlier (Checkland 1981; Wilson 1984, 1990) but a brief description will be given here for completeness.

Figure 2.2 illustrates both the process of using the FSM together with two ways of representing the concept. The first is merely a list of considerations/features which should be properly represented in any model of a HAS. The second is a way of representing the relationships between these features.

Thus the system which is defined by the particular RD resides at some position within a systems hierarchy extending from wider systems through to subsystems. The purpose is contained in the RD.

The first question within the iteration is: Does the model derived achieve the purpose defined? This is a crucial question since it determines the degree of defensibility of the model. If there are activities within the model which are *not* logically derivable from the words in the RD they should not be included (even if it is known that they occur in the particular part of the real world: remember, this is a model of the RD, *not* of the real world). Similarly, if there are words and/or phrases in the RD that have no representation in the activities within the model the model is incomplete. Complete logical consistency between the activities in the model and the purpose as specified in the RD is the first requirement of testing the model against the FSM.

Second, because it is a system and not just an aggregate, the activities need to have the complete logical connections (connectivity). Thus the second crucial question is: Have all the logical connections between activities been included?

The remaining features can all be addressed in relation to the 'monitor and control' activities. First, have they been included? Second, does the implied authority of the controller(s) cover the total 'resources' available to the activities and does this represent authority within the system 'boundary'? The 'monitor' activity is there to respond to the need to have some way of collecting information derived from the 'measures of performance' so that the 'decision taker(s)' within the 'control mechanism' will know if it is necessary to take control action and to which activity(ies) the control action should be directed.

This FSM is a generic model and represents a concept that should map onto any well-constructed HAS model irrespective of its resolution level. Therefore, for a subsystem to be a sub*system* it must also satisfy the FSM requirements.

Returning to Figure 2.1(a), we can assess its quality as a HAS by using the FSM. Its purpose is to invest spare cash, therefore the output of the transformation process (deliverable) is 'Spare cash invested'. The input is 'Spare cash to be invested' and so the only activities that are legitimate are those to progress from the input to the output. The arguments for including this set have been given previously and so we can proceed to question the connectivity.

Accepting that there will be options, the final activity, 'Implement the selected option(s)', must be dependent upon a 'select' activity, and implementation cannot take place without obtaining the cash. The select activity itself must have something to select from (options) and some reason for selecting some and not others (a criterion). Hence the activity is dependent upon the other activities. Similar arguments can be mounted for the activity 'Assess relative feasibility'. Other activities such as 'Identify ways of investing cash' and 'Determine how much cash is available' are not dependent upon activities within the model but require access to knowledge external to the system. Monitor and control activities are included and with a simple model of this kind with only one control system there is no inconsistency of the decision–taking process. This one controller has authority to take control action and allocate whatever resources are needed to all the activities within the boundary which encloses all the activities illustrated.

The foregoing has demonstrated that it is possible to develop a conceptual model from a transformation process. Thus the statement of purpose contained in the sparse RD, 'A system to invest spare cash' is described by the main verb 'to invest'. Adding the qualifying statement 'spare cash' provides a more specific meaning to what the system is for. The relationship between the RD and

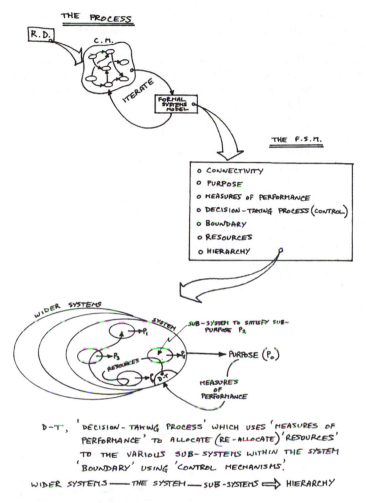

Figure 2.2   *The Formal Systems Model (FSM)*

the Conceptual Model (CM) is a 'being–doing' relationship. The RD tells us what the system 'is'; the CM tells us what the system must 'do' to be the one defined. This relationship must be retained irrespective of how complex the RD itself becomes.

The above discussion has been based upon a RD that is formed solely from the transformation process. In general this is too sparse to be of much practical value. What additional features need to be included in a RD for it to be well structured and potentially useful?

MULTIPLE PERCEPTIONS

Chapter One argued for the derivation of an 'explicit standard' to compare against an organisation unit when undertaking a strategic review. This would enable an 'audit trail' to be established and so produce recommendations for change that could be defensible. It was also argued that there would not be a single 'standard' since what the organisation unit was taken to be would be dependent upon the views (or perceptions) of it, based upon the concepts in the heads of all the observers of the organisation unit. These multiple perceptions therefore are a variable within 'soft' situations that cannot be ignored and must somehow be expressed in the RD chosen.

It is the case that there will be as many perceptions as there are observers and therefore to produce one RD for each observer's perception is totally impractical. The size of this problem and the variety implied can be reduced by making use of a variable which can be seen as a '*component of perception*'. This is given the letter W and originates from the German word *Weltanschauung*, which literally translates as 'world view'. There has been much discussion of an academic nature concerning W and the various ways it has been, or might be, interpreted (Davis 1989; Checkland and Davies 1986) but perhaps the most practical way it can be introduced within a RD is as *a belief*; not a belief attributed to an individual observer but as a belief statement associated with the words within the definition.

The relationship of this variable W to the multiple perceptions of the individual observers can be illustrated with reference to Figure 2.3. This shows an observer viewing a situation. The assumption being made is that we can illustrate the individual perception of that observer as being made up of a set of commitments to a range of Ws. This is a multi-dimensional picture since W is not a continuous valued function in a single dimension. However, as a means of illustrating the relationship of W to an individual perception we can represent it as a two-dimensional spectrum relating degree of commitment (C) to a W axis as at the top of Figure 2.3.

Suppose the situation being observed is a prison. We could take W to be characterised as follows:

W_1—a security orientation
W_2—a punishment orientation
W_3—a rehabilitation orientation

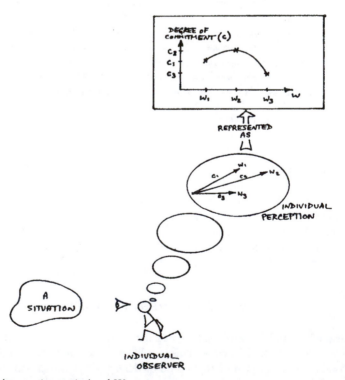

Figure 2.3   *Relation between 'perception' and W*

The representation shows that although the observer has some commitment to a prison being concerned with rehabilitating offenders, the greatest commitment is to a prison being concerned with secure containment of offenders together with their punishment. (The observer could, in these terms, be described as a 'hard-liner'.)

If on the other hand, the Ws are characterised as follows:

W_1—a security orientation
W_2—a rehabilitation orientation
W_3—a punishment orientation

then the observer would be more liberal-minded. He or she has an equal commitment to security but a greater commitment to the purpose of a prison being more concerned with rehabilitating offenders than with punishing them.

The simplest representation to use is to keep the orientations of the Ws the same and to change the shape of the commitment spectrum. This is illustrated for three observers of a prison in Figure 2.4. Here the W orientations are:

W_1—punishment orientation
W_2—security orientation
W_3—rehabilitation orientation

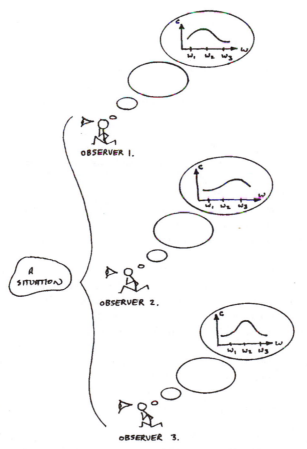

Figure 2.4 *W spectra*

The assumption is made here that no observer is 100% committed to any specific W. Observer 1 and observer 2 correspond to the two already mentioned above and here observer 3 is shown to have a major commitment to security and a minor commitment to both punishment and rehabilitation.

The above pragmatic thinking leads us to a way of reducing the variety mentioned earlier and gets away from thinking in terms of perceptions or viewpoints associated with individuals. What is now required is to define the population of observers relevant to the situation and to identify the set of Ws to which they subscribe. In an actual project for the Prison Department of the Home Office undertaken in 1983 around 50 people associated with the prison service were interviewed. They ranged from prison governors, prison chaplains and psychologists to personnel within the Home Office and prisoner aid societies. In all, twelve Ws were identified which were significant and distinct; a considerable reduction in the variety from the 50 perceptions associated with the people.

ROOT DEFINITIONS

The impact of the above discussion on the structure of RD is that a representation of W can now be added to the transformation process. Essentially what is being added is the belief that makes the transformation process meaningful.

The requirement is that each RD represents 100% commitment to a single W. Thus for the above example relative to the organisation unit being a prison, twelve models were produced from twelve Root Definitions. None of them represented a model of an individual perception since no individual had 100% commitment to a single W. All twelve models were capable of being mapped onto all 50 perceptions.

Taking an example from the prison study for a W related to a security orientation, the transformation process was 'to control the interaction between offenders and the community'. If we add 'by overseeing permitted contact both inside and outside the establishment and acting accordingly', the RD becomes:

> *A system to control the interaction between offenders and the community by overseeing permitted contact both inside and outside the establishment and acting accordingly.* (Note: 'Establishment' defines the physical boundary of a prison.)

The transformation process is as stated and the belief (W) contained in the definition is that: 'overseeing permitted contact and acting accordingly *will* control the interaction'. This is the statement of belief contained in the words used in the RD. It is *not* solely the belief of any one individual.

Thus each RD will contain a statement of T; the transformation process and a belief (W). These two elements are mandatory. The T is always explicit and is given by the main verb of the RD. The W is always implicit and is identified by answering the question: 'what *must* I believe for the definition to make sense?' Whether you hold that belief personally or not is unimportant.

In 1976 an Australian research student at Lancaster published an article suggesting a particular structure for a well-formulated RD (Smyth and Checkland 1976). He was arguing that if the FSM could be used to check the formulation of a conceptual model, then something similar could be used to check the formulation of a RD. The outcome of this particular piece of work was the derivation of a particular device (a mnemonic) to question the words used within a root definition. The mnemonic chosen was CATWOE and the elements can be defined as follows:

T—transformation process (described either as an input–output conversion or the process itself)
W—*Weltanschauung* (practically interpreted as the statement of belief within the RD)

C—Customer (the recipient of the output of the transformation process, either the victim or the beneficiary)

A—Actors (those individuals who would *do* the activities in the resultant conceptual model if they were to map onto reality)

O—Owner (a wider-system decision taker with authority over the system defined, with a concern for the performance of the system)

E—Environmental constraints (those features external to the system defined, which are taken to be significant)

One of the problems associated with using the English language for the intellectual process is that the words used need to be precisely defined. In everyday conversation we are too casual about our choice of words and the meanings that we attribute to them. Since English (or your own native tongue) is the modelling language within SSM more discipline is required in its use and this is not easy.

One of the major contributions made by the mnemonic CATWOE is that, if used properly, it provides a mechanism for testing the RD and ensuring that the words chosen are as precise as possible and that they represent the best choice for the meaning captured by them. Therefore to be useful:

CATWOE must be a test of the structure and words chosen in the RD

Bad practice has seen it degenerate into a woolly concept that adds to the RD. If it is not retained as a testing device then what useful purpose does it serve? It is the RD that leads to the CM and against which it can be defended. Thus if CATWOE appears as an intermediary between the RD and the CM all the logical defensibility is lost.

The proper relationship between the RD, the CM and the testing devices is shown in Figure 2.5. The aim of the first part in the development of a purposeful activity model (the chosen intellectual construct for all SSM-driven analysis) is to derive a properly formulated RD. CATWOE helps in this process. By considering elements other than just the T and W, a richer definition can be assembled which tries to capture the essence of the particular purpose being defined.

As stated previously, the T and W are mandatory; a meaningful purpose could not be defined without them. However, the remaining CATWOE elements can be included or excluded on the basis of the analysts' judgement in relation to the situation being analysed. What is important is that they are considered and a conscious decision made with respect to their inclusion or exclusion. How they are included within the definition is also important but practice in RD formulation and use will help in this latter aspect.

RD formulation cannot be mechanistic. The process is driven by the situation and the total intellectual structure into which the RD/CM pair fit. For example:

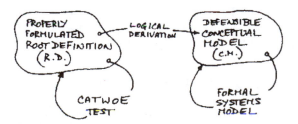

Figure 2.5 *The defensible intellectual relationship*

A system owned by O and operated by A, to do X by Y to customers C in order to achieve Z within the constraints E.

is one structure which utilises all the CATWOE elements. In some situations a different structure may lead to a more powerful intellectual device. This book contains a number of examples which were used to good effect over many years of practice. However, they are illustrative. You must develop your own style in using these ideas but retain flexibility. Do not be constrained by the above rigid format.

The iteration between RD and CATWOE is important though it doesn't matter where you start. Some practitioners start with CATWOE and then construct the RD. It is a defensible pairing that is required. It is usually the case, however, that a richer definition is obtained if the construction of the RD is driven by the situation rather than by the CATWOE elements.

Let us return to the security-oriented prison example and consider the other elements that could be included. Because of the nature of the transformation process 'to control interaction', it was already necessary to include 'customer' in order for the interaction to be defined. Thus:

T—to control interaction, and
C—offenders and the community

Also

W—overseeing permitted contact and acting accordingly will control the interaction

In addition we could take:

O—An 'Establishment' (i.e. some decision-taking process within the prison, not specifically
    defined)
A—Prison officers
E—Home Office policy

Introducing the CATWOE elements into a single sentence produces the following RD:

> *An 'Establishment'-owned system, operated by prison officers, to control the interaction between offenders and the community by overseeing permitted contact, both inside and outside the establishment and acting accordingly, while constrained by Home Office policy.*

A check against the CATWOE elements confirms that there is consistency between them and the words used in the RD. In the RD the additional words 'both inside and outside the establishment' are included. This is merely a qualifying statement about the words 'permitted contact' and is included to add richness and to be more specific. This does not alter the basic structure of the RD and hence the additional words do not appear as CATWOE elements. *It is legitimate to introduce additional words into the RD. However, it is not legitimate to include words and/or elements in CATWOE that do not appear in the RD.*

Violation of this rule is one of the most common deficiencies in the construction of RDs. If this rule is not applied, we might ask the questions, what is the purpose served by CATWOE and what intellectual device is remaining to use as a test of the structure and formulation of a RD?

CATWOE USAGE

Many examples exist in the literature related to SSM which illustrate incorrect usage of CATWOE. A few are used here to illustrate various aspects of the relationship of CATWOE to a RD taken mainly from student practice. The example is given followed by a brief discussion of the faults.

Example 1. Related to a RD representing a manufacturing company.

RD   A system to manufacture and sell a specific range of products at minimum cost in order to make a profit.

C—The market
A—Production Department and Marketing personnel
T—manufacture for sale
W—MD
O—not specified
E—profit

This example is probably the result of the casual application of the CATWOE test. The RD is sparse but is still a legitimate definition. It is initially poorly structured since the use of the word 'and' between 'manufacture' and 'sell' means that there are, in fact, two transformation processes.

Thus logic would require the resultant model to contain activities to do with both manufacturing *and* selling. The transformation process identified within CATWOE, i.e. 'manufacture for sale', only leads to manufacturing activities.

The Actors are specified as 'Production Department and Marketing personnel'. This may well be a reasonable choice of Actors but they do not appear in the RD. The RD would have to read:

A system, operated by Production Department and Marketing personnel, to ——

The Customer is also not specified within the RD although 'the market' appears within CATWOE. These errors arise because the student was still thinking about the real world to which the RD was seen to be relevant, rather than concentrating on the intellectual process itself.

The existence of two transformation processes makes the specification of customer difficult. The recipient of the output from 'manufacture' could well be the Sales Department whereas the recipient of the output from 'sell' would be an actual customer (within the market).

Although 'profit' is stated as a requirement within the RD it is not an externally imposed constraint. 'Minimum cost', however, is. The controller of the system can decide how much profit to make but cost *must* be minimum.

The fact that Owner is not specified within the RD illustrates the proper use of this CATWOE element. The student could now have decided whether or not it would be useful to include an 'Owner' and who the 'Owner' might usefully be. The iteration may have been done and the decision still reached to omit any reference to the wider system. Initiating iteration via the RD is what the CATWOE test is for, but it must be used properly. Whatever the decisions are, which are arrived at during an iteration, there should be a consistent pairing of CATWOE and RD.

The inclusion of MD as W, within CATWOE, is a common fault. Probably because of the 'profit' outcome the student has related the RD to the Managing Director. The implication of W within CATWOE is as a means of extracting the belief contained in the words in the RD not of attributing that belief to an individual (see Figures 2.3 and 2.4 to appreciate why this is not possible). W is a statement of *what the belief is* not of *whose belief it is*.

Any individual will probably subscribe to a number of beliefs. Any attribution to an individual will, in any case, be coloured by the range of Ws and degrees of commitment to them held by the analyst doing the attribution. In relation to this sparse RD the statement of belief is simply: 'Manufacturing and selling a range of products at minimum cost *will* make a profit'. Within this rather sparse RD the belief is merely a restatement of the whole of the words in the RD. In a richer and more complex RD this would not be the case.

Example 2.   Related to patient care

RD   A Hospital-owned system to comfort patients by undertaking regular visits within specified hours.

C—patients
A—relatives
T—provide comfort
W—visiting patients is a good thing to do
O—hospital
E—visiting time

One of the problems with this RD and CATWOE analysis is that different words have been used to describe the CATWOE elements than were used in the RD and there is also considerable ambiguity in the definition. In some cases the differences in the words may be regarded as trivial but as a general rule (given possible semantic problems), the same words should be used.

Thus 'visiting time' may be taken to be the same as 'specified hours' but it may not be, dependent upon who does the specifying. It may not even be a constraint if the system 'decision taker' is the one to do the specifying. The wording of the RD should remove the ambiguity and make this clear. The 'Owner' is 'Hospital' (or someone within the Hospital management structure). This is legitimate in terms of the CATWOE analysis but is it a relevant 'owner'. The wider system (given this owner) is apparently within the Hospital management processes and therefore, for the hierarchy to be coherent, we would expect the system also to be within these management processes. This raises the question as to who 'undertakes the regular visits'. The impression that this wording creates (particularly as A appears as relatives), is that the visitor is external to the hospital. However, this is not necessarily the case; it could be an internal visitor. Again this is ambiguity that should be removed.

In relation to the 'transformation process', 'to provide comfort' is not the same as 'to comfort'. One can *provide* comfort by ensuring that someone else does the comforting.

A is specified as 'relatives' but this word does not appear in the RD. Finally the W in this RD (i.e. the belief) is that 'patients *will be* comforted through regular visits'. The W specified in CATWOE is a value judgement about the acceptability of the purpose as a real-world activity. This is totally irrelevant as a technical requirement on the structure of a RD.

As a professional exercise I could produce a totally defensible RD (in terms of its structure) of a *system to cause unease within a community by random bombing*. To do this I would not have to believe that this is a good thing to do. The belief that would be contained within the RD is that random bombing *will* cause unease. Whether it is actually a good or bad thing to do is irrelevant to the structure of the RD.

Example 3. Related to service provision

> RD   *A Consultancy company-owned system, operated by skilled professionals, to satisfy clients' needs for technical advice by undertaking regular training and exploiting developments in new technology.*

C—clients
A—skilled professionals
T—to satisfy clients needs for technical advice
W—keeping up to date with skills and the technology is necessary to provide advice.
O—consultancy company
E—none specified

The only problem with this RD and CATWOE is that the W (and hence the RD) contains an inconsistency. The actual W contained in the RD is that: 'undertaking regular training and exploiting developments in new technology (Y) *will* satisfy clients needs for technical advice' (X). It would be possible to undertake training and exploit new technology without having any clients or without knowing what their needs were. Clearly, doing Y is insufficient to achieve X.

The W expressed in CATWOE sounds fine as a condition but it is not the W expressed in the words of the RD.

A more blatant and obvious example of this same fault appeared in a RD relevant to a manu-facturing company. It was stated that the system was: '*To increase company profit by planning to diversity the product range*'.

The outcome of planning is a plan. This will have no effect on profit unless something is done with the plan.

Some further examples are included in Chapter Three associated with the Albion Group case study and the responses to it produced by students and others.

The problems illustrated by these examples can be overcome by less casual use of the CATWOE test and critical evaluation of what it reveals about the words chosen in the RD. Adherence to a set of general principles and rules will also help.

GENERAL PRINCIPLES

- *Principle 1*   The characteristics of the situation that can be associated with the multiple percep-tions of those individuals impacting on the situation must be explicitly represented within the intellectual process to make the resultant analysis relevant to them and be more than mere opinion. These perceptions can be thought of as consisting of a number of 'orientations'. A practical interpretation of the variable W can be through a representation of these 'orientations'. In the prison example discussed earlier, a security orientation was considered. Within this orien-tation the articulation of the W within the RD was the belief 'overseeing permitted contact and acting accordingly will control interaction'.
- *Principle 2*   The characteristics of the situation under investigation that are represented by ambiguity, lack of clarity, complexity and a general messiness require the *intellectual process being used* to contain as much structure and rigour as is possible to avoid the analysis displaying similar characteristics.
- *Principle 3*   The intellectual construct representing the concept of a HAS consists of two com-ponents. The RD describes what the system *is*. The CM describes what the system must *do* to be the one described by the RD. Thus the only link between the RD and the CM is a being–doing relationship which can only be deduced on the basis of logic.
- *Principle 4*   The language of a HAS is our own natural language. For it to be useful as the language of an intellectual construct we must adopt more discipline in its use than we do in everyday conversation and try to choose words that are precise in meaning. Thus everyday words that are subject to multiple interpretations in the real-world manifestation should be avoided, particularly as transformation processes, e.g. to manage, to administer, to market, etc. Always ensure consistency in meaning, i.e. the same word should always mean the same within a specific context.

The above principles lead to the development of a set of rules that govern the structure and construction of the basic intellectual construct of a HAS. Such rules exist when the intellectual constructs are mathematically based. Similarly, rules need to be developed and applied in the construction of concepts based on HAS.

ROOT DEFINITIONS (RULES)

- *Rule 1*   A RD should be one sentence in which the major verb represents the transformation process. Additional sentences (outside the RD) may be used to define the meaning attributed to certain words within the RD if necessary.

- *Rule 2*   The mnemonic CATWOE (together with the defined meanings of its elements) is used as a test of the structure and words used in the RD. Once consistency between the CATWOE elements and the words used in the RD has been achieved, CATWOE has served its purpose and has no further relevance to the construction of the CM.
- *Rule 3*   The elements T and W must be identifiable in every RD. Thus they are mandatory. The elements C, A, O and E are included or excluded on the basis of the analysts' judgement. A well-structured RD should only have one transformation process.
- *Rule 4*   Words and/or phrases may be included within a RD to qualify other words and/or phrases to add richness or specificity to a RD without them being represented as CATWOE elements. They therefore do not affect the structure of the RD. However, words and/or phrases must not appear as CATWOE elements without also appearing in the RD.

CONCEPTUAL MODEL (RULES)

- *Rule 1*   The CM must be constructed from the words in the RD without recourse to the *specific* situation. Thus the inclusion of activities and/or sets of activities within the CM must be defended against specific words or phrases within the RD.
- *Rule 2*   Since each activity in the CM could be the source of a RD for expansion to a more detailed level, sufficient words should be used within the activity to be precise about the transformation process it describes.
- *Rule 3*   The CM should be defensible against the FSM. The major implication of this is that there should be adequate connectivity, reference to resourcing and *at least* one 'monitor and control' subsystem within the CM.
- *Rule 4*   Arrows within a CM are essentially logical dependencies and should have a consistent format. Arrows which represent accumulated dependencies (such as activity performance information and constraint information) may have a different format and labelled to indicate their content. Temporary dependencies as dependencies with unknown destination (such as control action) should be of a different format. In essence arrows which look the same should mean the same. Double-headed arrows are *not* permissible. (The desire to include them between two activities usually means that an activity is omitted. This is usually a feedback, updating or control type activity.)

CONCEPTUAL MODEL BUILDING

Figure 2.1(a) represented an example of a CM derived from a simple RD. The RD was based on a transformation process—'to invest spare cash'. For this to be a RD it must contain a W, however. In this case it is simply the belief that 'it is possible to invest spare cash'.

The same logic that led to this model must be applied when developing a CM from more complex RDs (containing more of the CATWOE elements and possibly additional phrases to enrich the RD and capture more of the 'essence' of the particular situation/perception). The rules articulated above must also be applied.

Perhaps the clearest way to illustrate the process is through an example based upon the CATWOE elements themselves. Let us start with the simplest RD.

$$\begin{bmatrix} \text{T} - \text{to do X} \\ \text{W} - \text{doing Y will lead to the achievement of X} \end{bmatrix}$$

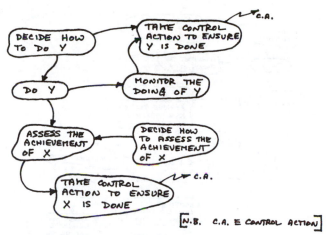

Figure 2.6   *A model of T and W*

The modelling can begin by making sure that activities exist to do Y and by then adding activities to make sure that these lead to the achievement of X. The resultant model is given in Figure 2.6.

Let us now add a customer (C) so that the RD becomes: *a system to do X by Y in order to satisfy the requirement of C.*

The RD is written to make C the beneficiary rather than the victim. (Note: there is no need to do the respective CATWOE tests as we are deliberately adding the CATWOE elements.) The model now becomes that illustrated by Figure 2.7.

Adding Actors (A) needs some explanation of the logic employed. We are developing a CM as a device for exploring the complexity and problems (concerns) in some real-world situation. Therefore our concept needs to 'work' if it is to lead to improvements (however defined) in that situation by identifying change to those features of the situation that do not work or do not work well enough. Since the actors are defined as 'those individuals who would do the activities of the CM if it were to map onto reality' they must possess the appropriate skills and be in sufficient

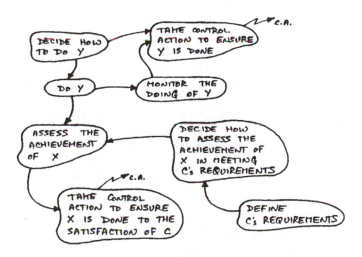

Figure 2.7   *A model of T and W, incorporating C*

Figure 2.8   *A model of T and W, incorporating C and A*

numbers to enable this to happen. Thus the Actors must have the *capability* of doing all the activities. Ensuring this leads to the activities contained in the model of Figure 2.8. Here it is assumed that not all the Actors will do all the activities, hence the 'Allocate' activity. It is also assumed that the human resources (HR) available to the system, as defined by the actors, will neither be too many or too few, hence the use of the verb 'to match'.

   Thus the controller can either 'redefine' actors if the total capability does not match or change the allocation if the individual capabilities (Actor to activity) do not match.

   The inclusion of environmental constraints (E) also requires some explanation. The FSM tells us that the system boundary is defined as representing the area over which the system decision-taking process has *authority*. There will therefore be features of the environment which significantly impact on the system, but which are outside this authority. The decision-taking process will therefore have to take them as given (i.e. as constraints) and ensure that the activities within the system conform to these constraints. This, in effect, reduces the degrees of freedom available to the decision-taking process. Within the models of Figures 2.6 to 2.9, the decision-taking process is represented by the various controllers. This means that the environmental constraints can be distributed throughout each system by ensuring that each controller is constrained according to the impact of the overall constraints on the set of activities under the authority of that controller. Thus, although every activity is constrained, the distribution of constraints can be accomplished through each controller by effectively reducing the degrees of freedom available to the controller.

   In Figure 2.9 the input constraints to each controller are represented by a solid broad arrow, annotated C, and the content of each arrow is determined by an assessment of the impact of E on each activity, a decision on how to react to the assessment and a notification to each controller of the collective impact on those activities under the authority of the particular controller.

   There needs to be a constraint controller in order to ensure that the constraints are not violated. This controller also has to be constrained, since it cannot take control action which, itself, violates the constraints.

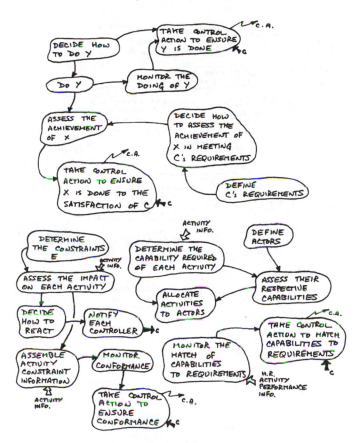

Figure 2.9 *A model of T and W, incorporating C, A and E*

It may help to explain this representation if we map it onto real-world budgetary control. Here the constraints E will be the total finance available.

'Assess the impact on each activity' represents the bidding process in which an estimate is made of the finances required for each activity within the budget holder's area. This has to be done for the total set of budget holders, hence the broad input arrow representing the information about all the activities. 'Decide how to react' produces the statement as to how the total finances are to be allocated to each budget holder (i.e. the budget). 'Notify each controller' is the activity through which each budget holder receives notification of their particular budget. Each controller is equivalent to the budget holder. 'Assemble activity constraint information' and 'Monitor conformance' produce the variances on finance available to each activity compared with finance consumed. 'Take control action to ensure conformance' is the overall budgetary control which ensures that each controller (budget holder) operates within budget.

Finally it is necessary to incorporate Owner (O). The definition of owner is that it is the decision taker of the chosen wider system. Using the FSM again identified the area of authority of the Owner to be the boundary of the wider system, which, of course, includes the system that we are modelling. Thus it can be assumed that if the system *does not* achieve what the Owner requires (i.e. it is not effective) then the Owner will take control action on the system. Hence to avoid such control action, the system decision taker must ensure that the system performs well enough to meet the Owner's expectations. Thus four additional activities are required to do this and the complete model is given in Figure 2.10.

Figure 2.10   *A model of T and W, incorporating C, A, E and O*

The RD corresponding to this is:

An O-owned system, operated by A, to do X by Y in order to satisfy the requirements of 'C' within the constraints E.

If we question the model of Figure 2.10. on the basis of the FSM we can justify it as follows:

- Connectivity: The logical dependencies have been checked and are appropriate. The activities to do with Actors, constraints and overall performance control are linked to all other activities through the broad arrows representing information dependency and/or constraint dependency.
- Purpose: This is clearly defined in the transformation process and through the activities representing 'to do X by Y'.
- Measure of performance:These are not specified explicity but each controller is preceded by either a 'monitor' or 'assess' activity and would lead to the specification of actual measures at the more detailed level of resolution.
- Decision-taking process: The controllers are identified explicitly and the purpose of each controller is described unambiguously.
- Boundary:The boundary is identified by the tototal set of activities in the model and the areas of authority of the controllers are defined.

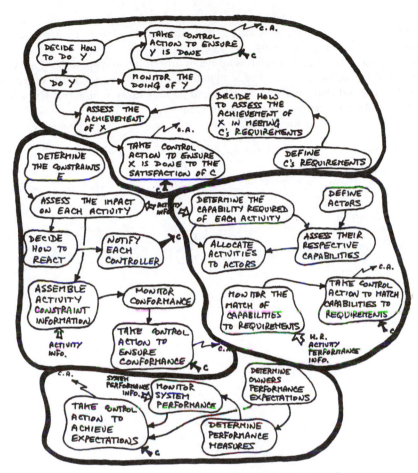

Figure 2.11 *A model of T and W, incorporating C, A, E and O decomposed into subsystems*

- Resources: Human resources are defined through the inclusion of Actors. Physical resources are not specified given the generic nature of the model. Every activity will require both human and physical resources but the latter were not emphasised in the RD.
- Hierarchy: The existence of a wider system has been identified through the specification of owner. The subsystems can be derived by mapping the boundaries of the area of authority of the individual controllers. See Figure 2.11.

Although the model of Figure 2.10 (and 2.11) is generic it should *not* be used as a template for all models.

As mentioned earlier, the structure of this CATWOE-based RD is one of many and does not incorporate any phrases or words to enrich the definition in relation to a specific situation. It has been included merely to indicate the logical assembly of a model. There is *no* real-world situation associated with this RD and therefore specific elements of the real world cannot be included in the model.

It is possible that another analyst could produce a different model from this RD (though this may be more likely in relation to a more real-world-oriented RD). However, if the model is equally defensible, then the differences should only be in terms of the words used to describe the activities (it is the meanings that are important), or in terms of the resolution level at which the model is assembled. Clearly a model containing 30 activities will be different from one containing 25 activities. Either will be acceptable as long as the anlaysts can defend each model in relation to the RD using general, *not specific*, real–word knowledge.

Thinking, which is transferable from this model to others, is based upon the CATWOE elements included in the RD, so that, if the owner is included there will be an overall control subsystem. If the Actors are included there will be an HR management subsystem and if there are constraints specified there will be a constraint management subsystem.

It is the case, however, that the activities may not be specified in precisely the same way:

It is always better to develop the RD and associated CM for the first time every time.

Chapter Three

Selection of Relevant Systems

RICH PICTURE BUILDING

The real world of organised activity is highly complex. The intention within SSM is to use the models of purposeful activity systems to help in structuring that complexity. Thus at some point it is necessary to make a transition from delving into the real world to try to describe and understand the nature of the situation to the intellectual processes that eventually contribute to that understanding. It is also necessary to undertake the transition back again in order to make something happen as a result of the intellectual activity. The concern of this chapter is with the first of these transitions.

The main concern here is, having had some immersion in the real world, how to use the knowledge gained to select those systems that it would be useful to model. It is also important to have some mechanism for deciding how to organise this initial immersion and when to make the transition.

'When to make the transition' is dependent upon the terms of reference (remit) in place at the start of the study and these also affect the choice of systems that are taken to be relevant. Clearly there is more scope for variety in this choice if the study is concerned with the identification of areas for improvement in an organisation than if it relates to deriving requirements for a data warehouse for a marketing function. Whatever the terms of reference are, however, some way of expressing the situation is required so that the state of current understanding is made explicit.

A useful way of achieving this is through what is known as a 'rich picture'. This is literally a picture of what the situation is taken to be. It includes the organisational entities of interest, the relationships between them, roles of apparent significance, issues, areas of conflict, etc. Symbols are used, where appropriate, to represent entities and roles: arrows, of various kinds, are used to express relationships. For the picture to be coherent, the symbols and arrows must be chosen with care. Those symbols and arrows, which *look* the same must *mean* the same.

One of the best examples of a rich picture is an Ordnance Survey (OS) map. This is an explicit representation of a piece of terrain, rather than an organisational situation, but its symbolism is consistent and this makes it easy to interpret. A rich picture of an organisational situation requires the same degree of consistency within the one picture, although Ordnance Survey maintains the consistency of meaning from map to map. Thus a square with a cross is always a church with a tower, it is never a church with a steeple. This transfer of consistency is not required from organisation to organisation as rich pictures do not need to be transferable, but consistency is essential within each picture.

The advantage of pictorial representation over text is that the information within the picture can be processed in parallel whereas, with text, it can only be processed serially, i.e. it has to be read. This is particularly valuable for that information which is concerned with relationships. Also *the interpretation* of the situation is made explicit through a picture whereas with text the interpretation of what has been read remains in the mind. This is particularly important when a group of analysts is involved. The construction of the picture allows differences of interpretation to be identified and permits agreement to be made on the interpretation to be taken. Thus the group of analysts can embark on the analysis knowing that they are all referring *to the same situation*. If differences of interpretation emerge during the analysis, commitments will have been generated and it will be that much more difficult to reach agreement. Little commitment has been generated at the picture-construction stage, since this is prior to the analysis, so that agreement over interpretation is relatively unemotional.

It is the construction of the picture that is important from the consistency of interpretation point of view, but it is the completed picture that is important as a source of inspiration on what purposeful activity systems it would be useful to generate. Assimilation of the significance of relationships, issues, etc. is what leads to the choice of *relevant* systems, i.e. it is based upon what the picture tells you. Here the old adage that a picture is worth a thousand words is demonstrated to be true.

Consider the example in Figure 3.1. Here a one-inch square picture, using OS symbols, represents a piece of terrain. It is actually less detailed than a real OS map but the amount of information contained in the picture is greater, by an order of magnitude, than what could be provided in a one-inch square of text.

In Figure 3.1 the textual description is also given. In order to illustrate the process of rich picture construction, consider a number of passages of text, together with their translation into a picture format. The extracts of text follow below and the pictures are given in Figures 3.2, 3.3 and 3.4 respectively.

The village is situated between 50 and 75 metres above sea-level, in a valley that runs North-East, South-West. A railway runs through the centre of the village and emerges from a cutting just prior to passing under a road bridge. The main road, which couples the two built-up areas, swings to the right to cross the bridge as it passes by the Hotel in a Northerly direction to then swing to the left to continue directly North. There is a footpath which goes South from the Hotel, across the road and passes a church with a steeple just before it bends to the left to go alongside the railway

Figure 3.1   *An OS map extract*

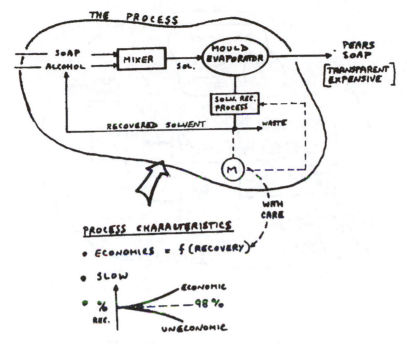

Figure 3.2 *Pears Soap—rich picture*

In a real situation, the process of rich picture construction is not one of translation but of representation. However, it is translation that is used here in order to illustrate how symbols can be used to represent entities and their relationships.

Words may still be used, but sparingly. The conversion of text into pictures should not be done by merely writing statements in boxes and joining the boxes by arrows.

Extract 1   Pears soap

Pears transparent soap, which is expensive, is made by dissolving soap in alcohol and allowing the alcohol to evaporate slowly. This is done in moulds which are the shape of the bars of soap: the natural shape achieved when the solvent evaporates is the oval with the characteristic depressions in it. The economics of the process depend entirely on recovery of the solvent for recycling. At least 98% has to be recovered if the process, which is in any case slow, is to be economic: hence the alcohol recovery has to be carefully monitored.

The picture corresponding to this extract is given in Figure 3.2. The picture is essentially in two parts. The extract describes a 'process' and the upper part of the picture is a process description. We are also told something about the process and so the lower part of the picture identifies the three features as the process characteristics. The above extract is a fictitious example used to provide a simple illustration. A more complex example is given in the second extract and this is also fictitious.

Extract 2   Slimline shoes

'Slimline', manufacturers of women's shoes, are hoping to improve their performance with a new range called 'Carefree'. (From a peak return on capital of 22% three years ago they have fallen to 15% then 11%.) The Managing Director discovers that the Production Department have introduced a new glue for

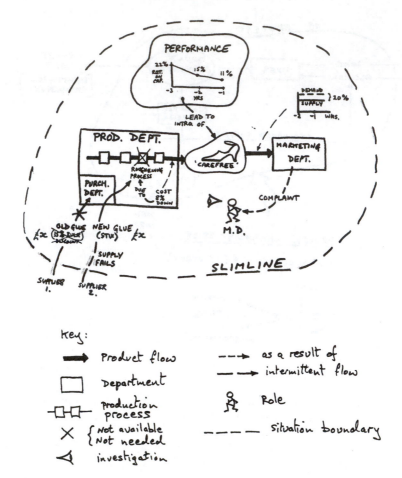

Figure 3.3 · *Simline shoes—rich picture*

sticking soles to uppers. This eliminates a sole-roughening process and has enabled them to achieve an 8% reduction in production cost. The MD, however, when investigating a Marketing Department complaint that for the last two weeks they have been 20% down on the supplies of shoes they need from Production, finds that the glue is in short supply. It seems that the Purchasing Section of the Production Department has cancelled an arrangement by which they received a 35% discount on bulk supplies of the original glue (this discount could not now be reinstated) and are buying the new glue ('STIX'), at the same price as the old glue, from a different supplier who has failed to meet delivery promises.

Figure 3.3 is the rich picture corresponding to this extract.

The final example is represented by an actual extract from a national newspaper.

Extract 3   Meccano

The workers at the Edge Hill (Liverpool) factory of Airfix Industries are currently staging a 'work-in'. This particular factory produces Meccano, the traditional construction toy, and Dinky toys, which range from model cars through all varieties of vehicles to agricultural implements. The situation has arisen because Airfix have stated their intention to close the factory, making some 940 workers redundant. Very little investment in new machinery has taken place over the last 50 years, resulting in production methods which are antiquated. The workers claim that they have a viable product and, given the opportunity, they intend running the factory as a workers' cooperative. This would require financial support from the government and a meeting has been arranged between local union officials and representatives of the Department of Industry to discuss the situation.

Meccano, which has been a household name in toys for most of this century, was invented by J.F. Hornby, a Liverpool businessman in 1893. As the business developed he added model trains and Dinky toys, all three products being highly successful. After the last war they suffered severe competition from other manufacturers, such as Lego, Triang, and Matchbox toys, resulting in the decline of the Meccano share of the market. Fifteen years ago, Hornby Trains Ltd was bought out by Triang, leaving the two product lines currently produced at Edge Hill.

The picture in Figure 3.4 focuses on the factory of Edge Hill in Liverpool. This represents the current state of affairs following growth and diversification since 1893. A number of arrows of different kinds are used and the meaning is explained in the key. This example is intended to illustrate the need to use different types of arrow to cope with the variety of meaning.

Although the extract makes no mention of a consultant, one has been included to make the point that, if we are being asked to interact in some way with an organisation, we should include ourselves

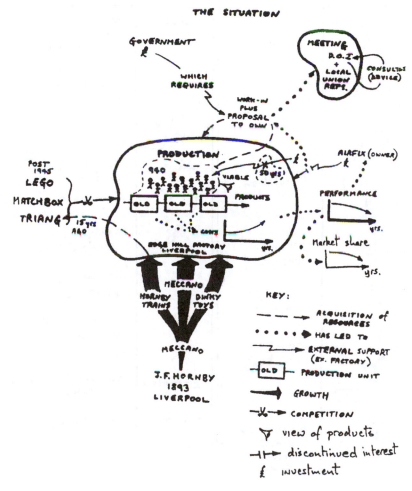

Figure 3.4 *Meccano—rich picture*

in the picture. We are part of the situation and our relationship to it is important. This illustrates that the consultant has been brought in by the Department of Industry (DOI) with the terms of reference: to provide advice to the meeting. Thus including the consultant (or ourselves, as consultant) we make clear who the client is and their expectations of us.

Because of the degree of variety contained in each problem situation, flexibility in the use of symbols and arrows needs to be retained. However, there are certain symbols which tend to appear in most rich pictures and a selection is given in Figure 3.5. This is *not* exhaustive and the freedom to use alternatives and to create new symbols to represent particular features must be maintained. The major offender to coherence in pictures is the use of arrows. They tend to be inserted casually so that arrows all look the same but have a multitude of meanings. Within badly constructed pictures, the same arrows can represent general relationships which are unspecified; they also represent information flows, material flows, communication, inputs of various kinds, statements about something and so on. If the same kind of arrow is used to illustrate all these facets of a situation the picture becomes unintelligible.

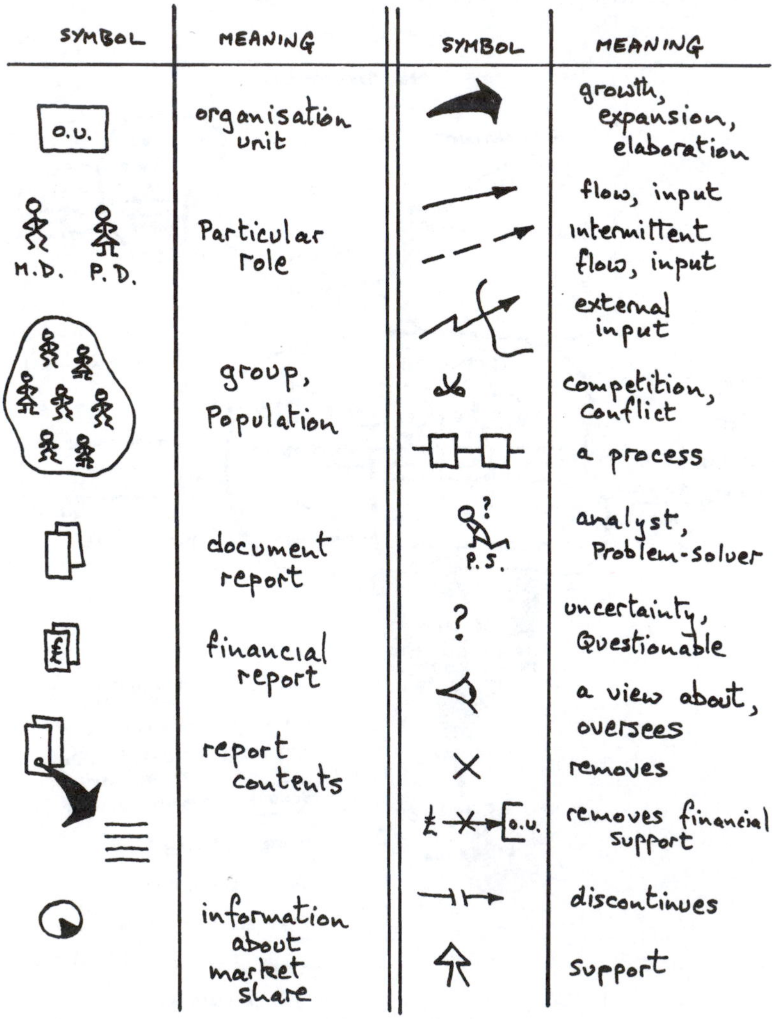

SYMBOL	MEANING	SYMBOL	MEANING
O.U.	organisation unit	(arrow)	growth, expansion, elaboration
M.D. P.D.	Particular role	(arrow)	flow, input
		(dashed arrow)	intermittent flow, input
(group of figures)	group, Population	(zigzag arrow)	external input
		(scissors)	competition, conflict
		(boxes linked)	a process
(document)	document report	P.S.	analyst, Problem-solver
(£ document)	financial report	?	uncertainty, Questionable
(document with arrow)	report contents	(eye)	a view about, oversees
		X	removes
		£→X→O.U.	removes financial support
(pie chart)	information about market share	→|↦	discontinues
		(arrow up)	support

Figure 3.5   *Common symbols*

Also more complex symbols than is necessary could be generated to represent characteristics. In the Meccano situation the process operating is old. It is much easier and quicker to insert the word 'old' than represent it as a process festooned with cobwebs. A pictorial representation can still include words but it must be a balance between symbols and words. The important aspect of picture construction is that it is capable of being processed as a total image. Individual words inserted into the picture do not destroy this facet. The insertion of sentences does, however, as the sentences have to be read.

A rich picture is an aid to the problem-solving group, i.e. the analysts. Thus it is essentially private to that group. It is not usually the case that the pictures are available to the personnel within the client organisation who are external to the problem-solving group.

It may be quite important in relation to a representation of power within the problem situation to include within the picture the following symbol:

M.D.

This tells us that the Managing Director is a big-headed individual (egocentric) who thinks that he is a gift from God (has a divine right), but it would not be diplomatic, or helpful, for this interpretation to reach the MD. Such a revelation could, in fact, terminate the project. Only in exceptional circumstances and for very good reasons should a rich picture find its way into the general domain and then it should be devoid of political and personal messages. The only exception to this is if the actual reason for its general release is to convey a political message.

Whatever else is contained within the rich picture, it should include reference to three roles; the problem-solving group, the client and potential problem-owners together with their relationships.

A generalised picture of these roles and their relationships is illustrated in the upper part of Figure 3.6. This shows an interaction between a problem situation and the activity of problem solving within a problem-solving system. The three roles are illustrated within their respective contexts.

The client is defined as the role that *causes* the interaction to take place between the situation and problem-solving activity. This role (client) provides the finance to enable the interaction to be funded and defines the terms of reference. The problem solver is the role that defines and undertakes the intellectual process leading to the formulation of recommendations and can be an individual or a group of analysts.

The role of problem owner(s) is the individual or group *nominated by the problem solver* to be usefully considered as potential owners of problems and who would provide useful insights into the range of perceptions of the situation that could provide the source of relevant systems. It must be emphasised that these are roles: any one individual could occupy all three roles.

This was the case in a project to be described later (Chapter Six) concerned with the organisation of a governing body for a secondary school in Cumbria. I was the chairman of the Governors and was concerned about the requirements of a governing body that was to take on the responsibility of the management of the school. I decided to use SSM as the intellectual process that would lead to an analysis of these requirements and an eventual structuring of the governing body into management

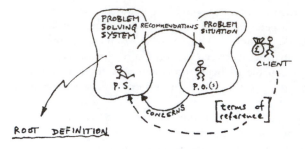

ROOT   DEFINITION

A CLIENT-OWNED SYSTEM, OPERATED BY PROBLEM SOLVERS,
TO MAKE RECOMMENDATIONS TO ALLEVIATE IDENTIFIED
CONCERNS WITHIN A PROBLEM SITUATION TO THE
SATISFACTION OF THE PROBLEM OWNERS, BY USING
APPROPRIATE CONCEPTS AND METHODOLOGIES WITHIN
DEFINED CONSTRAINTS.

CATWOE ANALYSIS

T — TO MAKE RECOMMENDATIONS TO ALLEVIATE
          CONCERNS

W — USING APPROPRIATE CONCEPTS AND
          METHODOLOGIES WILL LEAD TO
          RECOMMENDATIONS

C — PROBLEM OWNERS

O — CLIENT

A — PROBLEM SOLVERS   [may include finance,
E — DEFINED CONSTRAINTS   [terms of reference, time,
                                        etc.

Figure 3.6   *Problem solving/problem content*

groups. Thus I caused the analysis to take place (as the client). I did the analysis (as the problem solver) and it was my concern that drove the analysis (thus I was the problem owner).

This is only the case when you are solving your own problem. In general, different individuals or groups occupy the three roles.

The problem-solving system of Figure 3.6 is a purposeful activity system and can be derived through the mechanism of a root definition. This could be done in relation to any problem situation and be specific to it. Such an analysis is useful in defining the approach to be adopted, the skills and capabilities required in the problem-solving group and the management processes needed in the execution of the problem-solving activity. However, to indicate the kind of analysis a generic problem-solving system can be derived. A root definition is formulated in Figure 3.6 together with its CATWOE analysis. The resultant conceptual model is contained in Figure 3.7.

The top-left activity, 'Understand the nature of the problem situation', is the activity that is aided by the production of the rich picture. This understanding leads to the selection of concepts and methodologies believed to be appropriate. This is completely general and so the concepts could be mathematically based, or based upon any other discipline. Here, of course, we are concerned with concepts and methodologies which are SSM-based.

The essence of this chapter is the transition from the activity 'Understand the nature of the problem situation' to 'Select concepts and methodologies believed to be appropriate'. The rich picture aids the understanding so what is available to aid the selection?

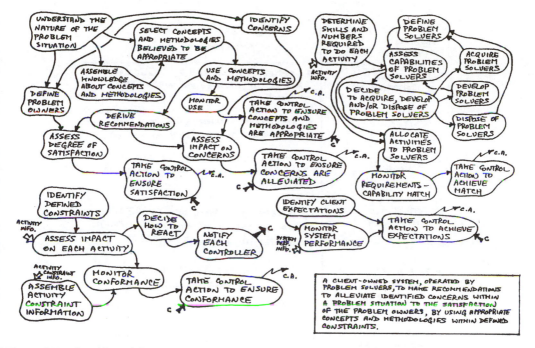

Figure 3.7 *A problem-solving system*

ISSUE-BASED/PRIMARY-TASK SYSTEMS

The distinction between issue-based and primary-task systems has been discussed previously (Checkland 1980; Wilson 1984, 1990) and will not be repeated here. However, a summary of the distinction is provided. As the name suggests, an issue-based system is one used to explore an issue such as a company role exploration system, a decision-making system, etc. It is a characteristic of such systems that should they map onto reality, they are unlikely to be institutionalised through some kind of department or section. Primary-task systems, on the other hand, would be expected to map onto some organisation unit. Thus a system to convert raw material into products (i.e a primary task system) would be expected to map onto a Production Department. The distinction between 'issue-based' and 'primary task', however, is a grey (not precise) one. To make the distinction more positive we could add that issue-based systems have *temporary relevance* whereas primary-task systems have *permanent relevance*.

Thus the problem-solving system of Figure 3.7 is an issue-based system, which is relevant as long as the particular problem-solving activity continues. The root definition that led to this system (Figure 3.6), however, represents the primary tasks of the problem-solving group, though this group, of course, has a temporary existence.

It is useful to make the temporary/permanent relevance distinction in order to initiate thoughts about choices of system following the rich picture assembly. An issue-based system that it is always useful to consider is the problem-solving system, itself, for the particular situation.

Other choices of system come from an identification of potential problem-owners. Taking the analysts to be a problem owner results in the problem-solving system being an initial relevant system. Consideration of other problem owners will lead to other choices of relevant system, which could be either primary task or issue-based.

For the publishing company example in Appendix 2, a series of problem owners could be considered. These are listed in Figure 3.8 together with the names of potentially relevant

POTENTIAL PROBLEM OWNER	CHOICE OF RELEVANT SYSTEM
• PUBLISHING COMPANY	A SYSTEM TO DIVERSIFY JOURNAL RANGE IN ORDER TO INCREASE INCOME.
• EDITOR	A SYSTEM TO MAKE QUALITY PAPERS AVAILABLE TO A WIDE AUDIENCE
• POTENTIAL AUTHOR	A SYSTEM TO PROVIDE ACCESS TO A PEER GROUP IN ORDER TO ENHANCE REPUTATION
• POTENTIAL AUDIENCE	A SYSTEM TO PROVIDE CURRENT 'STATE OF THE ART' SOURCE MATERIAL IN A SPECIFIC AREA OF INTEREST
• POTENTIAL ADVERTISER (MANUFACTURER)	A SYSTEM TO PROVIDE PROMOTIONAL OPPORTUNITIES FOR A RANGE OF ALLIED PRODUCTS
• POTENTIAL ADVERTISER (SERVICE PROVIDER)	A SYSTEM TO ASSEMBLE POTENTIAL CLIENTS IN A RANGE OF AREAS OF EXPERTISE
• ANALYST	A SYSTEM TO USE H.A.S. CONCEPTS WITHIN AN I.R.A.M. IN ORDER TO DERIVE INFORMATION REQUIREMENTS TO SUPPORT THE PRODUCTION OF A NEW TECHNICAL JOURNAL

Figure 3.8   *A publishing company (Appendix 2)*

systems. Note that these are *not* RDs but merely the names of systems that it might be worth considering.

The selection of problem owners and relevant systems must be particular to the specific situation. Examples only can be given to illustrate the process.

Appendix One gives a fairly complex example and describes a situation in which a Managing Director has brought in some SSM consultants to tackle a specific problem. As an example of these initial stages in relation to problem–solving activity let us examine this case. It is based upon a real project but the name and the technology have been changed.

THE ALBION GROUP

The reader is referred to Appendix One in order to read the unstructured case material. Although this book is about conceptual model building to support a soft systems-based analysis of complex organisational situations it is useful to continue the analysis to show how the resultant models were used. In this instance Albion is being used to illustrate the first stages of system selection. However, most analysis requires multiple system selection during the course of a project. Thus some selection may rely on the outcome of preceding analysis.

This case study is therefore taken through to recommendations to illustrate progressive systems choices.

We (as the SSM Consultant, Clark Kent) have received a very specific request from the Albion Group Managing Director (MD) to advise him on a warehouse expansion proposal, supported by relevant correspondence. However, he requires more understanding of the situation and in his second letter he talks about 'assessing the group, with particular reference to improving our overall profitability'.

If we initially take ourselves to be a problem owner we can derive an issue-based system to represent our problem-solving system.

Clearly we have to respond to his request for advice but, given his second letter, not in the context of Surface Stockists but in the context of the Group as a whole and Group profitability. Within this wider context our analysis could lead to suggestions for change to the Albion processes wherever they are located, to changes to information collection and dissemination and even to changes to Group policy

A RD which builds on these ideas is given in Figure 3.9 with an accompanying CM. The CATWOE analysis of the RD is as follows:

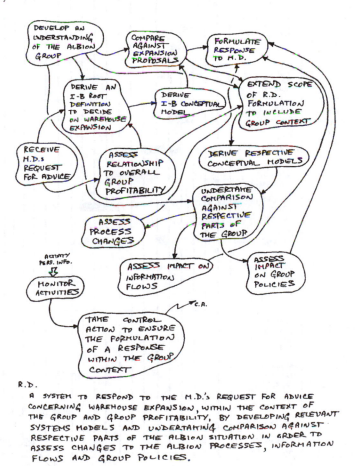

R.D.

A SYSTEM TO RESPOND TO THE M.D.'s REQUEST FOR ADVICE CONCERNING WAREHOUSE EXPANSION, WITHIN THE CONTEXT OF THE GROUP AND GROUP PROFITABILITY, BY DEVELOPING RELEVANT SYSTEMS MODELS AND UNDERTAKING COMPARISON AGAINST RESPECTIVE PARTS OF THE ALBION SITUATION IN ORDER TO ASSESS CHANGES TO THE ALBION PROCESSES, INFORMATION FLOWS AND GROUP POLICIES.

Figure 3.9 *Albion Group problem-solving system*

T—to respond to the MD's request
W—developing relevant models and undertaking comparison within the context of the Group and
    Group profitability *will* provide advice to respond to the MD's request
C—MD
A—not specified
O—not specified
E—not specified

The model represents the intellectual process that we could adopt to tackle the Albion project. Thus
we need to *do* each activity. If time was a constraint (which would be usual) we would need to
convert the intellectual process of Figure 3.9 into a schedule.

A possible schedule, assuming five time periods, is given in Figure 3.10. The monitor and
control activities in the conceptual model of Figure 3.9 represent the project management task.

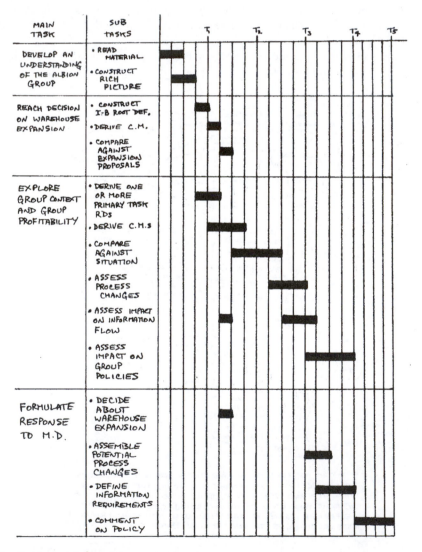

Figure 3.10   *Problem-solving schedule*

These are on-going activities for the duration of the project and hence do not appear in the schedule.

The activity performance information that the project control role requires (through the monitor activity) will include the quality of the deliverable produced by each activity (subtask), the degree to which the time taken adheres to the schedule and the resources consumed. This last measure (efficiency) would be particularly significant if cost was also a constraint.

Thus, taking each time period to be one hour, three quarters of an hour has been allocated to developing an understanding through reading and rich picture construction. This means that the degree of detail used in the picture cannot be excessive.

Figures 3.11 to 3.13 represent the construction of a picture within this time scale. It starts at the macro level (Figure 3.11) and, through progressive elaboration, the picture represented by Figure 3.13 was derived and used.

This picture is at a macro level and contains broad indications that more detailed data exist (which we can access if there is a need to know them). Further detail can be explored as the need to do so is generated by the analysis, in particular, the comparison.

It is always the case, when contemplating potential problem owners, to consider the client as a significant choice. That choice had already been made in deriving the RD for the problem-solving system and, in this case, it leads directly to the choice of an initial relevant system. It can be argued to be relevant since it is directly related to our terms of reference. This is another issue-based system to reach a decision about whether or not to expand the Surface Stockists warehouse.

The RD taken is as follows:

A managing director-owned system to decide whether or not to expand the Surface Stockists warehouse based upon the implications of this decision for the group as a whole.

The CATWOE analysis is:

T—to decide whether or not to expand the Surface Stockists warehouse
W—basing the decision on group implications *will* lead to a decision in line with the MD's expectations
C—not specified
A—not specified

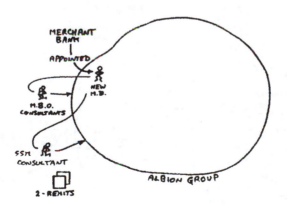

PROBLEM SITUATION EXPRESSED (1.)

Figure 3.11 *Relationships external to the MD*

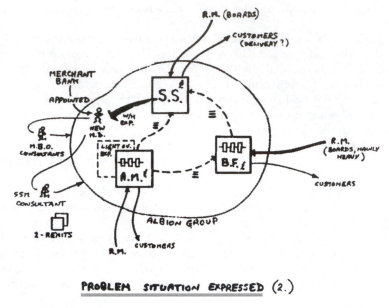

PROBLEM SITUATION EXPRESSED (2.)

Figure 3.12   *Internal/external group relationships*

O—MD
E—not specified

The conceptual model derived from this RD is contained in Figure 3.14.

The part of the real world relevant to the comparison of this model is the proposals for expansion (since this is what the MD was expected to base his decision on). Thus a simple comparison table can be constructed. See Figure 3.15.

The comparison tells us that considerable deficiencies exist in the support material for the proposed expansion and therefore the only recommendation to the MD, at this stage, is not to

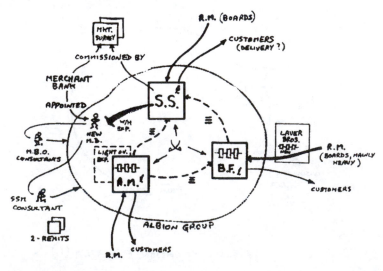

Figure 3.13   *Problem situation expressed*

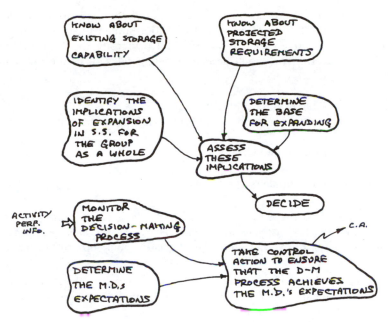

Figure 3.14 *Decision-making system*

make a decision until the information lacking is provided. We could specify the information requirements now but the schedule of Figure 3.10 delays this until time period 3, i.e. when we have completed further analysis. Thus the question arises as to what analysis to undertake.

The conceptual model of Figure 3.9 (our problem-solving system) and the schedule of Figure 3.10 require us to increase the scope of the investigation to assess group and group profitability aspects. Thus who could we take to be potential problem owners? The stockists' manager would be

ACTIVITY	COMMENTS ABOUT PROPOSALS
• KNOW ABOUT EXISTING STORAGE CAPABILITY	NO INFORMATION IS GIVEN ABOUT WHAT IS STORED NOW, HOW, STOCK TURNOVER RATE ETC.
• KNOW ABOUT PROJECTED STORAGE REQUIREMENTS	NO INFORMATION IS GIVEN ABOUT MARKET TRENDS OR FUTURE DEMAND PATTERNS
• DETERMINE THE BASE FOR EXPANDING (i.e. COSTS AND POTENTIAL RETURNS)	SOME COSTS ARE GIVEN RELATED TO ALTERNATIVE SCHEMES BUT GIVEN THE LACK OF THE ABOVE INFORMATION NO ESTIMATE OF POTENTIAL RETURNS CAN BE MADE
• IDENTIFY THE IMPLICATIONS OF EXPANSION FOR THE GROUP	NO RELATING OF STORAGE AT SURFACE STOCKISTS TO THE ACTIVITIES OF THE OTHER TWO MEMBERS OF THE GROUP HAS BEEN DONE
• ASSESS THESE IMPLICATIONS	WITHOUT THE PREVIOUS ACTIVITIES THIS CANNOT BE DONE
• DECIDE	GIVEN THE ABOVE DEFICIENCIES THERE IS LITTLE TO BASE THE DECISION ON.

Figure 3.15 *Comparison table*

an obvious choice given that it was his request for warehouse expansion that led to the SSM consultancy intervention. However, this would lead to a limited focus on Surface Stockists and not the group. As an alternative we could take the MD again to be the problem owner but with a group profitability concern. This would lead to a system relevant to the following CATWOE analysis:

T—to transform raw materials into finished boards
W—transforming raw materials into finished boards can lead to increasingly profitable sales
C—customers
A—component parts of the Albion Group
O—Tyzacks
E—competition from other suppliers

> *A Tyzacks-owned system, operated by the component parts of the Albion Group, to transform raw materials into finished boards of various grades in order to achieve increasingly profitable sales to customers while recognising the competition from other suppliers.* (Note: 'Finished' boards includes both 'surfaced' and 'unsurfaced'.)

This is a primary-task RD which would be expected to map onto the group as a whole. Thus it would take us into the maximum complexity of analysis immediately but would ignore our *actual* terms of reference, i.e. the advice on warehouse expansion.

This, of course, is modified by the MD's second letter, but we could interpret his concern here as one to do with the impact of the request on 'storage' within the group as a whole. Hence a system which examines the reason for storage might be a useful choice and would serve as a link between the specific warehouse expansion request and improvements to group profitability. All three parts of the Group supply customers and hence it could be useful to take the actual customers (internal and external) to be the problem owner.

If we take the reason for storage to be a mismatch between supply and demand we could construct the following RD:

> *An Albion Group-owned board transfer system to match the supply of finished board to both long- and short-term demand at a continuing level of service that is acceptable to customers, in relation to other sources of supply and with a performance that is beneficial to the group.* (Note: 'Finished' board has the same interpretation as in the previous RD.)

The inclusion of the term 'board transfer' limits the scope of the system to exclude the board production processes. This is a primary-task model which can be mapped onto the real world of the Albion Group.

T—to match the supply of finished board to demand
W—matching supply to demand at an acceptable level of service will lead to benefit to the group
C—customers
A—not specified
O—Albion group
E—not specified

The concepual model that results from this RD is given in Figure 3.16.

One of the major features of the real world which impacts upon the comparison with a primary-task model is that some form of structure always exists. Within a conceptual model the only structure is one based upon logic. Thus a comparison will yield comments about the real-world structure that may turn out to be problematic and part of the major findings from the analysis.

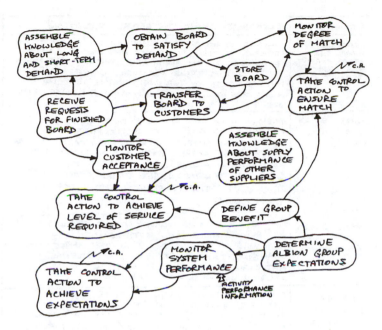

Figure 3.16 *A board transfer system*

In the case of the Albion Group not only is there an organisational structure within each element but the Group as a whole is geographically structured. Thus for comparison at the level of the Group it is the geographical structure that is taken to be of initial concern.

The conceptual model describes the processes (activities) that must go on to achieve some defined purpose (defined by the RD), irrespective of how and where they take place. It is in the comparison that these features become important. Thus, for Albion, the comparison could be of the form of Table 3.1.

Although not as explicit as this, the comparison tables of Figures 3.17(a) and 3.17(b) still recognise the real-world structure at the Group level.

These comparison tables lead to the following major conclusions:

(1) Material flow control both within and external to the Group has a number of deficiencies as indicated within the table.
(2) The base for Group contribution calculation needs to be chosen so that the heavy gauge becomes preferential. This will aid the flow control requirements in (1) above and help to move all Group members towards the future trend in demand.

Table 3.1 *Comparison table*

| Conceptual model | | | | Real world |
Activity	AM	BF	SJ	Consequences of separation
Identify customer demand	Believe it to be light gauge expanding light ovens	?	Market survey shows heavy gauge on increase	Inconsistency in view of future demand
Obtain board to satisfy demand	Pulp is output	No problems with light gauge, heavy gauge obtained from Laver	Problems with heavy gauge	Future problems will exist if supply internally is not sorted

ACTIVITY	COMMENTS ABOUT THE ACTUAL SITUATION
ASSEMBLE KNOWLEDGE ABOUT LONG AND SHORT-TERM DEMANDS	SURFACE STOCKISTS ARE AWARE OF THE FORECAST DEMAND PATTERN, IT IS NOT APPARENT THAT THE REMAINDER OF THE GROUP ARE. THE FORECAST SHOWS AN INCREASING TREND FOR HEAVY GAUGE AND A DECREASING TREND FOR LIGHT GAUGE YET ALBION MILLS ARE CONSIDERING EXPANSION FOR LIGHT GAUGE OVENS
OBTAIN BOARD TO SATISFY DEMAND	ALBION MILLS DO NOT DO THIS; THEIR RAW MATERIAL IS PULP. BOTH BETTERFINISH AND SURFACE STOCKISTS HAVE DIFFICULTY IN OBTAINING HEAVY GAUGE BOARD. BOTH ALBION MILLS AND BETTERFINISH ARE RELUCTANT TO SUPPLY HEAVY GAUGE. BETTERFINISH GET THEIRS FROM LAVER BROS. GIVEN THE FORECASTS THIS SITUATION MUST CHANGE.
STORE BOARD.	NOTHING IS KNOWN ABOUT STORING FACILITIES AT ALBION MILLS AND BETTERFINISH. NO ANALYSIS HAS BEEN DONE ON THE EFFECT OF CHANGING DEMAND PATTERN ON INTERNAL MATERIAL FLOW. THIS IS CRITICAL TO THE DECISION ON WAREHOUSE EXPANSION.
TRANSFER BOARD TO CUSTOMERS	COMPLAINTS HAVE BEEN RECEIVED ABOUT DELIVERY PERFORMANCE IN RELATION TO HEAVY GAUGE (SEE N.B.35) AND THERE ARE LONG LEAD TIMES WITH INTERNAL SUPPLY (N.B.32). THE NEED FOR IMPROVED DELIVERY PERFORMANCE IS RECOGNISED BY SURFACE STOCKISTS (N.S.11) BUT GIVEN PRESENT ATTITUDES TO HEAVY GAUGE LITTLE IS BEING DONE
RECEIVE REQUESTS FOR FINISHED BOARD	INTERNAL ORDERING IS PROBLEMATICAL. THERE ARE DIFFICULTIES WITH SMALL ORDERS PLACED ON BETTERFINISH (N.B.32) AND AN ARBITRARY ORDERING PROCEDURE AT SURFACE STOCKISTS. (N.S.34)
MONITOR CUSTOMER ACCEPTANCE	SURFACE STOCKISTS SEEM CONCERNED ABOUT CUSTOMER SATISFACTION (N.S.11) AND HAVE EMPLOYED CONSULTANTS TO DO THE ASSESSMENT. THERE IS NO EVIDENCE THAT THE OTHER MEMBERS OF THE GROUP TAKE THIS SERIOUSLY

Figure 3.17 *(a) Comparison table*

(3) Storage requirements are secondary to material flow control and are determined by it.
(4) Autonomy within the Group appears to be exacerbating the material flow problems, and the policy of 'internal competition is good for us' needs questioning.

The next stage in the analysis of Albion, with reference to the schedule in Figure 3.10, is to assess the impact of the analysis so far on information requirements.

In relation to the analysis of the decision on warehouse expansion, the information requirements are essentially things to find out. Since this was the result of the issue-based analysis and therefore of temporary relevance, there would not be a requirement for on-going information systems design.

The information deficiencies are therefore:

- Current state of storage and patterns of use
- Future storage requirements
- Costs and potential returns
- Inter-company storage (capacity and requirements)

ACTIVITY	COMMENTS ABOUT THE ACTUAL SITUATION
ASSEMBLE KNOWLEDGE ABOUT SUPPLY PERFORMANCE OF OTHER SUPPLIERS	THERE IS NO EVIDENCE THAT ANY MEMBERS OF THE GROUP DO THIS AS AN ON-GOING ACTIVITY.
DEFINE GROUP BENEFIT	THIS IS NOT DONE IN RELATION TO THE GROUP AS A WHOLE. CONTRIBUTION ASSESSMENT IS DONE BY EACH GROUP MEMBER, BUT AS THIS IS RELATED TO DIFFERENT BASES (i.e. per board, or per cu. ft.) THEY ARE NOT COMPARABLE. DEPENDENT UPON THE BASE CHOSEN AND ON HOW OVERHEADS ARE ALLOCATED, HEAVY GAUGE COULD BE EITHER THE HIGHEST OR THE LOWEST CONTRIBUTOR
MONITOR DEGREE OF MATCH TAKE CONTROL ACTION TO ENSURE MATCH TAKE CONTROL ACTION TO ACHIEVE LEVEL OF SERVICE REQUIRED MONITOR SYSTEM PERFORMANCE DETERMINE ALBION GROUP EXPECTATIONS TAKE CONTROL ACTION TO ACHIEVE EXPECTATIONS	BECAUSE OF THE AUTONOMOUS NATURE OF THE GROUP THESE ACTIVITIES ARE NOT DONE IN ANY CONSISTENT WAY.

Figure 3.17 *(b) Continued*

The outcome of the primary-task analysis will lead to a requirement for on-going information support. These will be classified as inter-company support (to ensure consistency of within-company information) and external information. Thus information will need to be provided on:

- Market demand (inter-company and external)
- Delivery performance (inter-company)
- Contribution (inter-company)
- Customer response (external)
- Competition intelligence (external)

The analysis of the board transfer system also led to a questioning of the current Group policy on individual member autonomy. This was anticipated in the problem-solving system and remains to be examined.

The significance of this aspect of Group policy can be examined by conceptualising two systems with opposing Ws, to map onto the Group as a whole. As an illustration we can take two simple systems as defined by the following two RDs:

RD1   *An Albion Group-owned system to supply finished boards to both internal and external customers in order to generate adequate Group profits by enabling each organisation unit to collaborate effectively.*

  T—to supply finished boards
  W—collaborating effectively will lead to adequate profits
  C—internal and external customers
  A—not specified
  O—Albion Group
  E—not specified

RD2   *An Albion Group-owned system to supply finished boards to both internal and external customers in order to generate adequate Group profits by allowing each organisation unit to compete against the remaining units.*

  T—to supply finished boards
  W—allowing competition among the organisational units will generate adequate profits
  C—internal and external customers
  A—not specified
  O—Albion Group
  E—not specified

The respective conceptual models are given in Figures 3.18 and 3.19.

Although the Albion Group case material (Appendix One) states that 'internal competition is good for us' and the word 'competition' has been included in RD2 it is not clear how it should be interpreted. Since Albion Mills, Betterfinish and Surface Stockists do not perform the same operations they are not *alternative* suppliers to the market. It is only Albion Mills who convert pulp to board; it is only Betterfinish that produces surfaced board and without these two Surface Stockists would have to get its board from external suppliers. This competition can only be interpreted as

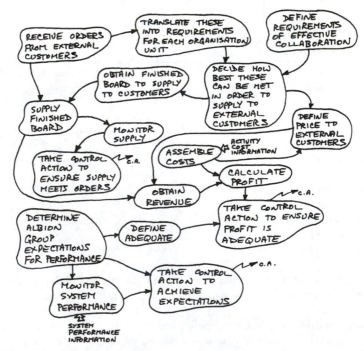

Figure 3.18   *Collaborative operation*

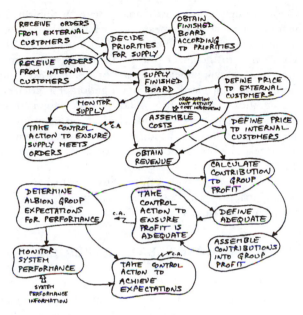

Figure 3.19   *Competitive operation*

freedom to set prices and freedom to decide whom to supply. Thus in the conceptual model for competitive operation (Figure 3.19) this is the reason for the activities 'Decide priorities for supply' and 'Define price to internal customers'.

The two models could be compared as a means of questioning current Group policy, but the only two conclusions that can be reached are:

(1) With collaborative operation, internal customer orders are determined in order to meet the total external supply needs; whereas with competitive operation they are determined independently by each organisation unit to meet only their own external customer needs.

(2) Given that both internal and external prices are independently fixed with competitive operation it is difficult to see how the Group profit controller (whoever that might be, but probably the MD) can affect the contribution of each organisational unit. This represents a control (authority) inconsistency in competitive operation. Thus Group profit is whatever they end up with having assembled individual contributions rather than something that can be centrally controlled to be adequate.

The new MD should seek to reduce the degree of autonomy by making price definition a Group concern and by instituting the base for contribution calculation to be consistent across the Group and that which makes heavy gauge the most profitable.

The two conceptual models could be converted into a simulation model and the two modes of operation evaluated using current demand, price and cost data.

However, in the real 'real world' (i.e. if Albion was an actual group and not a case study) it is likely that change to policy, particularly that which is history based, would turn out to be very difficult. Culture, entrenched attitudes, etc. would make change of this kind long rather than short term.

Formulating a response to the MD therefore would emphasise the product flow problems and the changes suggested. It would place the warehouse expansion decision to a lower priority and the comments about current policy would be integrated into the statements about authority requirements to bring about Albion Group product flow management. Within this analysis there has been a progressive development in system scope as a means of expanding the context of the investigation.

It would have been possible to have chosen the overall Group-oriented RD but, in my view, this would have been less convincing to the client (the MD). The systems chosen can be argued to represent a logical extension, i.e. warehouse expansion (storage) leads to material flow control (of which storage is a significant part) which leads to an investigation of internal competition (of which material flow control is a significant consideration). Thus the development of the analysis can be argued to stem from the initial terms of reference guided by the comments in the MD's second letter.

The example illustrates the significance of including yourself (as problem solver) within the rich picture together with your relationship to the client. Not only does this clarify your terms of reference (remit), and hence help in the interpretation of 'relevant', it also limits or extends the scope of the analysis. Clearly, if our client had been the Stockists manager, concerns at the Group level would have been totally inappropriate. Since the client was the MD, he has the authority to take action on any of our recommendations.

LESSONS FROM ALBION EXPERIENCE

The Albion case has been used extensively as a case study, both within the MSc course at Lancaster and within short in-house courses for a number of companies. It has proved to be a rich learning experience. It is worth quoting a few examples as a means of extending the 'RD – CATWOE' pitfalls at the end of Chapter Two.

Example 1. A RD was quoted as: '*A system to seek to satisfy market demand* . . . .' The conceptual model had in it activities concerned with producing and delivering a product. This was inappropriate modelling since to deliver a product customers are required. The RD was in terms of *the market*, not customers.

Seeking to satisfy a market must be about ensuring that a capability exists so that the system can supply what the market wants if called upon to do so (by actual customers). Actually doing the supplying is a different system.

Example 2. On one occasion a complex RD was produced along with the CATWOE analysis. These are as follows:

> *A shareholder-owned system, managed by a newly appointed MD 'who is recruited to maximise growth and profitability' of a Group 'that consists of three autonomous companies that import raw materials to produce and distribute prefabricated boards to meet market needs' whilst recognising time and resource constraints.* (Note: inverted commas have been added: they were not in the original RD.)

> C—shareholders and customers of Albion Group
> A—MD of the Group and employees
> T—maximising profit and growth of the company
> W—the Group can only survive in a competitive market if it is profitable
> O—shareholders
> E—time, resources, customer needs

First, the RD, as written, is not a RD. It is more a *description* of the situation. The first set of inverted commas contains a description of the MD and the second set a description of the Group. Thus we are told what the MD does and what the Group does but we are not told what *the system does*. Hence there is no transformation process. In the CATWOE analysis the T quoted is a definition of the responsibility of the MD. The W might well be a reasonable belief but not one contained in the RD. There is nothing about survival or about competitors. Since there is no T there cannot be any customers (C). In any case, 'shareholders' are only mentioned as 'owner' and 'customers' do not get a mention at all.

Actors are only included in the RD in the phrase 'managed by a newly appointed MD'; 'employees' do not appear and finally, with reference to the E, 'customer needs' do not appear in the RD as constraints.

This RD and CATWOE analysis is a good example of the difficulty of translating a concept in the head into an explicit and defensible written statement. It is probable that neither the RD not the CATWOE elements quite represented what the student had in mind and hence the lack of consistency was not apparent.

Example 3

A solution-oriented RD and CM are generally not useful. The RD chosen as an example began:

> A system to remove the competitive internal market throughout Albion Group by introducing a change programme.

Since, in the current situation, Albion are not introducing a change programme there will be nothing to compare the resultant conceptual model against. Hence nothing will be learnt about the situation. In general, during an investigation of a problematic situation, a solution–oriented RD has already made an assumption about 'the problem'. It is only useful to develop RDs and models of this kind if the investigation has already been undertaken and implementation of a desired change has been identified.

Example 4

Don't be casual about the way words are expressed even though they are precise. *A system to produce recommendations to improve profitability* ... is not the same as: *a system to improve profitability*.

Example 5. Maintain consistency in choice of words

During the construction of a conceptual model and the preceding RD the verb used to describe the transformation changed as its use went from RD to CATWOE to CM. The verb 'convert' in the RD became 'assemble' in CATWOE and 'produce' in the associated part of the CM.

The student may have interpreted the three words in the same way but there are subtle differences in meaning. Using the same word throughout will avoid possible misinterpretation.

Example 6. Avoid ambiguity in the structure of the RD

A student began a RD in the following way: *A manager-run system staffed by SS personnel* ... It is probable that the use of the word 'staffed' indicated Actor but the word 'run' could be either Owner or Actor. This ambiguity makes modelling difficult. On the other hand, 'A manager-*owned* system, *operated* by SS personnel* ... is not ambiguous'.

Example 7. As a final illustration, in a RD don't use 'e.g.' as a means of elaborating some of the words. 'RD ... while operating under constraints (e.g. time, money)'. It immediately raises the question, if these are examples then what else is there? It is essential that the RD should be specific.

SERVING SYSTEMS/SYSTEM SERVED

The Albion example has served to illustrate the use of the distinction between issue-based and primary-task systems in making the choice of those systems taken to be relevant. There is a further distinction that is useful to consider whether the nature of the problem-solving task is related to a certain class of concerns. These concerns can be described broadly as those related to service, or support provision.

Thus, information provision, training, manpower planning, general resource planning are examples of service, or support, provision. None of these are an end in themselves, they are all required to

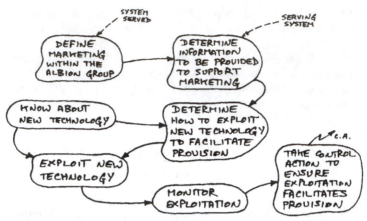

Figure 3.20   *Marketing information support*

enable other activity to take place. If this is the nature of the analysis to be undertaken the choice of relevant system becomes very clear.

The choice is based upon the following rule:

If the concern is with a service system always conceptualise the system served.

Suppose that we are required to determine the information systems needed to support marketing activity in the Albion Group. We might take the relevant system to be:

A system to facilitate information provision to support marketing within the Albion Group by exploiting new technology.

T—to facilitate information provision
W—exploiting new technology will facilitate information provision
C—marketing (personnel)
A—not specified
O—not specified
E—not specified

This is a rather sparse definition but it will serve to illustrate the need for the above rule.

The conceptual model in Figure 3.20 can be defended in terms of its logical relationship to the words of the RD. However, it is not very useful.

The information needed to support marketing is *dependent* upon the definition of what *marketing within the Albion Group is taken to be*. Thus we cannot elaborate this model any further until the definition of marketing is produced. Once this is known 'the information to be provided' can be determined. The top two activities in Figure 3.20 represent this relationship and, as illustrated, the 'serving system' is logically dependent upon the 'system served'. Thus the 'system served' must be produced first.

Clearly, there will be as many service systems as there are systems served. Therefore, if our concern is for a single service, like information support to a single organisation unit, we need to derive a single description of the system served. This provides us with a fundamental problem since, if we accept that W is an important variable in all organisational analysis, how do we take W seriously and still produce a single model? The answer to this question is the subject of Chapter Five.

Chapter Four

Business Process Re-engineering

INTRODUCTION

The world of business analysis is full of what are colloquially called buzzwords/phrases. 'The bottom line', 'competitive edge', 'base lining', 'downsizing' and 'refocusing' are a few examples. These vary from being precise and well understood to being woolly and capable of multiple interpretations. The same applies to the processes of business analysis. In some cases the process is never declared and remains in the heads of the analysts and in other cases it is explicit and well specified.

I believe that SSM should lie at the latter end of the above spectrum and it is that belief that has led to the production of this book.

In the body of this spectrum are a few examples of processes that are capable of multiple interpretation. 'Management by objectives' is a reasonably well-specified process but its application varies. Within the military, 'Joint Battlespace Digitisation' is neither well specified nor is its application understood with any degree of consistency. 'Business Process Re-engineering' tends to the latter of these two examples.

Business Process Re-engineering (BPR) is a term originally coined by an American consultancy company and it is generally accepted that the motivation behind the initiative was to sell more technology. Given this emphasis, it generally failed and was discredited. The following three reasons probably account for the majority of failures:

- The expectations were unrealistic.
- The whole approach was technology driven.
- Cultural issues were ignored.

Although there are some glowing success stories, it is generally the case (particularly in non-hi-tech organisations) that a technology-driven approach will ignore cultural issues and will, inevitably, meet with resistance to change.

It was believed (and senior executives were frequently convinced by consultants) that the advances in new technology could provide opportunities for radical change in the business not previously feasible, which would lead to major step changes in performance, particularly in profit and competitiveness. This was intended to be revolutionary, not incremental change.

The concept of radical change is not a bad idea. It can lead to fundamental examination of a business in terms of a reappraisal of business processes in relation to some future vision, but the degree of change will be that which is culturally feasible not that which the technology demands.

A more practical approach to BPR is hence called for, but what is it?

WHAT IS BPR?

If we are to adopt an approach to fundamental business analysis which is realistic then a definition of BPR which incorporates this view could be:

> BPR is the *realisation* of radical change to current business processes, as a means of improving overall *business performance* using proven new technology if appropriate.

This is my definition and the emphases are intended to clarify the orientation of the particular viewpoint taken. The application of new technology is not excluded, but it needs to be developed not developing and it needs to be secondary to the business intentions. The use of the word 'realisation' is intended to convey that, whatever the radical change is, it is capable of implementation and is hence culturally feasible.

Also 'business performance' need not necessarily be expressed in profit terms. A refocusing of long-term business aims may lead to diversification, or a customer orientation resulting in a more stable market position. In the long term this would have profit and/or cost implications but they may not be immediate factors in the relevant performance assessment. Flexibility and responsiveness to government initiatives may also be seen as appropriate performance measures in relation to the public sector. Whatever is seen to be an appropriate interpretation of business performance, it needs to be articulated at the start of a BPR study. Although the above definition is helpful it is not a complete answer to the question, what is BPR?

BPR is sometimes interpreted as Business Process Redesign as well as Business Process Re-engineering, but what is the difference? In order to avoid confusion, a distinction between them can be arrived at by considering the distinction between *What* a business process is and *How* it is done.

We can take Business Process Redesign to be concerned with the identification of alternative ways (hows) of doing the business processes (whats). The business processes are taken as given (i.e. current business processes) and the changes are essentially in terms of efficiency improvement.

Given the above interpretation, Business Process Re-engineering, on the other hand, can be taken to be a more fundamental reappraisal, concerned with exploring new business processes (whats) as well as identifying different ways of doing them (hows). The changes which result from this kind of investigation are improvements in effectiveness as well as in efficiency.

The former interpretation of BPR can start by identifying current business processes but the latter interpretation *must* start from an identification of future vision, mission, aims, etc. New business processes can only be derived from views about where the business wants to be, not from where it is now. Unfortunately a considerable amount of effort, time and cost can be incurred by deriving a detailed account of current business processes even when fundamental change is envisaged. A large initial interview task is embarked upon to produce this account which *achieves little more than educating the analyst*. What is required is much more modest interviewing to determining future business orientation.

In the Preamble to this book the point was made that all organisations (of whatever scale) are in transition. The current state is always undergoing change. This implies that the only defensible starting point for a BPR analysis is a definition of potential futures. This must be plural since uncertainty exists as to where an organisation will actually develop and hence a number of *potential* futures must be contemplated.

Although this represents an ideal view it is usually the case that if an organisation can be persuaded to think about its future it will, at best, contemplate a *single* desirable future rather than a set. This may be the best that can be achieved but it represents progress in the organisation's thinking.

Nevertheless, approaches to a BPR study can and do start from questioning the current situation.

BROAD APPROACHES TO BPR

There are basically two approaches to a BPR study: *bottom up* and *top down*. These can be sum-marised as in Figure 4.1.

Here the stages within each approach are designated with a ■, the bullets represent comments about each stage and on the right beyond the arrows, are the stage deliverables.

As already described, the bottom–up approach starts from where the business is now and leaves somewhat arbitrary (and piecemeal) the changes from the current situation. In this case a model to represent the business is constructed (a) by interviewing relevant personnel and (b) by assembling the descriptions of activity so obtained into an overall model of the business.

Irrespective of the modelling language used, this approach has three major drawbacks.

(1) Those interviewed will describe what they do on the basis of *their own interpretation of* their role in the organisation.
(2) The level of detail (resolution) at which these descriptions are made will be undefined and probably mixed. This is problematical since the distinction between a 'what' and a 'how' can only be described in relation to a specific resolution level.

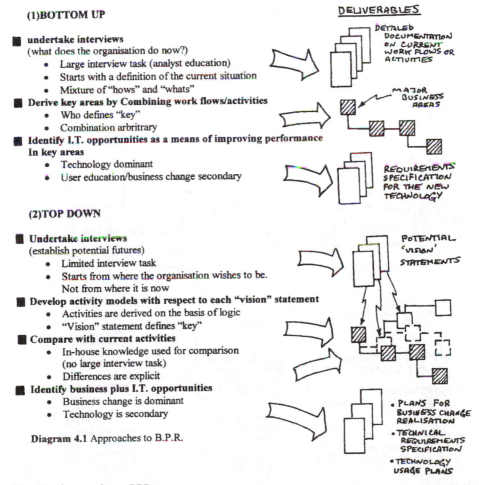

(1)BOTTOM UP

DELIVERABLES

■ **undertake interviews**
(what does the organisation do now?)
• Large interview task (analyst education)
• Starts with a definition of the current situation
• Mixture of "hows" and "whats"

DETALED DOCUMENTATION ON CURRENT WORK FLOWS OR ACTIVITIES

■ **Derive key areas by Combining work flows/activities**
• Who defines "key"
• Combination arbritrary

MAJOR BUSINESS AREAS

■ **Identify I.T. opportunities as a means of improving performance
In key areas**
• Technology dominant
• User education/business change secondary

REQUIREMENTS SPECIFICATION FOR THE NEW TECHNOLOGY

(2)TOP DOWN

■ **Undertake interviews**
(establish potential futures)
• Limited interview task
• Starts from where the organisation wishes to be. Not from where it is now

POTENTIAL 'VISION' STATEMENTS

■ **Develop activity models with respect to each "vision" statement**
• Activities are derived on the basis of logic
• "Vision" statement defines "key"

■ **Compare with current activities**
• In-house knowledge used for comparison (no large interview task)
• Differences are explicit

■ **Identify business plus I.T. opportunities**
• Business change is dominant
• Technology is secondary

• PLANS FOR BUSINESS CHANGE REALISATION
• TECHNICAL REQUIREMENTS SPECIFICATION
• TECHNOLOGY USAGE PLANS

Diagram 4.1 Approaches to B.P.R.

Figure 4.1 *Broad approaches to BPR*

(3) How these different interpretations are assembled into an overall model is not clear and hence the resultant model may be a mixture of 'whats' and 'hows'. The resultant model will also be quite detailed, to incorporate the information obtained by interviewing, and may lead to an incoherent comparison of current practices unless the what/how distinction is rigorously maintained.

Once the description of current business processes has been assembled, the major problem is to identify what changes to introduce. Knowing where the business is now provides little guidance on where the business wants to be. It may be a complete waste of resources to improve a current process where a more effective solution would be to introduce a completely new one.

The top-down approach addresses the crucial question of where the business wants to be as the first concern.

A strategic review is undertaken to explore the practicalities of future vision statements (or mission statements) in order to identify those business processes that need to be in place and which are culturally feasible. A comparison of these against what currently exists is driven by the business processes themselves. Thus large-scale questioning of the current situation is avoided in deciding the changes to be introduced. This is a much more efficient and rapid approach and makes use of the in-house knowledge about current processes to identify the changes to be adopted. The approach is summarised in Figure 4.2.

This second approach deliberately seeks to question 'what is being done' (as well as how) in the belief that major improvements in business performance can be obtained from such a fundamental reappraisal. The problem here is to decide what to take as given. If a 'mission statement', 'role statement' or future vision is the starting point, it is usually the case that they are stated in such broad terms that a number of interpretations of their meaning (perceptions) is possible.

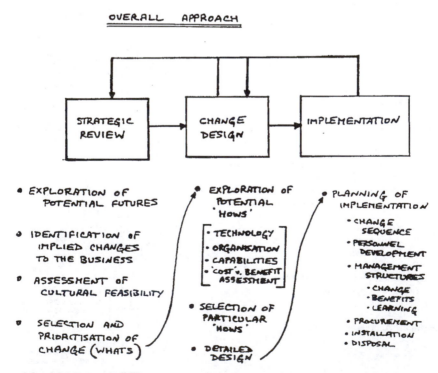

Figure 4.2   *Major stages in BPR*

Thus a major problem is how to develop a model that represents an agreed view as to what the business is all about which caters for these multiple perceptions. It may also be the case that a number of potential future business scenarios need to be investigated in order to explore the impact of implied degrees of change on the current situation. All these considerations require a statement of business purpose which can incorporate the multiple perceptions referred to above. Such a statement (and the resulting model of what the business has to do to achieve that purpose) is unique to the particular organisation concerned since it is totally dependent upon the 'perceptions of purpose' of the managers responsible for the strategic direction of the business.

Take the extreme example discussed earlier. If the business of concern is a prison, the question 'what is a prison for?' is not easy to answer. It could be:

(a) to punish offenders
(b) to rehabilitate offenders
(c) to control interaction between offenders and the community (a security perception) etc.

The immediate reaction, of course, is that a prison isn't any one of these but that it is a mixture of all of them, and other views. This is the case, but a trip round a number of prisons soon indicates that nobody (governors, visitors, chaplains, etc.) agrees on what the mixture is. Some prisons operate a hard regime which indicates a punishment orientation while, at the other extreme, some operate a very soft regime with an orientation to education and rehabilitation.

Although the degrees of emphasis may be more subtle than in the above extreme example, the same problem of multiple perceptions exists in all businesses.

Since the model of (whatever kind) is the basis on which the processes are re-engineered, it is of crucial importance.

PROCESS RE-ENGINEERING—A BUILDING SOCIETY

As an example of the application of a top-down approach suppose that a RD relevant to the future vision of a building society is:

> *An XYZ building society-owned system to provide a readily accessible service to customers, using other agencies, if appropriate, to support home transfer so that a balance can be achieved between customer satisfaction and a financial return to the society while recognising alternative services provided by the competition and the constraints arising from relevant legislation and the building society's policy.*

This states what the system is and, using the principles expounded in Chapter Two, a model can be derived using logic only which describes what the system must do. This is reproduced as Figure 4.3.

Although in a full study a number of such definitions would be taken leading to a corresponding number of models, as an illustration of the application, assume that Figure 4.3, is a legitimate member of this portfolio of potential futures. Hence, the model can be used to assess 'what' the society actually does and 'how' it does it. Two boundaries are mapped onto this model. The dashed boundary indicates potential new business processes whose desirability could be assessed via an investigation of how to do them and the potential business benefit that would arise. The full boundary describes existing processes. The assessment of these processes is done via tabular comparison illustrated by Figure 4.4.

Column 1 lists the activities from the model which are used to question the business under review. Columns 2, 3 and 4 are questioning if the activity is done, if so who does it (an organisational role, not necessarily a person) and the current mechanism. Column 5 makes explicit the criteria used to decide whether the current mechanism (how) is good or bad. Column 6 records the

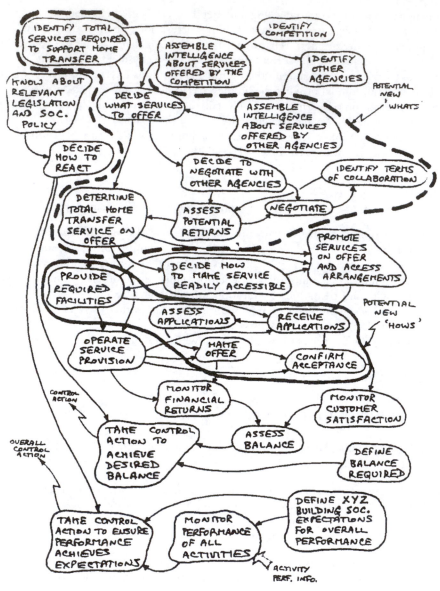

Figure 4.3   *Building society—conceptual model*

judgement and if there is scope for improvement. The criteria can be used to direct the change. Column 7 records the suggested change or changes if alternatives are feasible. The final column records arguments for change and cost/benefit assessment in financial, social or other terms.

  Given the model of Figure 4.3 part of an assessment is shown in Figure 4.5. In an actual study all activities would be considered, but for illustration only consider the activities within the full boundary. In this assessment all the 'whats' exist and therefore only changes of 'how' are considered. The table points the way to the kind of changes to be made and to those areas in which it would be beneficial to do a more detailed analysis. Column 8 has only been partially completed as there would obviously be social and policy issues raised by the changes identified. This example was part of a total BRR study for a building society and is used to illustrate the approach.

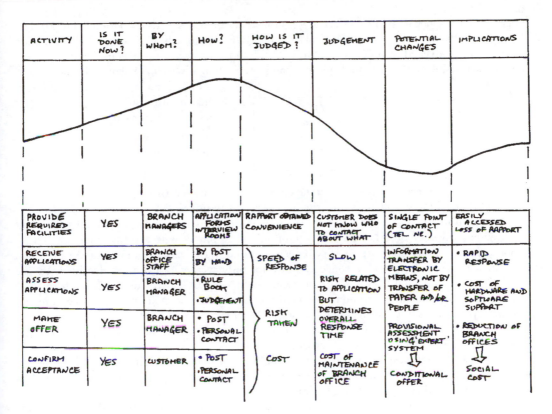

ACTIVITY	IS IT DONE NOW?	BY WHOM?	HOW?	HOW IS IT JUDGED?	JUDGEMENT	POTENTIAL CHANGES	IMPLICATIONS
PROVIDE REQUIRED FACILITIES	YES	BRANCH MANAGERS	APPLICATION FORMS INTERVIEW ROOMS	RAPPORT OBTAINED CONVENIENCE	CUSTOMER DOES NOT KNOW WHO TO CONTACT ABOUT WHAT	SINGLE POINT OF CONTACT (TEL. NE.)	EASILY ACCESSED LOSS OF RAPPORT
RECEIVE APPLICATIONS	YES	BRANCH OFFICE STAFF	BY POST BY HAND	SPEED OF RESPONSE	SLOW	INFORMATION TRANSFER BY ELECTRONIC MEANS, NOT BY	• RAPID RESPONSE
ASSESS APPLICATIONS	YES	BRANCH MANAGER	• RULE BOOK • JUDGEMENT		RISK RELATED TO APPLICATION BUT DETERMINES OVERALL RESPONSE TIME	TRANSFER OF PAPER AND/OR PEOPLE	• COST OF HARDWARE AND SOFTWARE SUPPORT
MAKE OFFER	YES	BRANCH MANAGER	• POST • PERSONAL CONTACT	RISK TAKEN		PROVISIONAL ASSESSMENT USING EXPERT SYSTEM	• REDUCTION OF BRANCH OFFICES
CONFIRM ACCEPTANCE	YES	CUSTOMER	• POST • PERSONAL CONTACT	COST	COST OF MAINTENANCE OF BRANCH OFFICE	CONDITIONAL OFFER	SOCIAL COST

Figure 4.4 *(Upper)*, **4.5** *(Lower) Comparison table*

BUSINESS PROCESS REDESIGN

Also within a building society (T.S.B. Homeloans), this study adopted the interpretation of BPR, identified earlier as Business Process Redesign. Hence it was taking the business processes as given and was looking for efficiency improvements. Also, as the business processes were spread across a number of specialist departments and at different geographical locations it was also looking for ownership definition and the improved use of IT as the interdepartmental communication mechanism.

The area of interest was the existing customer processes within Home Buying Services. As the focus was existing customers it was assumed that basic customer details were available and that the processes that were of interest were those required to respond to a customer-oriented event. These could be events like a request for a new mortgage, insurance claim, relocation, etc.

The business processes needed to respond to these events are event dependent and customer independent but, as they took place in different departments at different locations, there was no coherent definition of what they were and the sequence of processing was also not defined. This resulted in customer and event details being sent to the incorrect starting location, iteration and reworking of the details because parts of the processing were being done in the wrong sequence and considerable delays in completion since no individual had responsibility for the whole process.

Since the processes were being taken as given, the first task was to identify what they were. Also since the processes were event dependent it would be critical to identify the range of events relevant to existing customers.

There were three departments concerned with this area of business activity; Homeloans (H), Life & Pensions (L&P) and Network and General Insurance (GE). A workshop, involving representation from each, was convened in order to establish the full range of events to be considered.

The list derived is reproduced in Table 4.1 (template reference will be explained later).

→ Customer event	Via Interview Telephone Mail	Transparent event processing with total fulfilment from a single engagement

This particular project was being undertaken as part of a larger BPR project and this larger project had derived the vision above for this area of event response.

Thus the customer was to be unaware of the complexities of the processing required by the event and the whole process should be completed with only one contact with the customer.

Root definitions were constructed of systems to respond to the variety of events (taken one at a time) which recognised the above concept. Thus not only were the processes identified (by the resulting conceptual models) but also the information needed by each process. The information which was customer dependent could be specified and procedures (hows) put in place to ensure that this information was assembled during the single engagement.

Since the conceptual models are independent of both departmental and geographical arrangements, the responsibilities of the three departments could be specified in relation to the processes required and an overall responsibility for the monitor and control activities nominated for the respective events. It was also necessary to examine how each activity was currently undertaken and suggest changes that represented significant improvement.

The whole project was undertaken in a workshop mode occupying several days. Having identified the range of customer-driven events and derived the respective RDs the remainder of the activity was structured around two phases:

Phase 1   To derive event-driven activity models
Phase 2   To derive activity-based measures of performance and identify improved practices

Table 4.1   *Existing customer event listing*

Event	Template reference
Change of title (divorce/separation)	2
Death	2
Relocation (job change)	2
Change of personal circumstances (redundancy, unemployment, demotion etc.)	2
New mortgage	2
Further advance	2
Insurance/assurance claim	1
Tenancy	2
Second charge	2
Conversion	2
Redemption	1
Surrender/lapse	1
Arrears/non-payment of premium tax change	Non-customer driven
Customer progress enquiry	2
Tax Query	1

Workshop-Phase 1

Activity models were derived for the events listed in Table 4.1 and Figure 4.6 illustrates two of them.

Part-way through this phase it was realised that two generic models could be derived that could map onto all the others. Thus they could form 'Generic Templates' through which all the events could be examined and through which changes could be grouped to form recommended areas for detailed study and longer term vision achievement. These templates are reproduced in Figure 4.7 and referred to in Table 4.1.

The two models illustrated in Figure 4.6 represent the set of activities, at a particular level of detail together with the logical dependencies, that are necessary to complete the response to the event. The models contain monitoring and control activities to ensure that the respective responses achieve certain performance expectations and, for completeness, there are activities within the models to define what those expectations are.

Once the model is established, each activity can be examined to define how its performance might be assessed. Thus, if the 'current how' of doing the activity is said to be poor, the criterion (measure of performance) forms the basis for that value judgement and any improvement can be assessed against the same criterion. As an example 'Receive claim details' may be assessed against:

Accuracy
Completeness
Timeliness
Cost (of doing the activity)

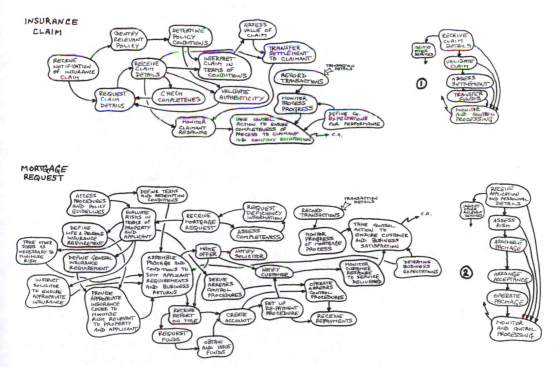

Figure 4.6 *Event response models*

Template 1.   Relevant to Insurance/Assurance Claims, redemption, tax, query, surrender/lapse.

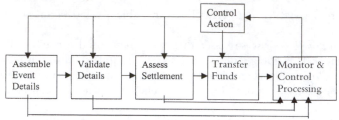

Template 2. (Relevant to all other events)

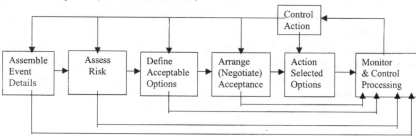

Figure 4.7   *Generic templates*

If a 'current how' incurs repeated contact with the claimant because of incorrect or only partial information, the activity will suffer in terms of increased time and added cost. Thus a 'future how' needs to be capable of overcoming this deficiency.

Workshop–Phase 2

The comparison of the conceptual models against current practices needs to be explicit in order to have a complete audit trail through analysis to recommendation. Each activity was questioned in terms of how it is currently performed, by whom and what measures of performance would be used to assess how well it was done. The measures were then used to identify problems with current 'hows' and to suggest ways of overcoming them, together with implications of so doing. This information was assembled into a tabular format to provide the required element within the audit trail. An example is given in Table 4.2.

Because the comparison was being done within a workshop with appropriate representation the expertise on current practices was immediately available and hence interviewing, to establish the current situation, was completely unnecessary. This made the process highly efficient in both time and cost.

Tables of the above format were initially produced for the activity models originally developed and then for the event-driven processes described by the appropriate templates. It was demonstrated by the group that this was an equally successful way of questioning the 'current hows' and of deriving changes.

Two kinds of recommendation were produced; those which could be implemented in the short term and longer–term recommendations which were beyond the scope of the current workshop. These were as follows:

Table 4.2 *Part of 'Assemble event details' which appears in each template*

Activity	'Current how'	By whom?	Measures of performance	Current problems	Improvements	Implications
Receive notification of death	Death Certificate	Branch homeloans (L&P)	Completeness Accuracy Timeliness Cost	■ Incomplete process ■ Information lack ■ Multiple responsibility ■ Communication gaps ■ Reworking ■ Inefficiency	■ Defined point of contact ■ Guided enquiry process	Customer shielded from complexity of processes Complete information obtained Rework removed
Identity requirements	Interview					

In the short term: Improve internal awareness of the various processes operated in all parts of the homebuying services (i.e. Homeloans, L & P, GI, etc.)

This would facilitate those processes which need to operate across organisational (and geographical) boundaries leading to a reduction in rework and wasted resource use. It would also help in a move towards the whole ownership and management of event processing.

In the longer term: Establish working groups to realise:

(1) A defined point of engagement
(2) Guided enquiry processes
(3) Shared systems and data

(1) The definition of point(s) of engagement would shield the customer from the complexity of the homebuying services and facilitate the bringing together of the various services required to effectively respond to the events.
(2) Guided enquiry processes would help to ensure that at the 'Assemble event details' stage all the information needed, to respond to the customer concern, would be collected.
(3) Shared systems and data would improve interservice communication and help to eliminate rework, inconsistencies, delays and wasted resource. They would also help to establish 'ownership' and hence integrated control of the whole process, to ensure validity of collected data.

The recommendations were accepted. They had been generated by the workshops and hence there was commitment to their realisation. The longer-term suggestions were taken on board by the wider BPR work and implemented in accordance with the total priorities for change. The SSM-based modelling had facilitated the analysis and structured the creative output of the individuals within the workshop. This was seen as a powerful and efficient contribution to the total BPR study.

CONCLUSION

It has usually been the expectation that the changes derived from a BPR analysis would be implemented through some form of IT-based solution. In fact it was probably this expectation that led to a new label (BPR) being applied to an old process of analysis (strategic review). There is a danger that any study which starts out with this expectation may miss significant opportunities which *do not* rely on the use of new technology. Thus it is important to differentiate between 'what' the opportunity is and 'how' it might be realised. IT is just one of the potential 'hows' and is therefore a secondary consideration in an investigation which is concerned with identifying radical change.

The approach described in this chapter is totally explicit and hence changes that are proposed can be traced back to their origins and an argument assembled to support their acceptance. This, of course, is also true of other approaches but the unique feature of SSM is that it takes seriously the multiple perceptions of the people in the situation together with the ability to model potential future scenarios. It provides a mechanism for constructing models pertinent to those perceptions which are themselves unique to that situation. Thus the origins of the recommendations are based upon the in-house values; not only the values which determine the acceptability of the changes proposed but also those which determine the unique set of business processes themselves.

The application of SSM to process re-engineering is also very efficient in terms of time due to the way it is used. Initial interviewing is a minimum since what is being questioned is not what people do (or how they do what they do) but the range of components of perceptions relevant to the particular group selected. It is these components that are used to develop the models, representing the activities to realise a set of potential futures.

Since it is a participative approach, SSM essentially provides the structure for the analysis. The in-house personnel provide the in-house knowledge and expertise relevant to the particular business, and the external analyst(s) provide the way of thinking about it. This thinking is made explicit through the general concepts of Human Activity Systems modelling. It is essential that 'defensibility' is maintained throughout and hence the rules and principles of model building, described in Chapter Two, must be observed. Referring back to the question posed at the end of the first section of this chapter, we can summarise an approach to BPR.

This approach is based on the assumption that the investigation of potential changes must be undertaken while retaining complete freedom on how such changes might be implemented. It also starts off by defining potential 'futures' for the organisation on the basis of role definitions which recognise the variety of the particular population of managers who would have responsibility for driving the changes forward. Most organisations, however, have difficulty in coping with the complexity of concepts derived as a means of accommodating the variety arising from a consideration of a range of potential futures together with the range of perceptions. Of course, these concepts represent an articulation of the thinking processes of the analyst and need never be declared to the organisation itself. However, if the 'analyst group' includes members of the organisation (important as a means of capturing domain knowledge within the group) this observation still applies.

Since there is *one* organisation the development of a *single model* helps in both the assembly of the 'audit trail' and in the processes of communication within the group. This is the same problem identified in the previous chapter when the concern was for a description of the 'system served'. Here we are looking for a 'standard' to compare against the current activities of the organisation.

This 'standard' is called a *Consensus Primary Task Model (CPTM)*, where the consensus is that of the analyst group (*not* the organisation) and represents a description of:

What we are taking the organisation business processes to be

Note: This may be what we are taking them to be *now* (if we are doing an audit of the current situation), or what we are taking them to be *in the future* if we are doing a fundamental review, as in a BPR study.

Using the above notion we can summarise the top-down approach to BPR as the following nine stages:

(1) Explore potential future role definitions through an analysis of relevant managerial perceptions.
(2) Construct a consensus primary task model for each potential future (or a combination).
(3) Compare model activities for all models against current processes.

(4) Decide which activities could lead to major performance improvements irrespective of the model from which they are derived.
(5) Define options for change.
(6) Define priorities for change.
(7) Assess information implications of changes
(8) Identify IT opportunities
(9) Select options for change on the basis of cost versus benefit. (Here cost is not only financial; social cost must also be included.)

The above approach is based upon a unique description of what the organisation is taken to do to achieve some 'seen–to–be–desirable' future. Thus the options for change which emerge at stage 5 are truly relevant to the particular organisation. Also, they can be defended on the basis of the audit trail that this approach provides. A further example of this process is given in Chapter Seven using a particular method of derivation for the CPTM. The project to be described is one that is underway at the time of writing and is being undertaken within the Met. Office.

Chapter Five

The Consensus Primary Task Model

INTRODUCTION

Chapter Three outlined a problem facing an analyst who is trying to derive a single model to represent the 'system served'. It was in the cases where the concern was for a service system of some kind that this problem was first encountered. However, once a defensible mechanism was derived for model combination, the use of a single, representative model as the basis of analysis, has become a powerful and efficient means of tackling a wide range of problem situations. The discussion of BPR in Chapter Four leads to the same requirement.

This single model is known as the Consensus Primary Task Model (CPTM). The choice of this label has, unfortunately, been the cause of much misinterpretation. It has been argued that consensus leads to a bland, unimaginative description of an organisation and that it is the radical, imaginative thoughts that people have that need to be captured. This kind of criticism is based upon the assumption that the consensus is related to the people within the particular organisation. *This is not the case.* The consensus is within the problem-solving group. It is an assumption about what the group take the organisation unit to be doing. This may or may not involve organisation-based personnel en route to the derivation of the CPTM but the CPTM itself is:

The consensus of the problem-solving group that this is what they are taking the organisation unit to be doing (now and/or in the future).

The CPTM has turned out to be a major development in the analysis of organisation-based problems. It represents a unique statement of the set of activities taken to represent the particular organisation unit of concern. Its importance is in the fact that it can provide the starting point for a whole range of investigations. Some of these were identified in the Preamble. For example, information requirements analysis is seeking to identify the information needed by an organisation, or part of an organisation, and hence a statement of what the information is to support, by way of the activities undertaken, is an essential part of the analysis. The CPTM gives an answer which is independent of who does the activities. It therefore provides a robust set of requirements independent of organisation structure (or restructuring). Because of this organisational structure independence, it is also a powerful tool in the process of organisational restructuring or organisational design.

As a statement of *what* the organisation unit is taken to do, it is a powerful and defensible basis for strategic reviews or BPR as discussed in Chapter Four.

THE CPTM—METHODS OF CONSTRUCTION

The concept of a CPTM has been in existence for around 18 years and during that time I have been conscious of the need to explore variety in the methods of construction in order to cope with the variety of situations to which it can be applied.

So far, four methods have been developed and used. They are described under the following headings:

A   Mission-statement based
B   W-decomposition
C   Wider system extraction
D   Enterprise Model assembly

A: Mission-statement Based

This is the most defensible method and the simplest to use. However, it is also the least likely to be adopted.

Organisations frequently derive mission statements but they tend to be woolly, imprecise and all-embracing. It is almost inevitable that the mission statement will be broad-based and imprecise since the statement has been agreed by a group of Managers/Directors each with their own interpretations of organisation purpose. Hence the words chosen must have been capable of satisfying their multiple perceptions. It is also usually the case that there is little commitment to them. They are usually issued to all employees who no doubt stick them on the wall/notice boards/filing cabinets, etc., where they are ignored while everyone gets on with doing their job.

This is the worst scenario. If the mission statement is well formed and really concentrates on the specific vision of the organisation, or organisation unit, then it can be translated into the structure of a RD and modelled in the usual way to create the CPTM.

B: W-Decomposition

This is the most complex and difficult method and starts with an identification of the range of Ws appropriate to the particular population associated with the investigation. Individual primary-task models are constructed for each W and these models are then combined into a single model using a neutral (non-contentious) model as the starting point. The process is described and illustrated later.

C: Wider-System Extraction

Although its significance was not appreciated at the time, an alternative way of constructing a CPTM has been used in several projects, dating back to 1976. Essentially it relies on two assumptions:

(a) A wider system, mission statements, job specification etc., relevant to (but wider in scope than) the role being explored can be defined and taken as given.
(b) An acceptable/feasible role can be identified by mapping various role boundaries on to the model developed from (a) above.

The activities within the boundary, eventually developed as a result of exploring acceptability as in (b), is then taken to be the CPTM.

D: Enterprise Model Assembly

At a very high level of generality any enterprise can be described in terms of four types of system. Thus a CPTM, which is an intellectual construct capable of representing any enterprise, can similarly be described in terms of four types of system. This means that a CPTM can be assembled from individual models representing the four types.

It is argued that in a model of any enterprise there will be a set of activities which represent its core purpose, i.e. its transformation process (T). There will be other activities (different in kind) which facilitate, or support, this process (S). Since the enterprise is bounded by some organisation boundary, other activities must exist which link its activities to its environment (L) and finally in a managed enterprise there will be activities to plan, monitor and control its destiny (P,M,C). This leads to the simple model below.

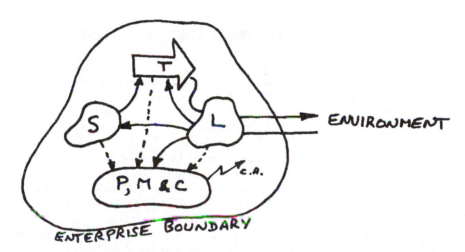

Thus, for example, if T is a transformation from a raw material to a product, S could be Research and Development, or product development; L could be product distribution and/or market intelligence gathering and P,M,C could be strategic (or production) planning, performance measurement and company (or production) control. There is not a single answer as to what these components are since, for the above example, T could also represent the satisfaction of a market demand. In this case the manufacture of a product would be part of S.

However, this simple model provides a basis for assembling a number of models, into a CPTM and, over the last few years, has turned out to be the most widely used of the four approaches.

ANALYSIS REQUIRING A CPTM

Chapter Four described an approach to BPR which was a top-down approach based upon a consideration of potential futures. In this there was a requirement to produce a 'standard' as a basis for comparison and it was argued that, since there is only one organisation (organisation unit), the approach gained credibility from having only one standard. This single standard is the CPTM.

Chapter Three introduced the notion of conceptualising a 'served system' as the source of a 'service system'. Again this requires a single answer to the question of what the analyst takes the served system to be. Examples of service systems are information provision, training, manpower planning, maintenance, capability and quality management, etc.

All these examples require an answer to the question 'to support what?' and that answer is provided by a description of the system served, i.e. the CPTM.

A further application requiring a CPTM is when the concern is for a particular 'how', as in the structure of an organisation (organisation unit). This may be the geographical as well as the departmental structure. Where a set of business processes are located is based upon what those processes happen to be, and their relation to the other business processes making up the total set.

A CPTM is an 'organisation structure-free' description of business processes onto which can be mapped boundaries representing actual and/or potential departmental roles and location.

This particular application is described in more detail in Chapter Nine and the application to service systems is described in Chapters Eight and Eleven.

MISSION STATEMENT-BASED APPROACH

As stated earlier, this is the most defensible method since the starting point for any subsequent analysis is a definition produced by personnel within the organisation itself. Because of that, it is also the least likely to be used for the reasons given earlier in section A. It should always be examined as a potential option since, as well as being defensible, it usually leads to a relatively simple model. This simple model is coherent and can be readily elaborated through expansion down the systems hierarchy.

The development of the model, once a well-structured RD is formed from the mission statements, follows the rules and principles expounded in Chapter Two.

A mission statement is usually in the format of a number of bullet points and the initial task, therefore, is to convert these into a single sentence representing the RD. Some of the bullet points may be seen to be at a more detailed level than others and may be left for inclusion as the model is elaborated. It is vital that they are not ignored completely since this would destroy the defensibility that we are seeking to achieve. It is useful to illustrate this initial conversion, from a mission statement into a RD: the process of modelling has already been covered.

The following example also illustrates the degree of consideration that can go into the formulation of a mission statement.

The company was TSB Homeloans and the activity referred to here was undertaken prior to the launch of the company. The MD had assembled a management team of four Senior Managers and they were setting out their views as to how the company should be established.

The extracts are taken directly from a set of papers produced by the management team at the time that the mission statement was being assembled. Some of the values expressed were used in the analysis of the company organisation structure, which followed the mission statement assembly. This is referred to again in Chapter Nine.

Extract 1–TSB Homeloans—Mission

The Homeloans Mission Statement was derived from the management team's perception of role, articulated at a pre-launch seminar. The statement was constructed from an understanding of the Total Quality Management principles of:

(1) Customer focus
(2) Process management
(3) Team working and
(4) Empowerment

and is as follows:

Together finding fulfilment from providing a low-cost, quality mortgage processing services to our colleagues in the branch network so they can deliver a quality mortgage product to their customers.

The Mission Statement was supported by a set of values expressed in high-level terms as follows.

(1) Provide a quality service to our customer.
(2) Deliver a personal service within the context of team working.
(3) Encourage staff to reach their full potential.
(4) Seek out ways of doing what we do better.
(5) Fulfil our responsibility to the local community.

Each of the value statements was supported by a process statement which in turn led to the introduction of a management system, i.e.

Value 1—Provide a quality service to our customer by:
(a) researching our customer needs
(b) keeping abreast of developments in the business and the marketplace
(c) agreeing service levels and performance standards
(d) establishing effective measuring and monitoring systems
(e) always exceeding expectations

Value 2—Deliver a personal service within the contest of team working by:
(a) accepting personal responsibility and accountability
(b) encouraging teams and individuals to support each other
(c) setting and communicating common goals
(d) encouraging the involvement of all staff in the development of the company
(e) creating healthy inter-team competition

Value 3—Encourage staff to reach their full potential by:
(a) providing career progression opportunities
(b) making available first-class training facilities
(c) rewarding staff for achievement
(d) valuing the courage of those who continually challenge assumptions

Value 4—Seek out ways of doing what we do better by:
(a) establishing a 'no-blame' culture
(b) encouraging and acting on suggestions from staff
(c) rewarding staff for initiative and creativity
(d) maintaining an 'open' communication system
(e) supporting 'champions'
(f) learning from our own and each others' mistakes
(g) declaring that there are no 'no-go' areas
(h) celebrating our success

Value 5—Fulfil our responsibilities to the local community by:
(a) attracting recruits from all sectors of the community
(b) providing employment opportunities for disadvantaged members of the community
(c) supporting and participating in local community activities

A number of these values tend to define a 'utopian' culture but nevertheless they were explicit, they drove the analysis of organisation structure and they led to a useable mission statement. As a result of internal debate among the senior managers, the following mission statement emerged:

Extract 2—Mission

To be the Branch Banking Division's centre of excellence for mortgage processing, delivering a sustained low-cost quality service to the retail network, thus complementing and supporting the profitable growth of TSB's Mortgage portfolio.

The phase 'centre of excellence' was not defined and two RDS were derived to interpret this while revisiting some of the value statements that had given rise to it.

During discussions with the management team about the mission statement, it was argued that the values surrounding 'excellence' were not absolute and that its achievement would not be unconstrained. Thus, others providing similar services would have to be recognised, i.e. competition and constraints would need to be specified related to the wider company, i.e. policy and the particular environment in which it was operating, i.e. legal.

The first RD definition that was produced was:

A TSB-owned system operated within legal and policy constraints, by appropriately skilled staff and suitable technological resources, which seeks to be a market leader in the provision of quality financial services to support the needs of the home-buying public in ways which satisfy customers' requirements for convenience and reassurance while being cost-effective in relation to the competition, achieving long-term profit in line with the banks' strategic requirements and ensuring staff motivation through the achievement of their potential.

The model corresponding to this is reproduced in Figure 5.1.

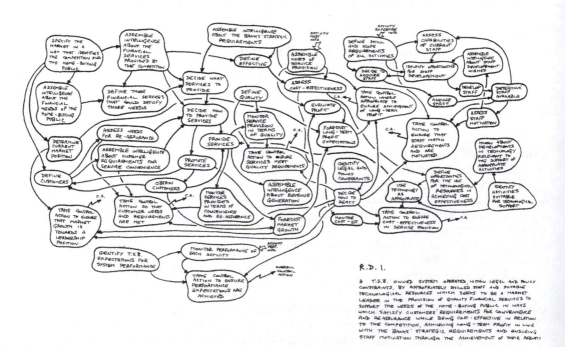

Figure 5.1 *A model of RD1*

It was argued that the activities in the model that resulted from this RD had not captured the essence of the phrase and also it contained activities outside the scope of 'Homeloans' (such as 'Decide what services to provide'). It was also recognised that money was likely to be a significant constraint and a second RD was produced which included reference to finance.

The second RD included the term 'centre of excellence' but it was removed from being the basic purpose (i.e. the T of CATWOE) as implied by the mission statement and introduced as part of the W. This RD was:

A TSB-owned system, operated by TSB Homeloans, to complement and support the profitable growth of the BBD Mortgage portfolio by developing a low-cost quality service to the branch network through the development and maintenance of a centre of excellence in mortgage administration, while recognising and responding to the services provided by completion and the constraints arising from legal financial and policy considerations.

(Note: 'Centre of excellence in mortgage administration' is taken to be achieved through the adoption of 'best practice' in relation to the service offered and delivered.)

Although 'best-practice' now requires definition, the model can cope with the derivation of its definitions. This was much more acceptable as the meaning of 'centre of excellence' would be the outcome of an adaptive process rather than a one-off definition. The model is reproduced as Figure 5.2.

It was decided that before the model was accepted, the activity 'Provide services' required some elaboration to make it specific to TSB Homeloans and so the final model used is that given in Figure 5.3.

At the other end of the spectrum, the following mission statement (an actual example) is totally non-specific:

To become recognised as the UK's leading authority on the application of technology for business advantage.

Apart from the generality of this statement, the emphasis (the major verb) is 'To become recognised'. Thus the major activities would be associated with the promotion of their capability. There is nothing in the statement to do with generating this capability by actually doing anything. They could become the leading authority on the application of technology by researching what every other organisation does.

To summarise: use a mission-statement as the source of a CPTM if it is sufficiently specific to lead to a model relevant to the particular organisation. Such a model will be defensible since the mission statement is generated by someone other than the analyst. Finally, the model will be relatively simple (e.g. Figure 5.3) and, as the basis for further elaboration, it will ensure coherence as the level of detail increases.

W-DECOMPOSITION

The example of 'a prison' as the organisation unit of concern has already been used to illustrate some of the underlying difficulties associated with organisational analysis. The example arose from an actual project and it happened to be the source of the W-decomposition approach to CPTM formulation.

In 1983 we were asked to undertake a project for the Prison Department of the Home Office in the UK. The project may be summarised as follows:

The concern: Do we get value for money from our prison service?
The expectation: Information systems to answer this question on a continual basis.

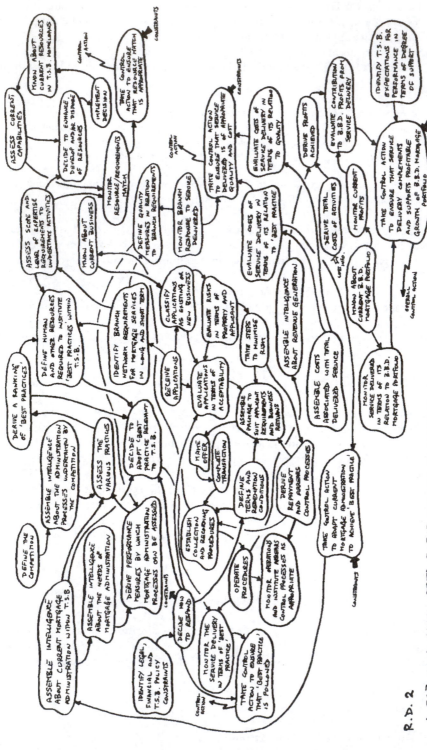

R.D. 2

A T.S.B. OWNED SYSTEM, OPERATED BY T.S.B. MORTGAGORS, TO COMPLEMENT
AND SUPPORT THE PROFITABLE GROWTH OF THE B.B.D. MORTGAGE PORTFOLIO
BY DELIVERING A LOW COST QUALITY SERVICE TO THE BRANCH NETWORK
THROUGH THE DEVELOPMENT AND MAINTENANCE OF A CENTRE OF EXCELLENCE
IN MORTGAGE ADMINISTRATION, WHILE RECOGNISING AND RESPONDING TO
THE SERVICES PROVIDED BY COMPETITION AND THE CONSTRAINTS ARISING
FROM LEGAL, FINANCIAL AND POLICY CONSIDERATIONS.

Figure 5.2   *A model of RD2*

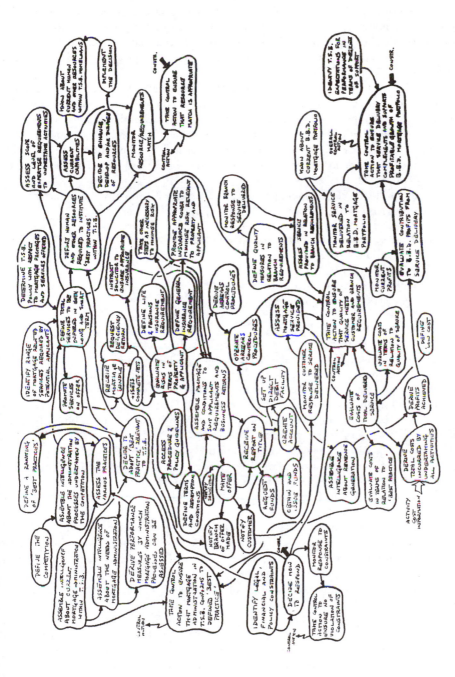

Figure 5.3 *A conceptual model relevant to TSB Homeloans*

Our problem: Cost can be accurately evaluated and 'value' requires an answer to the question:
                          What is a prison for?

The prison service consists of a variety of establishments, each operating a regime determined by the particular governor. Discussions with a number of governors and other prison officials indicated a variety of answers to the above question. The 'hardliners' believed that the inmates were there to settle a debt to society, while the more liberal-minded saw it as a process of education and rehabilitation.

The situation is complicated by the fact that no one individual is ever 100% committed to a single perception. Thus the 'punishment'-oriented governor operates educational processes while the 'education'-oriented governor operates punishment routines. Hence each individual has a spectrum of perceptions related to the situation with which they are concerned. This rather extreme example illustrates the added complexity arising from a consideration of multiple perceptions and it is this feature which makes each situation unique because its effect is determined by the particular group of managers/individuals concerned.

As a general rule, the problem of developing a single concept for a company while recognising the multiple perception spectra of the managers concerned requires three stages:

(1) Decomposition of the spectra by assuming that specific perceptions can be isolated and incorporated into root definitions of HAS.
(2) Logical modelling of the HAS.
(3) Recomposition of the perceptions through a process of accommodation resulting in a single HAS model, known as a consensus primary task model.

These stages are illustrated by Figure 5.4.

In the top-left of Figure 5.4. three managers are shown with particular orientations towards various parts of the spectrum of *Weltanschauung*. Here the legitimate range is from $W_1 \ldots W_n$ (where W_1 could be an orientation towards punishment and W_n could be an orientation towards rehabilitation). The decomposition stage is concerned with picking parts of the range (believed to correspond to distinct and significant Ws) and with developing RDs corresponding to these chosen Ws. In practice there may be any number of RDs, twelve being a usual upper limit, but only three are shown here for convenience.

Essentially the analyst is choosing to view the mission of the organisation in a particular way (as a human activity system) and, on the basis of a carefully produced RD, derives a logical model of what the system would have to *do* to be the one so defined. A second definition, based upon another perception, can be taken and modelled as a logical construct, and so on, as described in Chapter Two.

The second stage is concerned with the development of the conceptual models from the RDs and the selection of activities from these models which are desirable in some way. Desirability may be expressed in terms of feasibility or of necessity but it is defined and the choices are made in association with the group of managers to whom the range of Ws is relevant (in this case A_1, A_2 and A_3). Stage 2 in Figure 5.4 illustrates the derivation of a CPTM by a route which seeks to obtain coherence in the resultant model.

This process results in the mapping illustrated as stage 3 in Figure 5.4. The neutral primary task system represents that set of activities that the organisation must do to be that kind of organisation (i.e. a prison, to be a prison, must receive prisoners, store them for particular periods of time and release them). The larger shaded area represents the set of activities taken to be the single concept for the organisation (the CPTM) achieved through the accommodation (of Ws) process described above.

The process illustrated requires a number of assumptions to be made and it is worth examining each stage in more detail.

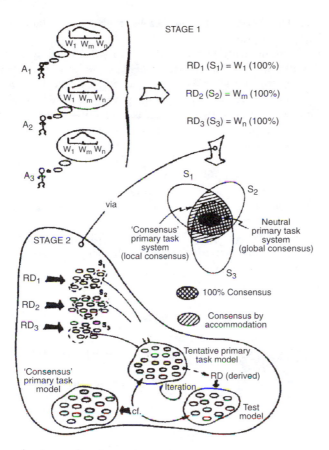

STAGE 1

$RD_1 (S_1) = W_1 (100\%)$

$RD_2 (S_2) = W_m (100\%)$

$RD_3 (S_3) = W_n (100\%)$

via

STAGE 2

'Consensus' primary task system (local consensus)

Neutral primary task system (global consensus)

100% Consensus

Consensus by accommodation

Tentative primary task model

RD (derived)

Iteration

'Consensus' primary task model

cf.

Test model

Figure 5.4 *A process of system condensation*

The various perceptions (Ws) used at the start of the process are those that are taken to be *legitimate* for the particular company or organisation as derived from discussions with the particular group of managers who the analyst takes as appropriate to the situation. While interviewing managers I try to be sensitive to illustrations of these Ws. For example, it is often the case that, as well as answering specific questions, the managers will volunteer information. Phrases such as 'I think you will find the following document(s) of interest' or 'By the way you will need to know.....', are examples of the introduction of such information. These are indicators that the manager finds them of interest or important. The question can then be asked 'what W must be implied by such an emphasis?' and answered by the analyst.

Significantly different Ws (but legitimate in the context described above) can then be chosen as the source of RDs of primary task systems. In the project for the prison service mentioned above the following perceptions were taken as relevant and legitimate for the range of UK prisons considered. In fact about eight definitions were used; these three are used for illustration:

- A system for the control of interaction between offenders and the community.
- A system to instil society's norms and values.
- A system to retain offenders

It is the case that the models derived from these definitions would contain different activities. Thus, while accepting that a complex changing mixture of perceptions can be simplified into a number of single perceptions the analyst now faces the difficulty of how to reduce these multiple models to a single model. The procedure described earlier for achieving this consolidation of models is based on the following assumptions.

The first assumption is that, no matter what kind of organisation is being considered, there will be a description of it that will achieve *global* consensus, i.e. a *neutral* or non-contentious primary task description. So for a prison, a neutral primary task description would be a *system* for the receipt, storage, and release of prisoners. Thus no matter if some governors believe that a prison is essentially about rehabilitation, and some believe that a prison is essentially about punishment they would agree that for a prison to be a prison it must, at least, take in prisoners, retain them for various periods and then release them. Similarly, for a refrigerator manufacturer to be such a company it must, at least, assemble components into finished refrigerators; an insurance company must provide financial guarantees in respect of certain defined happenings in return for regular payments, etc.

These definitions represent brief descriptions of the basic operators of the organisation under review, and hence the models derived from them are sparse representations of the activities undertaken by the organisations.

The second assumption is that less sparse models can be obtained in a way that is defensible through the addition of individual activities about which there is *local* consensus over their desirability. Diagram 1 illustrates this idea.

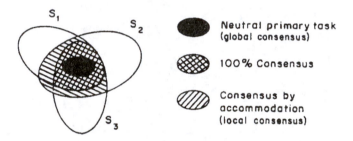

Diagram 1

The black central system (S_n) represents the 'neutral' primary task system, i.e. that set of activities that the particular organisation must do to be that kind of organisation. Systems S_1, S_2, S_3... represent those systems corresponding to the range of 'legitimate' perceptions as defined earlier (potential descriptions of the primary task of the organisation in that the system boundaries could map onto the organisation boundary). Given this restriction on choice of RD, it is to be expected that the set of activities within S_n will be common to S_1, S_2, S_3, etc, and can be taken to be part of the final primary task model.

Given the above two assumptions the procedure to be followed is in two stages. Each activity in systems S_1, S_2, S_3... (except those in S_n) are questioned to determine their desirability. Desirability is determined in discussion with the group of managers or others who the analyst judges to be the group most concerned with the output of the particular analysis being undertaken.

Those activities about which there is *local* consensus over desirability are added to those contained in S_n to form a 'tentative' primary task model. For those activities about which there is partial (rather than 100%) *local* consensus over desirability the analyst must use judgement on their retention or rejection. My criterion for retention is based on the resultant coherence of the model. If the activity is necessary (in a logical sense) in order to make the resultant model coherent then the activity is included, otherwise not. An iterative procedure is used to explore coherence, illustrated by Diagram 2.

Here it is shown that the selection of 'desirable' activities from three models CM_1, CM_2, CM_3... leads to the tentative primary task model which at this stage may be no more than an aggregate. Given the logical linking of RD and conceptual model (CM) it should be possible to reverse the

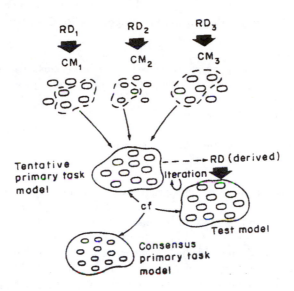

Diagram 2

process and derive an RD from the tentative primary task model. This is a difficult step and so a 'test' model is derived from the RD so formed. It is known that this is a coherent model and hence it can be used to compare against the tentative primary task model derived and so on. The iteration is continued until the test model is derived which is an acceptable version of the tentative primary task model in that it covers the scope of the activities and is also coherent.

During this process it may have been necessary to add activities to the tentative primary task model (i.e. those about which there is no 100% consensus) but also it may have been necessary to add others. For example, activities from CM_1 and CM_2 could in fact be conflicting if RD_1, and RD_2 represent conflicting perceptions. In this case an activity needs to be added which is concerned with resolving the conflict.

By adopting the above procedure any number of initial models $CM_1 \ldots CM_n$ can be reduced to a single model which, through the interaction with the relevant managers, can be taken to be a defensible 'consensus' primary task model relevant to the particular organisation in its particular social context. The boundary of this model is represented by the shaded area in Diagram 1.

The putting together of these stages results in the total process of deriving a primary task model illustrated by Figure 5.4. Since such a model is based upon an analysis of multiple perceptions (or Ws) it represents a taken-to-be or 'constructed reality'. It is similar to the 'selected target system' which is used as the initial stage in a conventional socio-technical systems approach (STS). The essential difference is that within STS, the target system is assumed to exist (i.e. to be reality).

To illustrate this process of construction let us return to the project that gave rise to it, i.e. the prison service. The full project will not be described but three of the systems will be used as an example. These are the three that correspond to the systems identified previously, i.e.

- A system for the control of interaction between offenders and the community
- A system to instil society's norms and values
- A system to retain offenders

These are not RDs but are merely labels to define the W-orientations.

The third system is taken to be a description of a non-contentious view and it was argued that for a prison to be a prison it must retain offenders. All prisons do this; the essential difference between a maximum-security prison and an open prison is the degree of security in the retention. In constructing a RD it is recognised that the retention is temporary. For this particular system the RD is as follows:

A system to retain offenders temporarily in appropriate secure surroundings in accordance with sentences defined by the courts while providing necessary life support and reacting to the requirements of parole and Home Office policy.

The CATWOE analysis is as follows:

C—offenders (more likely to be victims than beneficiaries)
A—not specified
T—to retain temporarily
W—it is possible to retain offenders in appropriate secure surroundings
O—not specified
E—requirements of parole and Home Office policy

There are some elements missing and this is deliberate. Since we are going to assemble all the system models (in this example, three) into a single model, it is not valuable or useful to specify all elements in every RD. Their inclusion requires activities in the conceptual model to recognise the words used to describe the elements and, hence, if the same words are used in each RD the resultant activities will be replicated. The CPTM still represents the minimum necessary activities and therefore the replication would have to be removed. It is more useful not to replicate the CATWOE elements in the first place.

The conceptual model derived from the above RD is given in Figure 5.5.

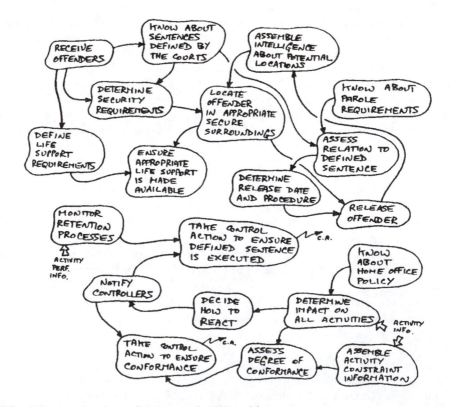

Figure 5.5 *Non-contentious (neutral) primary task (PT) model*

The second system that was developed was based upon the rehabilitation-oriented W. Its RD was:

A system to instil society's norms and values, through appropriate counselling, by example and other activities while fitting the offender for a specific role in employment, during the temporary retention period within the establishment so that, on release, the offender can be rehabilitated into society.

Here the CATWOE analysis is:

C—not specified (though offender is implied)
A—not specified
T—to instil society's norms and values
W—appropriate counselling, by example and other activities will instil society's norms and values
O—not specified
E—not specified

Again, since we know that the models are to be assembled into a single model, it is simpler to build this model directly onto the neutral model (Figure 5.5) than to construct the model from this RD independently and then do the assembly. We know that the activities of particular relevance in the neutral model are those to do with 'Receive offenders', 'Locate offenders in appropriate secure surrounding' and 'Release offenders'. This is because these activities define 'the temporary retention period within the establishment' contained within this new RD. Other activities within the new model may have other dependencies that need to be recognised but these should become apparent as the model is developed. Since the system constraints (E) were included in the neutral model, these constraints must be extended to the additional activities.

Figure 5.6 illustrates the combined model resulting from the two RDs. The activities within the boundary represent those derived from the above RD (rehabilitation-oriented) in addition to those related to 'temporary retention'.

An additional dependence was regarded as necessary and that was between the activity 'Assemble counselling and skill enhancing activities' and the activity 'Determine security requirements' since the former would be determined by how available the offender might be. The constraints in the neutral model are extended to the new activities by making each of the additional control activities dependent upon the activity 'Notify controllers'.

The same considerations apply to the third system. Here the RD is:

An Establishment-owned system, operated by prison officers, to control the interaction between offenders and the community, while retained in secure surroundings, by overseeing permitted contact, both inside and external to the Establishment and acting accordingly.

The CATWOE analysis is:

C—offenders and the community
A—prison officers
T—to control interaction
W—overseeing permitted contact and acting accordingly will control interaction
O—an Establishment
E—not specified

The elements of CATWOE in this RD now include those elements excluded previously. It has been necessary to include (c) again since the transformation refers to 'control of *interaction*', thus there must be at least two customers and the community was not specified previously. The Actors will do all the activities in the assembled model and the owner will have a concern for the

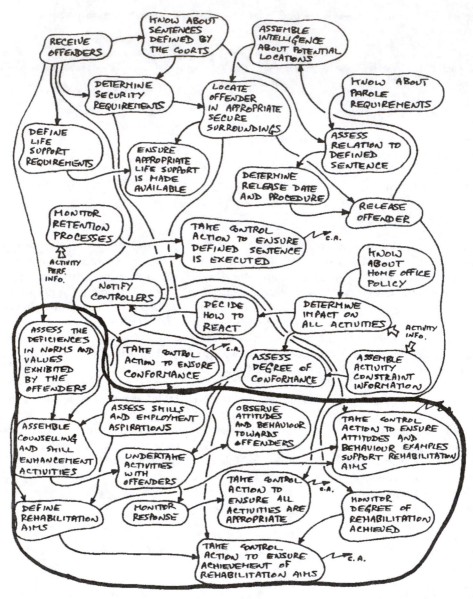

Figure 5.6   *The addition of rehabilitation*

total performance. The complete assembled model from the three RD's is given in Figure 5.7. Again the boundary represents the additional activities from the above RD.

The constraints have again been extended by making the additional control activities dependent upon the activity 'Notify controllers'.

In this particular example the iteration described by Diagram 2 has not been carried out. This is because we don't have access to the relevant population of managers and hence the three complete models have been assembled into the total model of Figure 5.7. This is frequently the quickest route if access to the relevant managers is limited. The procedure then is to decompose the final model into its subsystems and then to question the desirability or otherwise of the subsystems rather than the activities. This way, model coherence is maintained. Figure 5.8 represents the total model

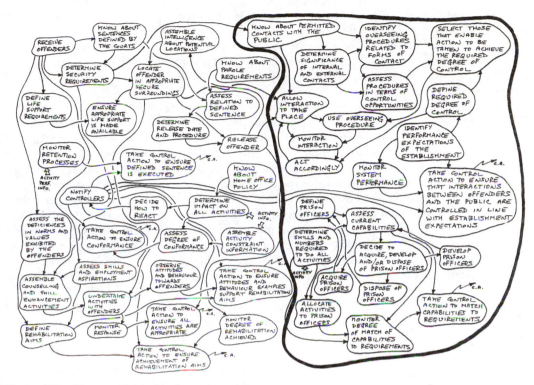

Figure 5.7 *The assembled model relevant to a prison*

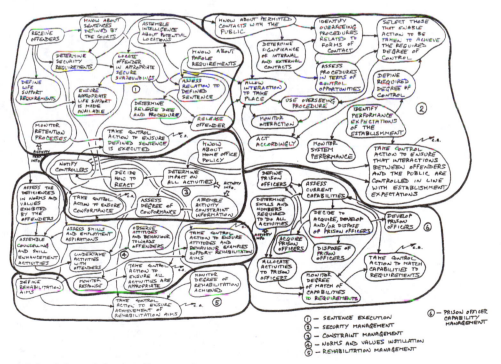

① — SENTENCE EXECUTION
② — SECURITY MANAGEMENT
③ — CONSTRAINT MANAGEMENT
④ — NORMS AND VALUES INSTILLATION
⑤ — REHABILITATION MANAGEMENT
⑥ — PRISON OFFICER CAPABILITY MANAGEMENT

Figure 5.8 *Subsystem decomposition*

decomposed into six subsystems. Remember that a subsystem requires at least one control activity for the set of activities to be a subsystem (see discussion of the FSM in Chapter Two).

The removal and/or addition of a subsystem does not destroy coherence whereas removal of individual activities could. Conflicting activities could only appear within a subsystem if there is also an activity to resolve the conflict. Thus if a subsystem structure can be maintained, the model will remain coherent.

The resultant set of subsystems (in this case that illustrated by Figure 5.8) becomes the CPTM.

This method relies on the ability easily to form a *non-contentious* primary-task model since all the other models are assembled around it. It also relies on the ability to interact with the managers in an organisation that make up the population of interest. The discussion about activity and/or subsystem desirability is not carried out in the language of the models but in domain language. For this reason it is useful for a member of the organisation to be part of the analyst group.

The impact of such discussions should not be distortion of the model to try to make it *fit* reality. We are deriving a concept to map onto, or question, reality and hence it is important that the model remains coherent. All we are trying to ensure is that the *scope* of our concept allows us to question the existing reality or the desirability of some potential future. This is what is required if we are using the CPTM as part of a strategic review. It is representing the scope of some potential future that is important if we are deriving the concept of a 'system served' to act as the source of a service system.

The next chapter examines the wider-system extraction method of deriving a CPTM and Chapter Seven deals with the most frequently used method based upon the 'enterprise model' assembly.

Chapter 6

CPTM—Formulation Using Wider-system Extraction

INTRODUCTION

The use of this approach to the construction of a CPTM relies on being able to define and construct a *defensible* wider system. Once this has been achieved the mechanism chosen for extracting the system of interest must also be defensible.

Once again a desirable starting point for the wider-system development is an existing mission statement. If this is not available, a definition of purpose, which is non-contentious, is a usable alternative. If neither of these is available then this method of constructing a CPTM may be infeasible and one of the alternative approaches will need to be adopted.

In the next chapter a project is described in which the terms of reference were specifically to do a 'marketing audit'. It was agreed, at the start, that marketing represented an interface between the company and its environment (specifically, this was the community since the company was a theatre). Hence 'marketing' could not be isolated and would have to be viewed as an integral part of the total theatre activity.

The approach to devising this total theatre model (i.e. the wider system) used the 'enterprise model assembly' method and will be described in more detail in Chapter Seven. However, having produced a description of the total set of activities it was necessary to decide which could constitute a 'standard' for marketing. This 'standard' would then be used to question what was currently done, how it was done and what was missing, i.e. to carry out an explicit audit by having the 'standard' as the basis.

Thus given the total set of activities, those that could be said to operate at the interface between the planning and operational aspects of the theatre and the community represented the definition of 'marketing'.

These activities were identified in consultation with the chief executive and hence agreement to both the mechanism of extracting the relevant activities and the activities themselves was achieved through involvement. The chief executive understood the concepts being used and was a member of the problem-solving group. This involvement provided the required defensibility and, hence, the 'standard' that was used as the basis for the audit was accepted without further question.

The above example represents a combination of two approaches to CPTM construction. The 'enterprise model' was used to extract the system of interest. The use of the 'enterprise model' will be further discussed in the next chapter.

To further illustrate the 'wider-system extraction approach', three examples will be taken related to very different organisations.

THE ROLE OF DATA MANAGER

Within the Engineering and Technical Centre (ETC) of a company in the petrochemical industry the use of personal computers (PCs) had proliferated to the extent that each engineer had his own. This was used to produce, analyse and store data, which effectively became 'owned' by the individual engineer. It was the case, however, that the data was not the personal property of the originator; it belonged to the organisation and was shared by others. The individual ownership of data produced particular structures and interpretations of it, which led to inconsistencies and misuse when the data was shared. The company believed that a change in attitude was required which would result in a shift from individual to corporate ownership. Their response was to make a structural alteration and appoint a 'data administrator'. The intention was that the appointment of a central responsibility for data would bring about the desired change. The big question, of course, was 'what could the role and responsibility of this data administrator be?' within the current situation in the company. It is current philosophy in many organisations, as it was here, that 'each manager should have a PC on his/her desk' and if that is the case then this problem of individual data ownership is one that must be faced generally. In order to answer the question posed above we had to decide how to think about it.

Within this situation, the role of data administrator could be taken to lie somewhere on a spectrum which extended from a mere storekeeper (with responsibility for the capture, storage and availability of data) to the other extreme of 'information manager' (with a responsibility for the planning, progress, maintenance and control of an information network).

The latter role could be taken to represent the wider system and somewhere between this and the 'storekeeper' role would be the role of data manager.

This particular incumbent of the role had been in post for about 18 months and had attempted to do what he felt was necessary. On the basis of this experience he was dissatisfied with what he was trying to do and so was the Head of ETC, hence the project.

Myself, the incumbent and two members of the MSc course at the University of Lancaster formed the problem-solving group and the first task was to make the incumbent of the data manager role conversant with the concepts and approach that we were going to adopt. It was felt, particularly in this project, that the involvement of the data manager would lead not only to the defensibility that we were seeking but also to commitment to the role definition that would emerge.

Together we developed a RD and conceptual model to represent the wider system, i.e. the role of information manager. A simplified version of this appears as Figure 6.1.

In order to satisfy ourselves as to its scope and legitimacy, the data manager mapped onto it the tasks that he had been trying to do for the previous 18 months. The resultant mapping is illustrated in Figure 6.2. The boundary crosses some activities, as he argued that he was only partially attempting to do them. Also he was attempting to do too much.

However, the mapping achieved what we required. The activities within the model were legitimate (since he was already trying to do most of them) and the scope was adequate (since he introduced no new activities and what was there was greater than the role he could reasonably be expected to achieve).

The procedure to identify the activities appropriate to the role of data manager was to map various role boundaries and explore the feasibility of the set of activities as a job specification. The first part of the feasibility assessment was to define the skills required of each activity and to relate these to the current skills of the incumbent data manager, together with his career-development intentions. The second part of the assessment was to explore the implied responsibility associated with the set of activities and the degree of authority that was culturally feasible for this role within ETC.

Each boundary, which was drawn on the model, represented a reduction in the area of responsibility. The set of activities within the boundary could be seen as a reduced job specification and the interactions between these activities and those outside the boundary represented the communication

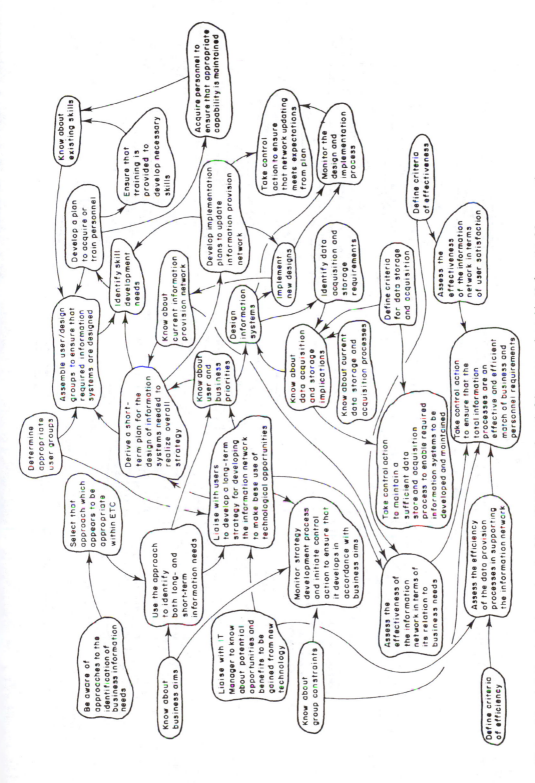

Figure 6.1 *Activities appropriate to the role of data administrator at the end of the spectrum denoted by 'Information Management'*

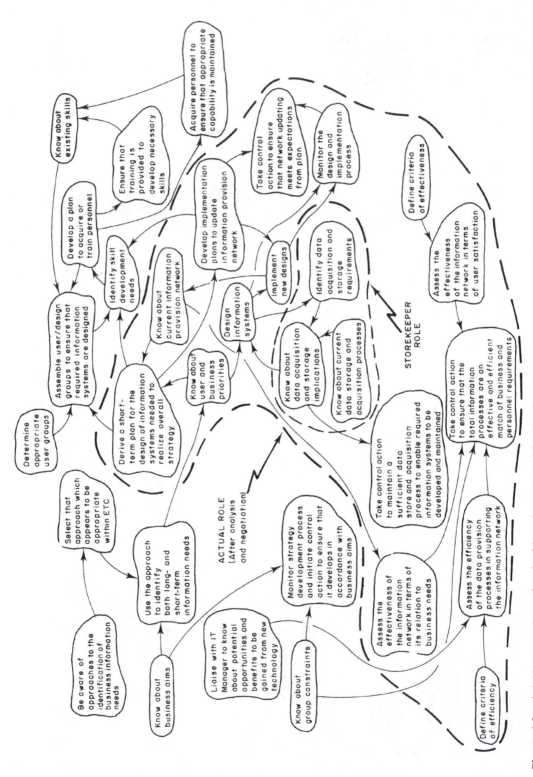

Figure 6.2 *Activities appropriate to the role of data administrator (defined by the incumbent)*

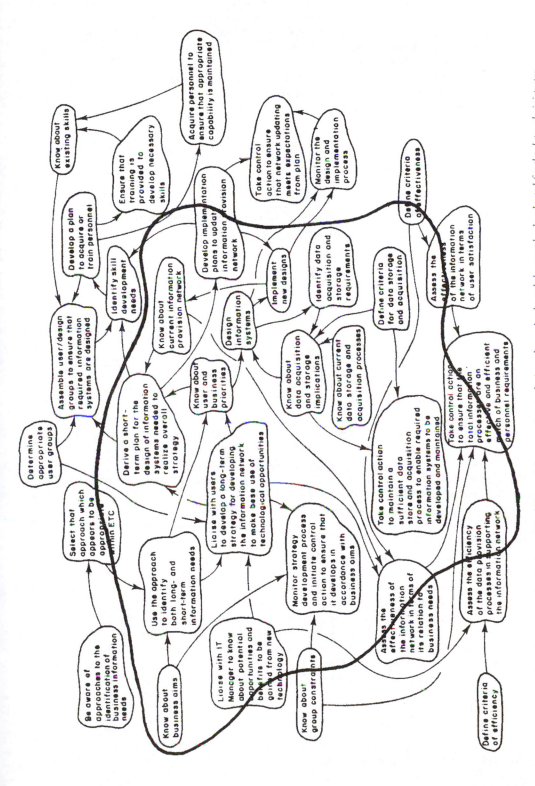

Figure 6.3   Role boundaries mapped onto the model of Figure 6.1 appropriate to the 'storekeeper' role and the actual role adopted for the data administrator

processes and procedures that would need to exist to link the data administrator with those other managers who were undertaking these external activities (if, in fact, they were undertaken). A particular boundary was derived using this procedure and this is illustrated in Figure 6.3.

Having defined the activities within the role of data administrator it became important to turn attention to those activities outside the boundary. It was necessary to identify the existence or otherwise of those activities on which the role depended since, if they were not in existence, it would become difficult to undertake relevant activities within the role. The nature of the dependency also needs to be examined. If the dependency is of the nature of information then the source of the information must be identified and ways must be discussed of ensuring that it could be provided. If the dependency is of the nature of a material flow then the absence of such material would represent a constraint on subsequent operations.

In this project the dependencies were of the nature of information and that which was immediately available was specified. The inability to obtain information from activities that did not yet exist obviously reduced the effectiveness of the activities requiring such information. The identification of these activities represented the source of recommendations for the future adaptation of the information management role in total.

THE ROLE OF A GOVERNING BODY

At the time of this project the education scene in the UK was changing very rapidly, particularly at the level of primary and secondary education. At the academic level a national curriculum was being imposed and the local management of schools was being encouraged. The impact of both of these changes was to move the responsibility for education and its management away from the local education authorities to the school and its governing body. Activities such as hiring and firing of teaching staff, the employment of services (such as catering and cleaning) and the detailed definition of school activities (within the constraints of the national curriculum) became the responsibility of the governing body and senior school staff. However, the precise definition of the responsibility of the governing body was not clear. The local authority still retain some responsibility (for example, the maintenance of buildings and the allocation of government finances), but precisely where their responsibility ends and where that of the governing body begins was problematical.

In my role of chairman of such a governing body I decided to use systems ideas to attempt to define the actual responsibilities of the governing body, *vis-à-vis* the other interested parties. Since I was in the multiple role of client and problem solver and, taking the governing body as a whole to be in the role of problem owner, it seemed important to me to ensure that we undertook those management activities that would produce maximum benefit to the school. If we could do this properly then we could be forward-looking and proactive in our role rather than reacting to issues as they arose, which tended to be the *modus operandi* of the governing body. In order to define the management activities that we should be involved in it seemed useful to undertake a systems analysis relevant to the exploration of our role.

Figure 6.4 attempts to illustrate a view of the school as a particular kind of transformation process together with those organisational entities with which it interacts. Children are seen to enter the school, some with enquiring minds, others less so. They are transformed into enlightened children though some may see less light than others. However, we will concentrate on the intended transformation. The other organisational entities are shown as elements of the school environment and in order to relate them to the school there needs to be a set of liaison and management activities as illustrated in Figure 6.5.

These activities will be those required to do the following:

(a) To translate general government policy in relation to education and school management into that appropriate to the particular school.

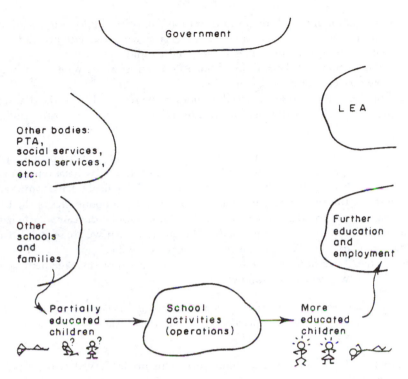

Figure 6.4 *The school seen as a transformation process and the relevant elements of its environment*

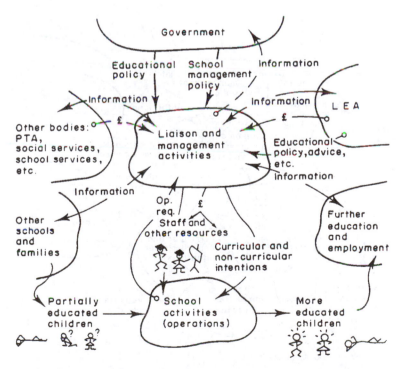

Figure 6.5 *A linking process between the school and the environmental elements (op. req. = operational requirements)*

(b) To process the relationship with the local education authority (LEA) in terms of information transfer, financial management, and those school services which were to be available centrally.
(c) To process information related to other schools and families.
(d) To process information and the additional finances, contracts, etc., with other bodies such as PTA and those services not centrally provided.
(e) To manage the provision of resources to the school, to be responsible for the development and management of the school's strategy and to provide performance and other information as required.

This is in effect, a rich picture of the situation although the inclusion of the 'liaison and management' activities is partly conceptual. These liaison and management activities will *not* represent the area of responsibility of the governing body since the school and the LEA will also have some involvement.

Figure 6.6 illustrates this situation by mapping the organisational boundaries of the LEA and the school. Given that there is no other organisation involved, it must be the case, that what is left can only be the responsibility of the governing body. The questions that we are seeking to answer are, where do these boundaries lie? What is this remaining responsibility?

To investigate these questions a system relevant to these liaison management activities was derived. The RD that was taken is as follows:

> *An LEA and community-owned system for the translation of government education policy into a formal secondary education process that meets the needs of the local community, while recognising financial, LEA and local constraints and the needs of the premises in which it takes place.*

The conceptual model is illustrated in Figure 6.7. This model served two purposes. First, it enabled us to identify the expertise required to be able to undertake the activities. This is illustrated by the boundaries mapped onto the conceptual model in Figure 6.8.

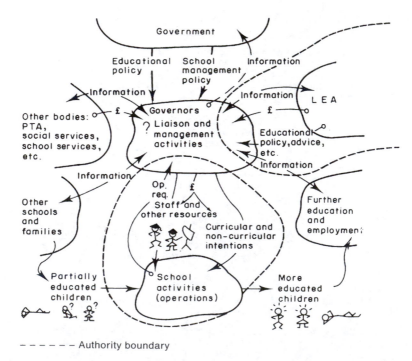

- - - - - - Authority boundary

Figure 6.6   *Mapping of authority boundaries*

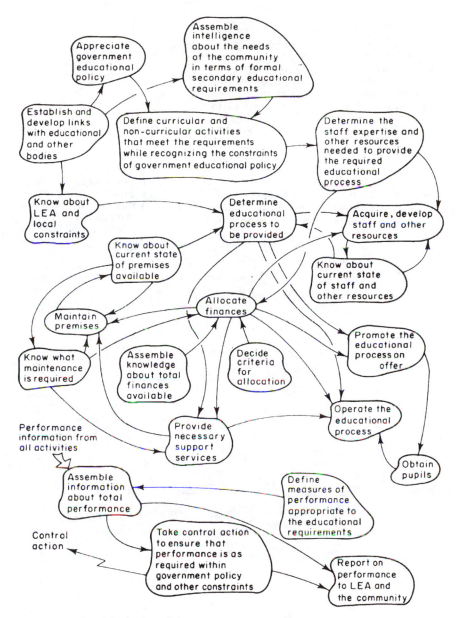

Figure 6.7 *Conceptual model relevant to liaison management*

The mapping of Figure 6.8 shows a requirement for six different kinds of expertise:

(1) Education and teaching skills
(2) Financial management ability
(3) Promotional expertise (i.e. advertising etc.)
(4) Buildings and ground maintenance
(5) Contracting and job definition ability
(6) Performance, assessment and reporting skills

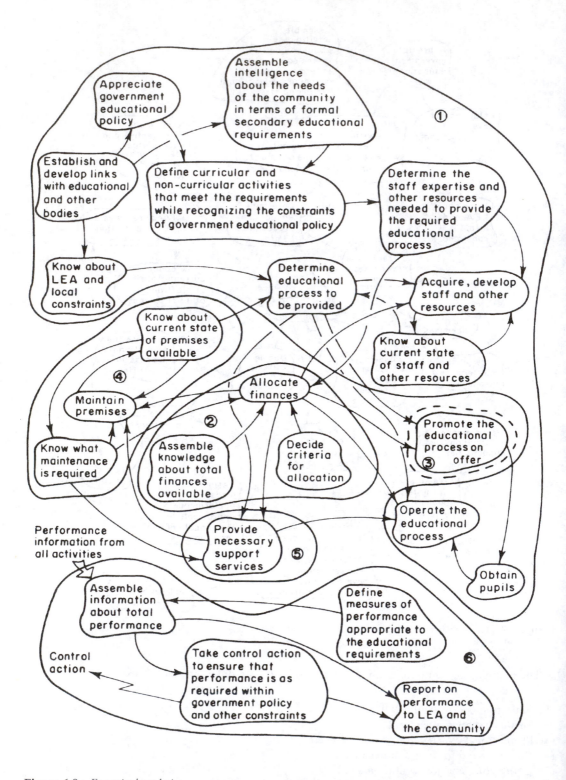

Figure 6.8 *Expertise boundaries*

Traditionally members of governing bodies have been elected on the basis of their political and organisation affiliations and their general popularity with parents and staff. This could no longer be the case if the governing body was to be an effective management unit requiring the above range of expertise. It is necessary to ensure that this expertise is available through the elected members.

The second use of this model was to identify the role of the governing body, which was the original intention. The organisation mapping of Figure 6.9 illustrates the LEA and school responsibilities. What is clear from this mapping is that whereas some activities are wholly contained within these boundaries a large number are shared between organisations. The argument is that what is contained within these boundaries is the responsibility of the relevant organisation and what

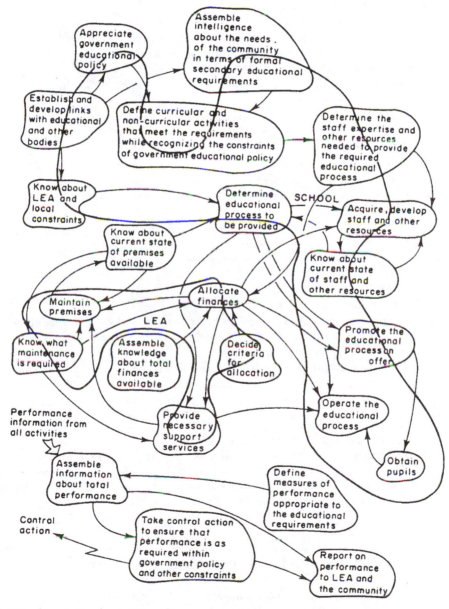

Figure 6.9 *Organisational mapping*

is outside these boundaries is the responsibility of the governing body. Apart from the activities, associated with performance monitoring, control, and reporting, all the other activities are shared with either the LEA or the school. This is to be expected since, as illustrated by Figure 6.6, the role is essentially one of liaison.

Given the expertise requirements, as illustrated by Figure 6.8 a number of suborganisation units was suggested as a way of structuring the governing body. The governing body as a whole must be responsible for the total task but these subunits could usefully be seen as advisory bodies to the main body, each with their own particular expertise. Four such units (i.e. subcommittees) were defined on the basis of the mappings in Figures 6.8 and 6.9. Their responsibilities were as follows:

- *Education and promotional subcommittee:*
  To liaise with the school in order to
  (a) ensure a common understanding of government and LEA educational policy
  (b) derive plans for the schools' curricular and non-curricular development
  (c) define staff and other resource needs
  (d) promote the school and its activities
- *Buildings and contracts subcommittee:*
  To liaise with the LEA and other service-providing bodies in order to
  (a) ensure that the premises meet the required standards from aesthetic, utilitarian, and health and safety viewpoints
  (b) ensure that these support services (meals, grounds, etc.) are provided in such a way that they are both appropriate and satisfactory
- *Financial management subcommittee:*
  To liaise with the LEA and other fund-generating bodies in order to
  (a) negotiate the allocation of responsibilities for financial control with respect to the school
  (b) define criteria for the allocation of funds
  (c) maintain an updated account of funds available and potential sources
- *Performance and reporting subcommittee:*
  To liaise with the other subcommittees in order to
  (a) ensure that performance is consistent with overall aims
  (b) identify problems or general areas of concern which prevent individual responsibilities from being achieved
  To liaise with whoever is appropriate in order to
  (a) define measures of performance which represent the total educational process and its management
  (b) to report on performance (to the LEA, the school, the community, the governing body in total, potential employers, etc.).

The resultant structure was implemented and worked effectively.

This project description was taken to its conclusion in order to demonstrate the interaction between organisation and skill mapping. Skill mapping had been used in the previous example but, here, it was the combination of the two that led to the system definition: the 'liaison and management' activities being the wider system.

THE USE OF AN ADDITIONAL CONCEPT

The final project description, related to the construction of the CPTM using the 'wider-system extraction' approach, was undertaken in 1976. It is a good illustration of utilising a concept from another field entirely to provide the mechanism for extracting the system of interest from the wider system.

The project is also an example in which the process of analysis (i.e. the problem solving) consciously changed direction during the analysis in response to features of the situation not anticipated at the outset.

We had originally viewed the need for the existence of the particular organisation unit as a continual issue since the unit of interest was a management services function. However, the exploration of the issues turned out to be problematical given their variety and eventually it was the structuring of the conceptual model, which was achieved through the use of a particular concept from control engineering, that was felt to be crucial to the progress of the project. Success in the project was assessed in two ways. First, it was seen as one way of introducing systems ideas and methodology to the personnel within the management services function of the company and, second, in terms of the degree and quality of debate about the nature, organisation, and activities of the services function itself, that it generated. Because of the first of these requirements, the project was preceded by a seminar to introduce systems ideas and the senior personnel took part in other seminars that were organised in parallel with the project. Since, through the seminars, the personnel became familiar with the particular systems language used, they were also actively involved in the analysis.

The project was undertaken for the Management Services Branch (MSB) of the South West Region of the Central Electricity Generating Board (CEGB) and the client was the head of the branch. We were asked to undertake a study of 'The management requirements of the Management Services Branch' as a means of both developing understanding of the nature of the branch and through which the Lancaster systems approach might be demonstrated. The phase 'management requirements' was deliberately vague in order to allow considerable scope for the project and flexibility in approach. The team responsible for the project consisted of two students from the Master's degree programme, a senior manager from within the Branch, and myself, as project manager. It was recognised by the team that any discussion generated by the findings of the study would be constrained to personnel within the organisational boundary of the branch but that access to other parts of the CEGB Headquarters and the South West Region was permissible in order to assemble as complete a picture of the role and working of the branch as was feasible within the timescale of the project (approximately 16 weeks). Given the nature of the 'problem-content system', an issue-based analysis was initially considered appropriate and the activities in the problem-solving system were as listed below. This effectively represented the intellectual development of the project and it was seen to consist of two phases. This approach was agreed with the branch management at the start of the project.

Phase I

(1) Assemble a picture of management service activity as viewed from within the branch and from outside (i.e. by their clients).
(2) Define 'a system' to realise management service needs within the Region.
(3) Select RDs for this system which reflect the views express in (1).
(4) Develop conceptual models from these RDs and examine the significance of any major differences which result.
(5) Decide to (a) accept a particular view; (b) accept a modified view or (c) progress separately the models produced in (4) to identify the implications of the differences.

Phase II

(6) By comparing the conceptual model(s) derived in (4) with the actual situation, identify areas in which more detailed analysis would be beneficial. These may be in the context of defining 'management requirements' in specific areas as indicated in the previous phase.

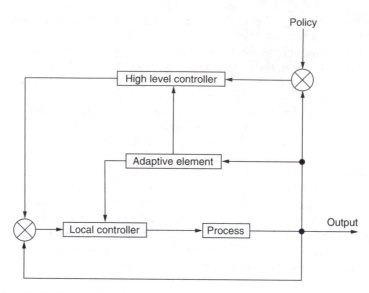

Figure 6.10   *Simplified: adaptive feedback controller*

(7) Set up a seminar with branch managers to discuss the areas of concern resulting from the investigation.

Activities (2) to (5) turned out to be difficult since, as already mentioned, considerable variety was encountered while doing activity (1), about the purpose of the Branch. The approach which replaced these activities was arrived at by considering the question 'what system does the Management Services Branch serve and hence of which is it a part?'

The system chosen was the South West Region electricity provision system of the CEGB. A broad-level activity model was produced and those activities discarded which were seen to be executive decision-making activities and those concerned with operations management. What was left, it was argued, could be viewed as a management support system. The relevant system in this case was derived by reduction from a wider system. The process of reduction was based upon making an analogy between the CEGB electricity provision system and a general model of an adaptive control system (Figure 6.10).

Figure 6.11 represents the translation of this adaptive control system into the structure of the wider CEGB system.

The RD of this wider system was derived from the published set of objectives for the south-western regional organisation of the CEGB, and this was argued as reasonable since the role of the CEGB was not being questioned, only the role of the MSB within it.

Figure 6.12 represents a notional set of activities for the wider CEGB system. Each activity was examined in turn to identify whether or not it could be allocated to either the higher-level regional control system or to the operations management system. These are shown within the shaded areas. The remainder could be viewed as management support activities. In addition to this process of reduction, further activities were discarded from this management support set which, within this particular situation, could *not* be seen as MSB activities.

These were, for example, activities concerned with the accounting and personnel functions.

Thus, by this process of reduction, a set of activities remained which could be viewed as a set appropriate to the MSB.

However, when compared against the formal systems model, it was seen to be deficient as a model of a HAS. It represented a set of activities, but none of these were concerned with the

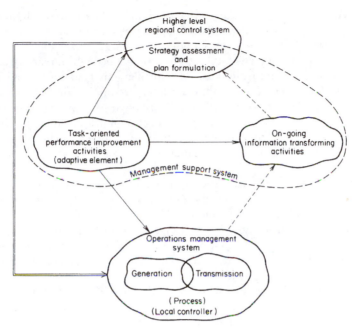

Figure 6.11 *The Central Electricity Generating Board as an adaptive control system. Key:* ⋯→, *performance information* →, *actions to improve performance:* ⇒, *demand and expectations for performance*

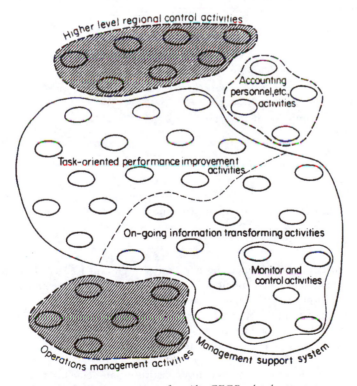

Figure 6.12 *A management support system as part of a wider CEGB-related system*

monitoring and control that was necessary if the set could also be said to be a human activity system. Thus control activities were added which were appropriate to the area of decision taking represented by the boundary of the remaining support activities.

Returning to the activities of phase I, RDs were also obtained which reflected the views of senior managers within the branch and from these RDs further activity models were derived.

Apart from providing insight into the different interpretations of the branch's role, these models were used to 'validate' the derived model described above. By comparing the models from the manager's RDs with the one derived by reduction, it could be established whether or not the derived model *at least* contained the others. Once the derived model had been validated it could then be used as a tool to compare against the actual branch situation to identify areas for improvement or for more detailed investigation.

Here the word 'validate' is used in a particular sense. It is not validation in the sense of confirming that the model was an adequate representation of reality but, on the basis of the mapping, it was confirmed that the model was *legitimate* and of *adequate scope*.

Views were also sought from outside MSB, again with the intention of identifying possible activities missing from the derived model. In the event this proved less valuable as a means of validating the scope of the model but was extremely valuable in assessing the effectiveness of some of the 'across-boundary' MSB activities.

Having produced broad observations from a comparison of the total MSB model with the actual situation, the next stage was to concentrate on specific areas for a more detailed analysis. It was argued that the 'on-going' activities could readily be seen as necessary regional management support activities (see Figure 6.12) but that the task improvement activities represented a part of MSB role that was *needed to be seen to be effective* if it was to survive. Thus effort was concentrated on this particular area and, because the 'management' of the branch was crucial to effectiveness, the branch control activities were also examined. The necessary activities for a task-oriented improvement system and an MSB control system are given below:

Task-oriented system

(1) Establish a means for identifying areas for improvement.
(2) Ensure that skills are available to analyse and reach recommendations about improvements.
(3) Make known the existence of this capability.
(4) Take steps to obtain improvement tasks.
(5) Allocate the tasks.
(6) Carry out the tasks.
(7) Make recommendations on improvements and how to implement them.
(8) Monitor implementation and review recommendations.
(9) Control the system to ensure that the specific tasks, their identification, and their execution are done effectively and contribute to the improvement in performance of the region.

MSB control system

(1) Decide on measures of performance and expectations relevant to each subsystem.
(2) Monitor performance of management activities based upon mapping the above subsystems.
(3) Identify areas for improving the management of these activities.
(4) Know and be competent in the application of modern management techniques and approaches so that the management of the identified activities can be improved.
(5) Select from (4) and apply where appropriate to improve total MSB performance.

A listing of activities such as the above does not constitute a model. The connectivity must also be included. However, the listing is given here to illustrate the nature of the activities being considered.

Comparing these activities with the picture of the branch derived from both internal and external sources led to the identification of areas of concern within which specific recommendations could be made. A summary of the comparison at this level of detail together with generalised comments about the activities is included to illustrate the kind of areas highlighted for debate.

Task-oriented system

Activities (1), (3) and (4) were all concerned with projecting to present and potential clients the capability of the branch as a problem-solving resource. Particularly as a result of outside questioning it appeared that activity (3) was not well done. Activities (1) and (4) were related to the decision on where the branch effort should be directed in seeking and obtaining problem-solving assignments. It was apparent that this decision was not taken corporately in the light of a disciplined survey of branch capability and future desired direction.

It was suggested that a useful aid to carrying out corporate strategy evaluation of this kind was a device that we called an 'experience matrix'. This was a particular recommendation that emerged from the comparison and will be discussed later.

Activity (2) suggested a need to assemble the appropriate skills once the 'marketing' decisions referred to above had been taken. A particular deficiency was seen to exist in that skills were assembled more on a technique orientation rather than on a problem-solving orientation. Activity (5) was seen to be done on a limited scale. Because of the technique orientation, problems tended to be allocated according to the technique that was likely to be of use and, hence, the resources used tended to be restricted to that particular expertise. Allocation also tended to be partial, i.e. the project manager and 'doer' were not always given full access to the problem situation.

Activity (6) seemed to be adequately performed, except (as mentioned above), for the need to be involved in the problem situation as much as possible if the resultant 'solution' was going to be appropriate.

Activity (7) was deficient in the sense that 'how to implement' was rarely seen as another problem to which a problem-solving expertise should be developed. It was apparent that the reason for some on-going activities living on in the MSB was due to a failure to implement, the distinction here being the difference between designing and then operating a procedure.

Activity (9), which was concerned with the control of activities (1)–(8), is complex in the sense that a mixture of resolution levels of control is implied. Activities (1)–(4) were related to group effectiveness and hence should be the concern of the overall branch controller whereas activities (5)–(8) were related to within-group, individual task, effectiveness and hence should be the concern of section managers. There appeared to be a mixing of these levels within the then current branch control with, particularly, the involvement of the Head of Management Services in the lower-level task control.

MSB control system

Activities (1)–(3) were concerned with the identification of the different kinds of activities going on within the branch and the development of measures of performance that were appropriate to them. This was not done in any *explicit* way and hence it was not possible to state whether or not it was done well. It was decided to make recommendations on the structure and components of measures of performance so that, if necessary, modifications to any existing measures could be made.

Activities (4) and (5) were concerned with keeping abreast of modern developments in problem solving and other management activities and selecting and developing, if necessary, those particularly pertinent to the branch and the region's needs. The only deficiency to be noted here was that the process was rather *ad hoc*. There was no formal survey of what was available or under development in outside establishments and hence no rigorous selection of those worth monitoring.

As a result of comparison of these and more detailed models for the 'task-oriented' and control systems, the following areas of concern were established within which detailed recommendations were formulated: (a) understanding, by MSB staff of the role and capabilities of MSB; (b) understanding by clients and other functional areas of the role and capabilities of MSB; (c) development of resource skills within the branch; (d) development of external linkages between the branch, headquarters and the region; (e) development of MSB marketing policy; (f) organisation structure of the branch; (g) measures of performance for control.

It is not really appropriate to discuss the detailed recommendations here, but one that may have more general applicability is the experience matrix.

Derivation of an Experience Matrix

As an aid to creating a greater appreciation of the extent of the branch's capability, as well as providing a vehicle by which conscious decisions could be made on the allocation of marketing effort, it was suggested that the matrix be construction. This showed, in the one picture, the areas of work undertaken by the branch as a whole and also the degree of effectiveness achieved. This is reproduced as Figure 6.13. The vertical scale a listing of existing and potential clients and the horizontal scale was a listing of task areas. The elements of the matrix could be filled by a symbol for each project (the density of such symbols in any one element indicating the degree of experience in that area) or by a number (on a scale from 1 to 7, say) indicating the outcome of the project. Such a scale could be

1 = enhanced understanding
2 = improved organisation of information
3 = new organisation structure and/or processes
4 = improved level of service or quality
5 = better utilisation of resources
6 = reduced operating costs
7 = increased productivity

Although one matrix only was considered, it is clearly possible to develop others which separately show level of activity in specific projects in particular client areas, or outcome in relation to

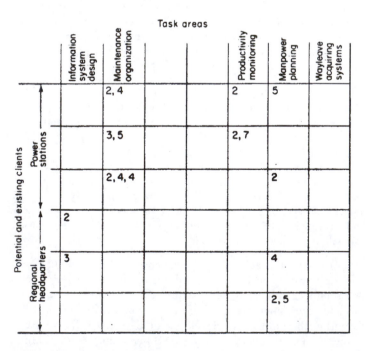

Figure 6.13   *An experience matrix*

particular clients, or outcome in relation to particular kinds of projects. The analysis of these matrices could provide information on how effective the branch was in relation to certain clients or in relation to particular kinds of projects.

The total picture could demonstrate those areas (both client and project) in which the branch had experience and those in which it had not. Thus decisions could be made on where, and how, to direct marketing effort and on what skills were required in order to provide the total problem-solving/advisory capability.

Such a matrix would have to be constructed for a particular historical period and subsequently updated. In this case the previous three years was suggested as a suitable period over which to survey existing branch capability and type of activity.

The methodology derived at the start of the project, listed previously as a two-phase analysis, was consciously modified as it was being used. Phase I, in particular, was changed as difficulty was experienced in using the issue-based models derived from the variety of views that existed about the role and activities of the MSB identified from the initial interviewing of branch staff and their clients. It was at this stage that the control analogy was used to extract a relevant model from a primary task model of the wider system related to electricity provision for the region as a whole. The resulting methodology that represented phase I is illustrated by Figure 6.14.

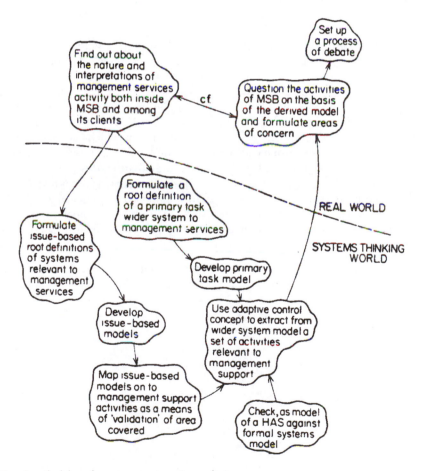

Figure 6.14   *A methodology for management service analysis*

CONCLUSION

This chapter has concentrated on the 'wider-system extraction' approach to CPTM construction and a few examples have been described as a means of illustrating its use. The model building has been included within the context of each project both to illustrate what was done and also to place each model within a particular methodology. The concepts being used and the methodology cannot be separated in actual problem solving. The CEGB project described above demonstrated that, as the methodology adopted in phase I of the project changed, so did the models and the way they were used.

A crucial feature of this approach is the drawing of the boundaries to explore the content of 'the system' within the wider system. Four critera have been used as an aid to deciding how to place these boundaries and the chapter concludes with a description of them.

(1) **The use of an alternative concept**   An alternative concept was used in the CEGB project. Essentially the concept that was used was that of an adaptive control system. This was mapped onto the model derived from the mission statement of the CEGB and those activities that represented the adaptive elements were taken to be relevant to the role of the Management Services Branch: the focus of the investigation.

(2) **Expertise requirement**   For a particular boundary mapping to be feasible the assumption is made that personnel exist (or can be acquired) with the expertise necessary to do the activities within the boundary. This assumption can be reversed and used to define the boundary implied by the existence of a particular expertise set.

(3) **Wider–system feasibility**   Although something like a mission statement may be used as the source of a wider-system model, activities may be implied which do not exist in the actual organisation. This is problematical if a boundary is drawn around activities, some of which may be missing. It is also problematical if the derived system boundary includes activities that are present, or are seen to be desirable, but that depend upon activities outside the boundary that do not, themselves, exist. Such missing activities outside the derived system boundary may raise questions about the feasibility of the wider-system model on which the mapping is based.

(4) **Decision–taking power/authority allocation**   Since any role, however derived, has to lie within some power or authority structure within an organisation, this can be used as a criterion for deciding on boundaries that are feasible in relation to this particular context. If the model has been partitioned into subsystems, each subsystem boundary represents an area of authority of the subsystem controller. Thus the mapping can be carried out in relation to a feasible set of controllers and the derived system boundary drawn around the appropriate number of sub–systems.

The criteria used in any situation must be based upon the political and social context in which the investigation is being undertaken. The actual critera are likely to be some combination of the above set rather than any particular one.

Chapter Seven

CPTM—Assembly Using the Enterprise Model

THE ENTERPRISE MODEL

The Enterprise Model was first used as a way of thinking about the different management processes within an organisation (Wilson 1984, 1990). Over the last few years it has been used increasingly as a device for ensuring that the total range of systems required within a CPTM have been considered and included. Thus as an 'aide-mémoire' it has been extremely useful and its application has proved highly successful.

For convenience, it is introduced again here.

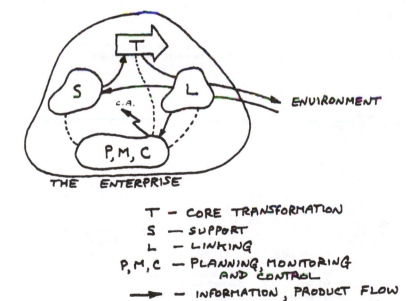

The Enterprise Model

As the above diagram illustrates, there are four types of system to consider. The transformation process (T) represents the core purpose of the organisation (or organisation unit) under consideration. It may be usefully considered as the non–contentious (i.e neutral) primary task model as used within the W–decomposition approach described in Chapter Five. However, it doesn't need to be. It is up to the analyst to decide what would be the most useful. In a sophisticated application, the analyst may use the W–decomposition approach to derive the model for the T. This could be useful if there is no clear concept to represent the core purpose of the organisation. (see the description of the West Yorkshire Police project described later).

However, once the T has been decided the other elements become more straightforward. S represents that system (or those systems) needed to facilitate or support the transformation. These systems are usually concerned with ensuring that the necessary capability is in place through the provision of human and physical resources. The support also goes beyond the transformation to the enterprise in total. The whole concept represented by the CPTM must be capable of working (even if the part of the real world it is intended to represent, does not). Thus the other elements (i.e. L and P, M, C) must also have the necessary capability. L represents those linking systems which provide the required interfaces to the environment of the enterprise. If the CPTM is intended to represent an organisation unit rather than the organisation in total, then some of the interfaces required may be internal as well as external to the organisation.

The environment that is important is everything *outside* the organisation unit and those features need to be represented that have significant impact on the OU.

P,M,C represent the planning, monitoring and controlling systems that ensure that the enterprise is adaptive and is capable of developing in response to internally generated future vision as well as external messages provided by the linking systems.

As a simple illustration, suppose that we wished to develop concepts to represent the marketing and sales functions within a manufacturing company.

The systems, for which we could produce RDs, are named in Figures 7.1 and 7.2. Here only the Enterprise Model elements are shown.

The connections between the elements are formed, as logical dependencies, when the models are assembled. These two models, of course, are based upon a single perception of what the functions of

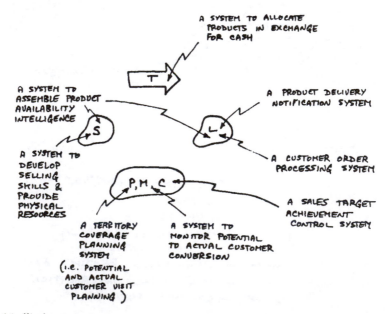

Figure 7.1   *A 'selling' system*

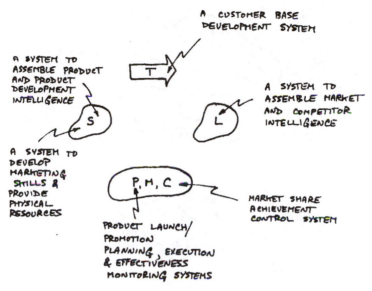

Figure 7.2 *A 'marketing' system*

marketing and selling mean to me. Any analyst can form their own models based upon interaction with a specific group of relevant people within a specific manufacturing company. The models are neither right nor wrong but they are explicit and they represent what the analyst is taking the respective functions to be.

METHOD OF ASSEMBLY

The procedure to assemble the models is similar to that adopted for the W–decomposition approach except that, in this case, there is not a neutral (non-contentious) model that forms a common set of activities in each system. Thus the activities are additive from the models representing each type (i.e. for T, S, L and P,M,C). The simplest approach is to model one system first, usually the T or P,M,C, and then to take each other RD in turn and add the activities, with appropriate connectivity, to the first model derived and so on. The procedure is illustrated in Figures 7.3 and 7.4.

Referring to Figure 7.3, the Enterprise Model at the top identifies the set of RDs taken as definitions of the four elements. In this example only one RD is taken to represent each element. In practice more than a one-to-one representation will be required. For example, in Figure 7.1 eight systems are defined whereas in Figure 7.2 six systems are taken to represent the total concept.

In stage 1 a selection is made of the system to start the modelling process. Here RD4 is taken but, in practice, it could be any. Having started with the PMC system, the RD corresponding to the T is taken next. As the conceptual model for RD1 is developed, it is added to the model from RD4 and the total logical connectivity added as the model is constructed. Stage 2 is completed when the sets of activities and the connectivity appropriate to the combination of the two models is complete.

In stage 3 the next system to be added is chosen and in this example it is the system required to facilitate, or provide support for, the T, i.e. RD3. Here the same procedure is adopted.

As activities appropriate to RD3 are derived they are added to the total model existing at the end of stage 2. Once this is complete, the final model is constructed from RD2 and added incrementally as in the previous stages.

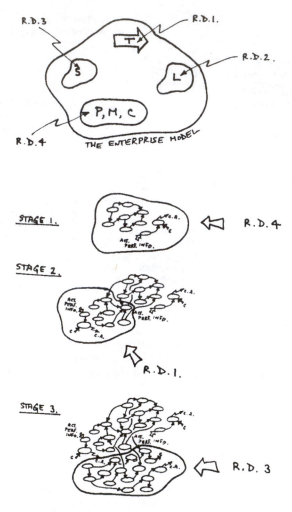

Figure 7.3   *The CPTM—initial stages*

Irrespective of the number of RDs representing the four Enterprise Model elements the complete CPTM is obtained by the sequential addition of both activities and connectivity as each RD is taken in turn.

Where to place the activities on the page is obviously a practical consideration and is important when it comes to locating the connectivity and performing the subsystem decomposition later on. This requires prior thought and here one is effectively planning the layout. The first aspect of this planning is to form some idea of what kind of subsystems are likely to arise from the total range of RDs being developed. Understanding the structure of each RD is a helpful first consideration by thinking about the CATWOE elements. The T (of CATWOE *not* the enterprise model) will give rise to at least one subsystem and so will the W. The specification of a customer (C) will usually produce a subsystem to do with responding to the deliverable(s) of T. The E will lead to a constraint management subsystem and so on.

The next consideration will be to think about how one subsystem relates to another in the context of the Enterprise Model. Figure 7.5 attempts to illustrate this consideration for a CPTM relevant to a manufacturing company.

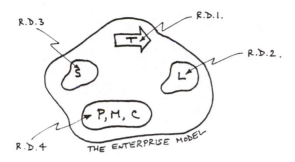

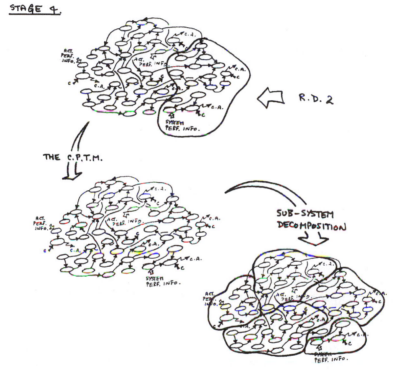

Figure 7.4 *The CPTM*

First, however, we need to derive the set of RD relevant to the various CPTM elements. The following set, together with the expected subsystems, leads to the arrangement in Figure 7.5.

T   A system to convert components into a range of quality finished products to satisfy the needs of a variety of customers according to a derived schedule.

Subsystem
   T1   Product assembly
   T2   Component acquisition
   T3   Product quality control
   T4   Customer response assessment
   T5   Schedule management

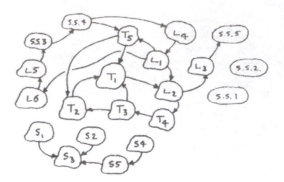

Figure 7.5 *Subsystem relationships*

L   A system to distribute finished products to customers in response to generated orders in order to
acquire revenue.

Subsystem
    L1   Customer order processing
    L2   Product delivery
    L3   Revenue collection
    L4   Product promotion

S   A system to ensure physical resource capability matches the requirements while making best use
of relevant developments in technology.

Subsystem
    S_1 Requirements derivation
    S_2 Current physical resource assessment
    S_3 Resource matching
    S_4 Technological intelligence assembly
    S_5 Technology exploitation

PMC   A company-owned system operated by suitably skilled personnel to realise the desired
strategic development of the company by defining the product range to be made available
through an assessment of market and competitor intelligence, while constrained by company policy and the finances available.

Subsystem
    SS1   Overall performance control
    SS2   Human resource management
    SS3   Product planning
    SS4   Plan realisation management
    SS5   Constraint management
    L5   Intelligence assessment
    L6   Intelligence assembly

In Figure 7.5 a number of subsystems appear to be unconnected to the remainder. This is because
they impact on *all* the remainder. All subsystems need to be resourced; with both physical and human

resources (S_1 ... S_5, SS2) and all subsystems are subject to overall performance control (SS1). The constraint management subsystem (SS5) will also impact on all the others, through their control activities, but in this case the finance available will be dependent upon the revenue collected (L3).

We can use this example to illustrate the process of CPTM assembly detailed in Figures 7.3 and 7.4.

Although we could choose to start with any of the RDs let us take that derived for the PMC element. The RD actually overlaps into the linking element, since it requires the assembly of market and competitor intelligence, and into the support element, since the human resources are specified through the inclusion of Actors.

Given the complexity of the overall CPTM, illustrated by Figures 7.5, a further practical consideration is the size and aspect ratio of the paper onto which the model is to be developed. The subsystem layout suggests an aspect ratio appropriate to 'landscape' and the number of subsystems (22) suggests an AO-size paper. This makes an illustration in book form difficult since the aspect ratio is essentially 'portrait' and the page size is A5.

We can start to model the RD for the P,M,C element by choosing to ignore (initially) the phrases for Owner, Actors and (E) constraints. The resultant model is in Figures 7.6 and 7.6(a). This latter model illustrates the four subsystems L5, L6, SS3 and SS4.

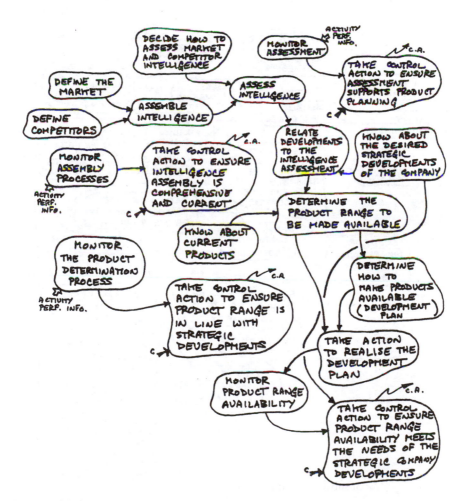

Figure 7.6   *Model of P,M,C*

As in Figure 7.3, the RD for the T element is taken next. The resultant activities are then added to the model of Figure 7.6.

In order to assess whether or not the customers' needs have been satisfied (i.e. subsystem T4) it is necessary to receive orders and to get the products to the customer. Hence the activities appropriate to the linking system have been included at the same time (i.e. subsystems L1, L2, L3 and L4). The resultant model is reproduced as Figure 7.7.

Stage 3 of the process illustrated in Figure 7.3. can be completed by taking the RD relevant to the support (S) element of the enterprise model and extending the model of Figure 7.7 by adding the activities of Figure 7.8.

This model covers the scope of subsystems S_1 to S_5 but the detail has been reduced so that only two subsystems are represented; one concerned with matching physical resources to requirements and the other related to technology exploitation.

The CPTM can now be completed by adding the subsystems related to Human Resource Management (SS2), constraint management (SS5) and overall performance control (SS1).

The complete CPTM is reproduced as Figure 7.9 with the subsystem decomposition in Figure 7.10.

Since it was known at all stages of the assembly of the CPTM, that the system was constrained (i.e. the E of CATWOE had been specified), it is useful to include the constraint (C) arrow in each

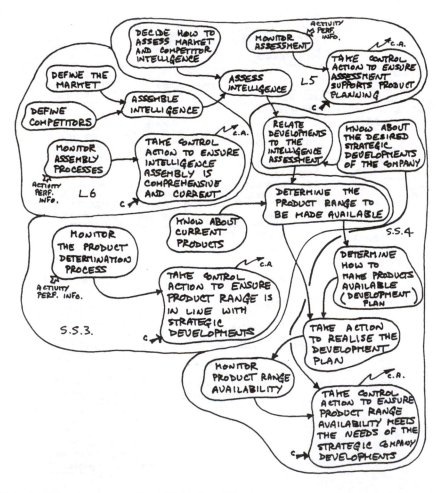

Figure 7.6   *(a) Subsystem decomposition of P,M,C model*

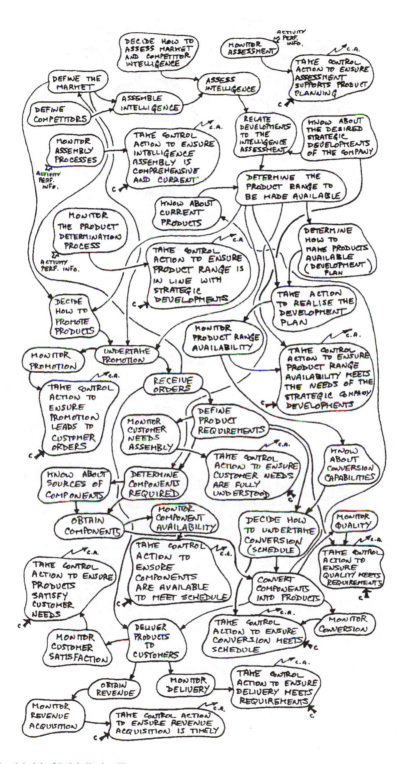

Figure 7.7 *Model of P,M,C plus T*

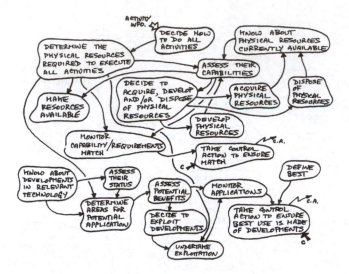

Figure 7.8   *Model of S*

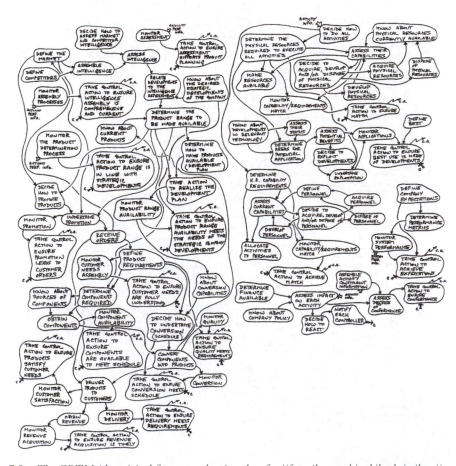

Figure 7.9   *The CPTM (the original figure may be viewed on ftp://ftp.wiley.co.uk/pub/books/wilson/)*

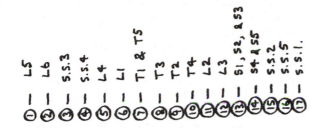

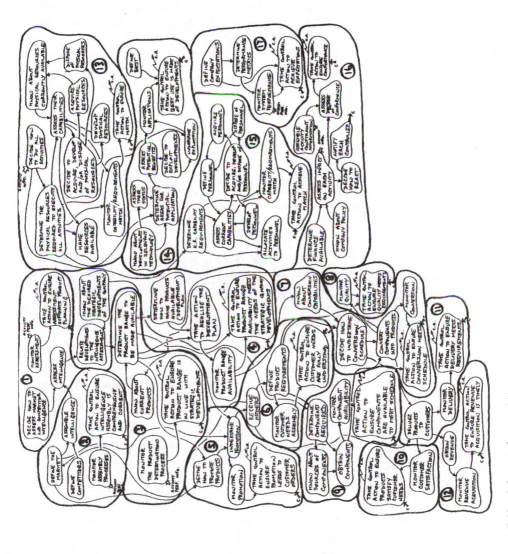

Figure 7.10 *Subsystem decomposition*

controller as the model is developed. That way no controllers are missed. Omissions might happen if the inclusion of constraints is left until the whole model is assembled.

The process of model assembly may, initially, appear complex, but after a little practice it is relatively straightforward. It does, of course, rely on the basic ability to form a defensible conceptual model from a root definition. Thus the rules and principles expounded in Chapter Two must be followed and sufficient experience accumulated at the level of developing a single RD and associated model before attempting the assembly of a CPTM.

The real skill that needs to be developed is to ensure that the range of RDs representing each of the enterprise model elements are consistent and fit well together.

Since it is known at the outset that a single (CPTM) model is to be produced it is not necessary to replicate all CATWOE elements in each RD formed. Customers may differ from RD to RD and hence they would need to be specified appropriately. The Owner is best specified only once since the Owner that is appropriate is that relevant to the wider system with respect to the CPTM rather than any one of the enterprise model elements. Environmental constraints are essentially those impacting on the CPTM and need to be included within one RD (usually the P,M,C, definition).

However, there may be constraints that are of limited concern. Technological standards, for example, may only be related to those activities to do with exploiting new technology. Hence they should be introduced explicitly within that subsystem. The overall constraints (again usually specified within the P,M,C definition) will have general applicability (like company policy, the law, etc.) and will limit the degrees of freedom of each controller via the broad arrow annotated with C.

It was mentioned in Chapter Four, in the discussion about BPR, that a study is currently underway within the Met. Office. Since the enterprise model assembly method is being used extensively, futher discussion had to be delayed until this method had been described. It would now be useful to continue the discussion as an actual illustration of the use of the enterprise model.

THE MET. OFFICE

Although it is essentially a BPR study, this terminology is not used. In 1999 the Met. Office embarked upon what they termed a major BPI exercise (where BPI is Business Process Improvement). This was to be undertaken in two phases. Phase I was a determination of the major business processes required by the Met. Office to achieve its strategic vision. Phase II was concerned with undertaking a detailed review of each division within the Met. Office in order to derive changes (not necessarily radical) to bring about the improvements that were desirable and also feasible. The link between phase I and phase II is an organisation mapping. This is a necessary intermediate stage to relate the current organisation groupings (Divisions), to the business processes (i.e. CPTM activities).

The Enterprise Model assembly method was used to construct a model that was taken to be the CPTM relevant to the Met. Office and its future vision. Eight RDs were derived to represent the four Enterprise Model elements and the total model was obtained using a process similar to that described in Figures 7.3 and 7.4. The final model contained about 300 activities and was decomposed into 35 subsystems. This is too large to display here but it is the process that is being illustrated. The 35 subsystems represented the major business processes. They could be defended as 'major' since they could all be shown to be necessary in achieving the future vision. The internal project manager was conversant with SSM modelling and the model logic was discussed and agreed. Thus at the end of phase I we had derived the major business processes (the required deliverable) and we had achieved organisational 'buy-in', in the form of a senior Met. Office manager.

As part of phase I and to enable us to move to phase II we went through an organisational mapping. This served to define (for each division within the Met. Office) those major business processes that they currently undertook. This also helped with the 'buy-in' process since the mapping showed that the model was at least wide enough in scope to accommodate all divisions. The mapping was actually done by using large acetate sheets and forming coloured boundaries for each division by using overhead projector pens. This is a very graphic method which illustrates areas of potential overlap (and possible duplication) together with gaps in the current responsibilities. The mappings were converted into matrix representations for reporting and communication purposes. These are given in Figures 7.11 and 7.12.

Phase II is being done sequentially. The order in which the various parts of the organisation are reviewed is being driven by the respective managers. All are aware of the BPI exercise and we are responding to their readiness to be involved.

Essentially we are moving down the organisation hierarchy rather than the systems hierarchy. This is necessary if we are to generate the commitment of the various managers to the changes

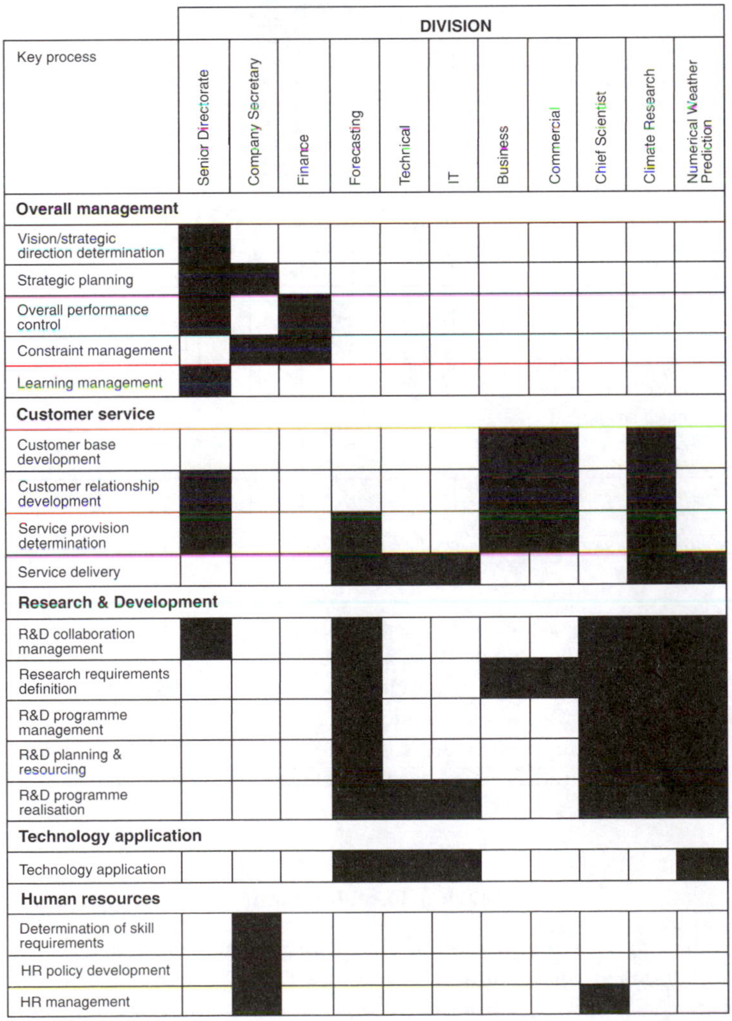

Key process	DIVISION										
	Senior Directorate	Company Secretary	Finance	Forecasting	Technical	IT	Business	Commercial	Chief Scientist	Climate Research	Numerical Weather Prediction
Overall management											
Vision/strategic direction determination	█										
Strategic planning	█	█									
Overall performance control		█	█								
Constraint management	█	█									
Learning management	█										
Customer service											
Customer base development	█						█	█		█	
Customer relationship development	█						█	█		█	
Service provision determination	█				█		█	█			
Service delivery					█		█				
Research & Development											
R&D collaboration management	█				█		█		█		
Research requirements definition					█				█	█	
R&D programme management					█						
R&D planning & resourcing					█			█			
R&D programme realisation					█						
Technology application											
Technology application					█		█				█
Human resources											
Determination of skill requirements		█									
HR policy development		█									
HR management		█								█	

Figure 7.11 *Organisation/process matrix*

Key process	DIVISION										
	Senior Directorate	Company Secretary	Finance	Forecasting	Technical	IT	Business	Commercial	Chief Scientist	Climate Research	Numerical Weather Prediction
Observation activities											
Determination of requirements					■						
Programme management					■						
Planning & resourcing					■						
Work plan execution					■						
Sub-contract management					■						
IT provision											
Determination of requirements					■	■					
Programme management						■					
Planning & Resourcing						■					
Work plan execution						■					
Sub-contract management						■					
Works Services											
Determination of requirements			■								
Programme management			■								
Planning & resourcing			■		■						
Work plan execution			■								
Sub-contract management			■								
Change management											
Programme management	■										
Project management	■										

Figure 7.12　*Organisation/process matrix continued*

emerging. The organisation mapping was the mechanism used to relate the organisation hierarchy to the systems hierarchy so that when RDs are derived for systems to map onto the various organisation units we know what scope of activities we need to represent. Some models represented a re-use of the activities in the Met. Office model since they were at a useful level of detail already. In other cases, minor expansion of some areas of the existing Met. Office model was all that was required. However, several models have been developed as more detailed CPTMs, using the Enterprise Model assembly method.

Market Development

As an example of the latter, an examination of the customer service-oriented activities illustrated in Figure 7.11 was undertaken for Commercial and Business Divisions. In this, eleven RDs were derived to represent the elements within the enterprise model. Figure 7.13 illustrates the structure and the level of complexity of the resultant model.

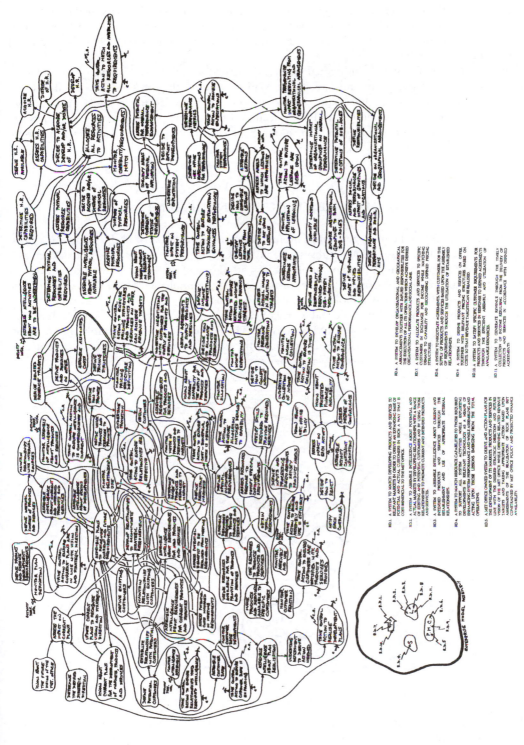

RD.1. A SYSTEM TO MATCH DEVELOPING PRODUCTS AND SERVICES TO RELEVANT MARKETS IN ORDER TO CREATE AN EXPANDING BASE OF POTENTIAL AND ACTUAL CUSTOMERS IN SUCH A WAY THAT IS COST-BENEFICIAL TO THE MET.OFFICE.

RD.2. A SYSTEM TO USE INTELLIGENCE ABOUT POTENTIAL AND ACTUAL MARKETS BY DEVELOPING PRODUCTS WITH A RANGE OF EXISTING AND POTENTIAL CUSTOMERS AND BY USING THOSE RELATIONSHIPS TO PROMOTE CURRENT AND DEFINED PRODUCTS AND SERVICES.

RD.3. A SYSTEM TO ASSEMBLE INTELLIGENCE ABOUT CURRENT AND INTENDED PRODUCTS AND SERVICES THROUGH THE ESTABLISHMENT AND USE OF APPROPRIATE INTERNAL RELATIONSHIPS.

RD.4. A SYSTEM TO MATCH RESOURCE CAPABILITIES TO THOSE REQUIRED TO SUPPORT ALL SYSTEM ACTIVITIES WHILE EXPLOITING DEVELOPMENTS IN RELEVANT TECHNOLOGY AS A MEANS OF ENHANCING SYSTEM PERFORMANCE AND WHILE ASSEMBLING AND ACTING UPON THOSE LESSONS EMERGING FROM THE TOTAL OPERATION.

RD.5. A MET.OFFICE OWNED SYSTEM TO DERIVE AND ACTION PLANS FOR THE DEVELOPMENT OF ITS MARKETS, PRODUCTS AND SERVICES IN LINE WITH THE DESIRED STRATEGIC DIRECTION AND FUTURE VISION OF THE MET. WHILE DERIVING RELATED REVENUE TARGETS AND TAKING APPROPRIATE ACTION BASED UPON ASSESSMENTS OF THE REALISATION OF SUCH PLANS MET CONSTRAINED BY MET.OFFICE POLICY AND PROJECTED FINANCE AVAILABILITY.

RD.6. A SYSTEM TO DEVELOP ORGANISATIONAL AND GEOGRAPHICAL ARRANGEMENTS TOGETHER WITH RELEVANT FACILITIES FOR THE EXECUTION OF ALL ITS OPERATIONS WHICH ACHIEVE DESIRED ORGANISATIONAL PERFORMANCE AND SOCIAL AIMS.

RD.7. A SYSTEM TO ALLOCATE PRODUCTS AND SERVICES TO SPECIFIC CUSTOMERS IN ACCORDANCE WITH INCOME MATCHING DEMAND TO CAPABILITY AND RECOGNISING DEFINED PRICING STRUCTURES.

RD.8. A SYSTEM TO NEGOTIATE AGREEMENTS WITH CUSTOMERS FOR THE SUPPLY OF PRODUCTS AND SERVICES BASED UPON THE FAMILY OF REQUIREMENTS THROUGH THE UTILISATION OF ESTABLISHED RELATIONSHIPS.

RD.9. A SYSTEM TO DEFINE PRODUCTS AND SERVICES ON OFFER TOGETHER WITH RELEVANT PRICING STRUCTURES BASED ON COSTS SO THAT REVENUE TARGETS CAN BE REALISED.

RD.10. A SYSTEM TO SATISFY SPECIFIC CUSTOMER REQUIREMENTS FOR PRODUCTS AND SERVICES IN RESPONSE TO DEFINED AGREEMENTS THROUGH THE EFFICIENT ASSEMBLY AND UTILISATION OF AVAILABLE RESOURCES.

RD.11. A SYSTEM TO GENERATE REVENUE THROUGH THE TIMELY COLLECTION OF INCOME RESULTING FROM THE DELIVERY OF PRODUCTS AND SERVICES IN ACCORDANCE WITH DEFINED AGREEMENTS.

Figure 7.13   *Market development model (the original figure may be viewed on ftp://ftp.wiley.co.uk/pub/books/wilson/)*

In this figure the relationship between the eleven RDs and the four elements of the Enterprise Model is also illustrated. The individual activities were the source of questions about current practices and the assessment, based upon this model/real-world comparison, was the source of recommendations for change.

Two other areas for which individual 'Enterprise-based' CPTMs were developed were for Human Resource Management and Constraint Management. Although these are specific to the Met. Office they represent illustrations of expansions in detail of the models arising from the specification of A and E within any RD. Because of their more general applicability they are included here. Further discussion of human resource management appears in Chapter Eight as an area of particular interest.

HUMAN RESOURCE MANAGEMENT

Within the Met. Office the management of human resources is undertaken in the Centre as well as in Divisions. The HR management subsystem, in the CPTM, relevant to the Met. Office as a whole, was developed from the statement of Actors within one of the RDs. This is not sufficiently detailed to be used as the comparison device for further analysis in phase 2 of the project. Thus, the 'Management of HR' requires elaboration in order to be useful.

To cope with the complexity of the real world of HR management, it was necessary to develop a CPTM for this particular part of Met. Office activity. The Enterprise Model assembly method was, again, chosen as the most appropriate to use since the original subsystem had been accepted as relevant and all we were seeking to do was to maintain a consistent expansion. The structure of the model developed is given below:

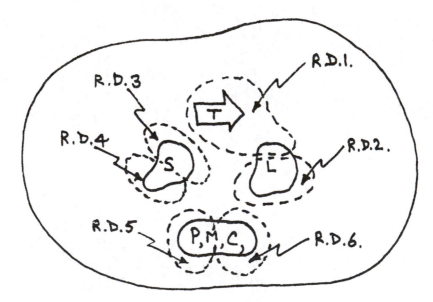

The RDs corresponding to this model were:

RD1   A system to satisfy specified opportunities for staff by acquiring selected candidates with the required skills, competences and other characteristics through both internal and external acquisition which can be permanent and/or temporary, in a timely and cost-effective manner while recognising the need to adopt the requirements of 'open and fair' competition, MOD recruitment guidelines, personnel procedures and employment legislation and constrained by finance availability.

RD2   A system to assemble intelligence about relevant competition in order to assess comparative levels of remuneration and other terms of employment to facilitate the maintenance and acquisition of Met. Office personnel.

RD3   A system to match physical resources to requirements in order to facilitate the operations of HR management while exploiting developments in relevant technology, on the basis of authorised business cases, as a means of enhancing performance.

RD4   A system to seek to improve the operations of HR management by extracting lessons from those operations, storing and disseminating the learning as appropriate.

RD5   A Met. Office-owned system, operated by HR Department personnel and line managers in association with the unions and the Pay and Pensions Agency, to maintain the required roles within the Met. Office as the roles change in response to planned departmental and strategic developments and as staff changes give rise to vacancies, by specifying opportunities, both now and in the future, for recruitment and staff development while seeking to balance organisation needs and those of the individual with respect to career development and conditions of contract.

RD6   An HR-owned system to derive policy in line with Met. Office HR-related policy developments together with its dissemination to all staff associated with HR matters in order to ensure consistent interpretation and action across the Met. Office while, in particular, realising the adoption of performance-related pay.

N.B. MOD = Ministry of Defence.

The CPTM resulting from these RDs is given in Figure 7.14 together with the subsystem decomposition in Figure 7.15.

Sixteen subsystems have been defined and these are:

(1) Personnel requirements specification
(2) Policy derivation and dissemination
(3) Opportunity planning
(4) Opportunity specification
(5) Promotion and candidate introduction
(6) Candidate selection
(7) Needs (organisation and individual) balancing
(8) HR personnel management
(9) HR expectations management
(10) Physical resource management
(11) Learning management
(12) Constraint management
(13) Appointment cost–benefit management
(14) Performance-related pay adoption
(15) Competitor intelligence/HR policy management
(16) Overall performance control

This was the model that was used to derive HR-related recommendations across the Met. Office in relation to both the Central and Divisional areas of activity.

Constraint Management

As with HR management, constraint management is dispersed across the whole of the Met. Office divisions. Within the overall model relevant to the Met. Office, the constraint management

Figure 7.14   A model for HR management (the original figure may be viewed on ftp://ftp.wiley.co.uk/pub/books/wilson/)

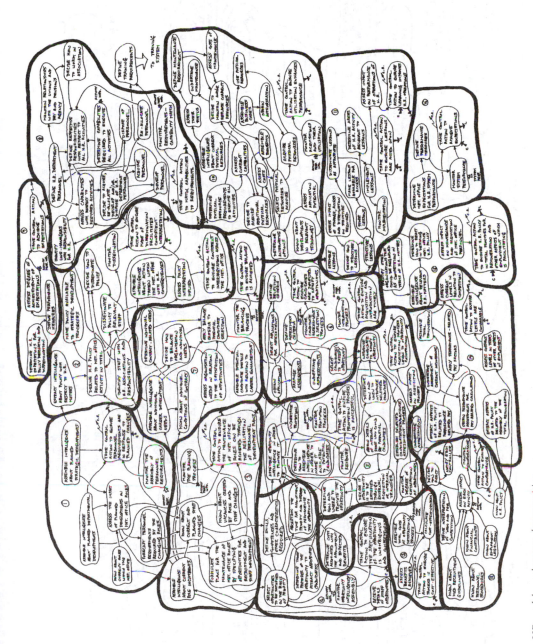

Figure 7.15 *HR model—subsystem decomposition*

Figure 7.16   Constraint management

subsystem had been represented by the simple generic model resulting from the specification of E in one of the RDs. Again, this was not detailed enough to be useful in phase 2 of the project.

The word 'constraint' required elaboration because there are essentially two kinds of constraint.

(a) There are those constraints whose impact can be minimised. An example is the constraint of locality. If an organisation is operating within an area occupied by a number of high-tech enterprises paying high salaries there is little that the specific organisation can do other than attempt to match salaries or compensate through other aspects of employment conditions. Thus it could seek to minimise the impact of the constraint of locality.
(b) The second kind of constraint are those that must be obeyed. These are the more common kind and are the ones most usually quoted. Examples are the law, regulations, standards, etc.

Both of these interpretations were introduced into the RD that was used as the source of the model. Only one RD was produced to elaborate this area of activity since the model could be more generic as it would be replicated across the divisions rather than split between different kinds of organisation. The RD used was:

A Met. Office-owned system, operated by suitably skilled personnel with required degrees of authority, to ensure conformance to those constraints derived and developed by relevant regulatory bodies and to minimise the impact of those which could be avoided, by allocating appropriate responsibility within the Met. Office and by establishing auditable procedures for their execution and reporting as necessary, while reacting to finance available and to those discretionary elements of company policy concerned with HR, quality, security, technology and others which may appear from time to time.

This definition resulted in the model of Figures 7.16 and 7.17.
The subsystems of Figure 7.17 are:

(1) Constraint intelligence assembly
(2) Responsibility allocation
(3) Procedure establishment
(4) Reporting
(5) Policy response management
(6) Personnel appointment
(7) Overall performance control

Although this model was derived for use within the Met. Office, it has general applicability as a detailed model of constraint management that could replace the generic model of constraints included in Figure 2.9 of Chapter Two.

GUIDANCE

Given four methods for the production of a CPTM an obvious question to consider is how to select the method to be used. What guidance is available?

Looking back over the situations in which a CPTM was developed and trying to generalise those situations, leads to the following suggestions:

(a) **Mission statement** This is the most defensible method since the starting point is a 'definition of purpose' arrived at by personnel in the situation itself. There is already some commitment to it and the production of the mission statement (or vision) will already have achieved accommodation of the variety of Ws that those personnel (unknowingly) possess. This feature also makes it the least likely method to be adopted since the accommodation may have resulted in a statement that is so woolly that the words in it are capable of multiple interpretations and it

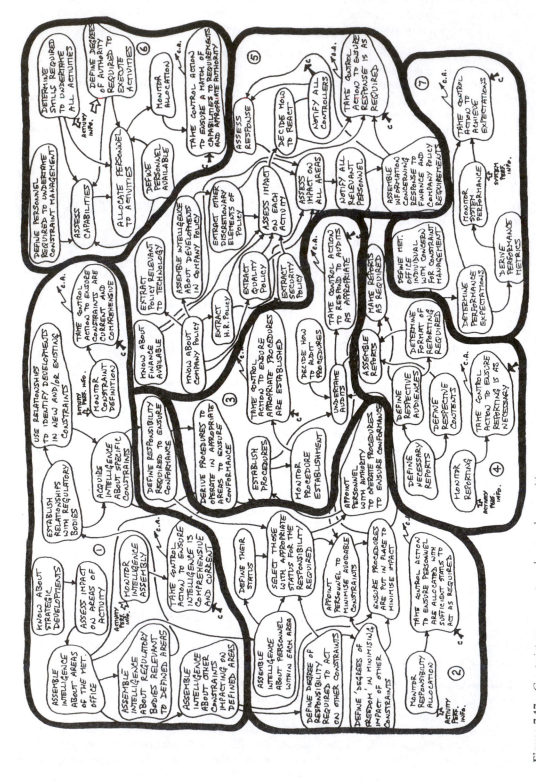

Figure 7.17 Constraint management—subsystem decomposition

will, therefore, be useless as a single statement of purpose. The other drawback is that the in–house commitment may be superficial. However, if a mission (or vision) statement is sufficiently precise to be useable, it is the simplest (a single RD) and the most defensible method.

(b) **W-decomposition** This is the most difficult method to be used since the combination of the resultant W-dependent models has to be based upon a well-specified non-contentious (neutral) RD and model. The conditions under which this seems to be an appropriate method are as follows:

- W differences are slight (subtle).
- A well-defined neutral (non-contentious) primary-task model can be derived. For example, a hotel, to be a hotel, must provide temporary accommodation and associated facilities, of a specified standard, at published rates. (This is not defining, but is a necessary requirement.)
- There is ease of access to relevant stakeholders.

(c) **Wider–system extraction** This method is relatively easy to use once a wider–system model has been derived. It may be the case that a mission statement can be the source of the wider system (as in the CEGB case, described in Chapter Six). However, the wider system itself may be derived using any of these methods. In Chapter Nine a project is described which used the 'Enterprise model' method to derive the wider system.

Once the wider system has been described the process of extraction relies on a defensible method for mapping the system boundary and, hence selecting the activities regarded as relevant. The suitability of this method relies on the acceptability of the selection criteria. These may be based on the following:

- The use of an alternative concept (the CEGB example in Chapter Six)
- The mapping of a defined set of skills
- The definition of an area of authority
- Wider-system feasibility (i.e. the activities outside the system boundary on which the system activities depend are present within the organisation or can be implemented)

(d) **'Enterprise Model' assembly** This is the most widely used method and is the most acceptable from the client 'buy-in' point of view. Of course, the client must have some initial appreciation of the status and purpose of the models being generated in order that acceptance can be pursued. The method, apart from being based upon a very simple generic model of any enterprise, is an appropriate method given widely differing Ws. With a little practice, it is a relatively easy method, but relies on the ability to construct a logically defensible conceptual model from a RD.

The above statements are derived from observations on experience and represent only broad guidance. The overriding message is to use that method with which you feel most comfortable and which seems to be appropriate for the situation in which you find yourself. Declaration of the intellectual processes to be used at the start of a study and the contribution of the models within that process will allow conscious learning and adaptation to take place. What you will eventually do may be a combination of methods. The healthcare project (in Chapter Nine) is an example of the combination of the 'Enterprise Model' method and 'Wider-system extraction'.

A project which used a combination of W–decomposition and the Enterprise Model assembly methods was undertaken for the West Yorkshire Police. This was essentially a strategic review and a brief description follows since it also used a particular selection criterion in a wider-system extraction mode to define organisation sub-roles.

THE WEST YORKSHIRE POLICE

Recently, the West Yorkshire Police undertook a major strategic review and organisation study. The project was already underway when I became involved and the situation, on joining, can best be described through a brief account of its early history.

A large group of managers had been involved in a number of 'brainstorming' sessions as a means of identifying those areas of activity of major interest for the strategic review. The outcome of these sessions was the definition of five areas:

- Organisation
- Policy dissemination
- Resources
- Buildings
- Personnel

For each of these areas a Task Force had been established to undertake the detailed review and the whole project was under the control of a chief superintendent. His concern at this stage was the considerable overlap in the areas defined. As he pointed out, 'you cannot examine resources without considering buildings and personnel; and policy dissemination must consider organisation'. Thus, 'how do we define the terms of reference of the various task forces to avoid duplication?' was a question he needed to answer. Also, he was concerned that the process of brainstorming may have missed areas that were not current issues, but which, nevertheless, should be addressed within a strategic review.

A further worry that he had was the lack of any defined approach. So far they had relied on brainstorming, which was fine as far as getting individual commitment was concerned, but of no use as a vehicle for doing the actual review.

As part of his own knowledge development, he had pursued a couple of Open University courses and in one of these there had been reference to SSM. He felt that it might have something to offer and I was invited to visit him to discuss its relevance. The outcome of this visit was the setting up of a 3-day workshop for himself and 10 of the members of the strategic review team in order to explore the ideas and how they might be used within the West Yorkshire Police.

It was also an extremely useful session in presenting the language of conceptual model building. They were not likely to become practitioners in this process in 3 days, but they would be able to understand the models and participate in their use later on.

Two members of the group plus myself were given the task to progress the review down to a level at which we could be definitive about the terms of reference of the task forces and also to undertake an organisation study.

It had already been decided, within the Force, that the West Yorkshire area was to be split into 15 geographically separate areas; each under the control of a superintendent. These were termed 'Basic Command Units' (BCUs). Three major Areas were to be defined, under the control of an assistant chief constable (an Area Commander), with the task of overseeing five of the BCUs each and finally there was to be a Headquarters.

The major questions associated with this organisational philosophy were related to the tasks to be undertaken within each BCU and each Area, the 'job specifications' of the superintendents and the assistant chief constables and the function of the Headquarters.

To undertake the strategic review and to answer the organisation questions, we needed, first of all, to answer the fundamental question: 'What do we take the organisation to be doing?' (see Figure 1 in the Preamble). We needed to develop a CPTM to map onto the organisation as a whole.

Formulation of the CPTM

The first task in thinking about the construction of a CPTM is to form some views about the potential purposes to be pursued by a police force and, in particular, the West Yorkshire Police.

We (the three team members), in discussion with the project manager, derived six purposes that we felt might be relevant but, before proceeding to consider RD, we decided to involve a greater number of members of the police force. We circulated every member of the West Yorkshire Police with an invitation to visit a specific room in the Headquarters, over a 2-day period, in order to participate in the strategic review. It was our intention to generate some commitment to the review by initiating this early involvement in the process as well as achieve our aim of 'opening up' the thinking about 'purpose'. This turned out to be extremely useful, in both respects, and our initial list of six potential purposes was increased to 14. They were not all of the same level in that they could not be taken to map onto the Force in total, but they provided elements of the 'Enterprise Model'. It was this feature that led us to use this particular method of assembly. However, there were other features of the list that caused us to consider the W-decomposition method as well. The total list, as it emerged from the wider discussions, was to:

- Maintain community well-being (1)
- Facilitate transfer of goods and people (2)
- Respond to and manage incidents (3)
- Identify and apprehend those violating the law (4)
- Maintain security of people and property (5)
- Recognise and defuse situations which could lead to a breach of the peace (6)
- Educate the community with respect to security (7)
- Assemble community intelligence (8)
- Develop communications (9)
- Develop resources (10)
- Develop CID expertise (11)
- Plan Force development (12)
- Assess performance of BCU and Areas (13)
- Manage role maintenance (14)

An examination of the above set led us to segregate the list as follows:

T—(1) to (6)
L—(7) and (8)
S—(9) to (11)
P,M,C—(12) to (14)

The W-decomposition method was used to develop a CTPM to represent the T. Within this the neutral (non-contentious) model was derived from a RD based upon:

A system to identify and apprehend those violating the law

It was argued that for a police force to be a police force, irrespective of what else it might be, it must be describable as that.

Having now produced a model to represent T the remaining purposes were structured as RDs and the total model produced using the Enterprise Model assembly method.

It is difficult to illustrate the resultant model, given the size limitations of the page but a subsystem decomposition resulted in nine subsystems. This was a fairly coarse decomposition, with several control systems in each subsystem. The coarseness was deliberate in order to use the model as a source of recommendations for the definition of the organisational groupings. The nine subsystems were:

- Strategic control (1)
- Resource development (2)
- Community education (3)
- Force operational planning and control (4)

- Communications development (5)
- Transfer of people and goods (6)
- Community intelligence assembly (7)
- Crime prevention (8)
- Community well-being management (9)

There is no significance underlying the names of these subsystems. They were merely chosen to give a broad indication of the basic purpose of each subsystem.

The organisational philosophy mentioned earlier effectively defines 15 different communities corresponding to the 15 BCUs. Thus, if we examine the model and identify those groups of activities that are community dependent we can define the role of a BCU. The activities that this represents will, therefore, need to be replicated 15 times to correspond to the total operational task of the whole West Yorkshire area. These activities are represented by subsystems (7) and (9). Subsystem (3) also refers to the community, but it was argued that 'community education' was regarded as a Headquarters task within West Yorkshire.

Further examination of the model yields a group of activities with the responsibility for operational planning and control; subsystem (4). Thus these could define the role of an Area and represent the job specification of an Area Commander (an assistant chief constable). These would have to be replicated three times to give the total set of activities, at this level, within the total area of West Yorkshire.

The remaining activities within the model need only occur once and therefore could represent the role of Headquarters. Thus the subsystem decomposition was the source of the organisational recommendations. They were largely accepted, though to cope with the size of the task for a superintendent, the number of BCUs was increased to 18, thus reducing the geographical area over which they had responsibility.

Having made our recommendations with regard to the organisational arrangements we proceeded to the broad-level strategic review. This involved a comparison of the activities within the CPTM against the current activities of the Force. A comparison table was created for each of the nine subsystems and in it we added a column to record the current allocation of task force responsibility. The format is shown in Table 7.1.

The tables were completed over a 3-week period by other workshop members. It was important that they were involved since they understood the 'systems' language and also the domain (West Yorkshire Police) language. The fourth column provided the feedback to the task forces regarding their terms of reference. If, say, task force numbers 3 and 5 appeared this would indicate duplication for that particular activity and one of them would have that activity removed from their consideration. If, on the other hand, no task force number appeared against a particular activity the question would be asked, 'why not?'

It may have been that the activity had not been raised during the brainstorming sessions, or it might have been decided that the activity was of little importance to the review. If the former was the case, the activity would be introduced as the responsibility of one of the task forces. In allocating activities in this way, an attempt was made evenly to load the five task forces.

Table 7.1

Activity	Does it currently exist?	Current mechanism 'how'	Task force responsibility	Assessment	Comments
Taken a subsystem at a time	Yes, no, in part	Existing procedure (if existing)	1 . . . 5	Good (no change) Poor (further analysis) Does not exist (explore change)	Impact of assessment re IT, Org, HR, etc.

The discussion of this particular case has gone beyond the model building in order to illustrate the way in which the CPTM and its subsystem decomposition have been used to tackle two different kinds of problem.

The process of analysis adopted was extremely efficient. It occupied 11 days of my time and this included the 3-day workshop. There was a large intermittent involvement of members of the West Yorkshire Police Force during the two days set aside at Headquarters to explore potential purposes. There was an involvement of 10 members of the task forces for the 3-day workshop plus about 1.5 days each over a 3-week period to complete the comparison tables and 8 weeks' involvement of the other two members of the team. The total elapsed time of the project was 8 weeks for both the strategic review and the organisation study.

THE DUKES THEATRE

In order to develop the Enterprise Model, six RDs were derived. The choice of these six came from a series of interviews with staff within the theatre ranging from the Artistic Director to the staff within the box office. Thus a wide range of views and expectations were explored. The chief executive was a member of the problem-solving team as was the marketing director. Both of these individuals wished to participate fully in the analysis and therefore initial sessions were concerned with them gathering an appreciation of the language and status of the systems models. Both were also new appointments and saw the involvement as a way of understanding the particular situation at The Dukes Theatre. An additional member of the problem-solving group was an ex-theatre director, who was an associate and who had been a 'caretaker' chief executive of The Dukes Theatre while the new incumbent was being acquired. Thus I had an associate who was familiar with the situation and who understood the 'domain' language. I regard this as a necessary requirement of a problem-solving group as I find it unrealistic, as a consultant, to become a domain 'expert' as well as an SSM practitioner.

The resultant CPTM is presented in Figure 7.18 together with the structure and RDs. The major outcome of the comparison, which led us to abandon the extraction of a marketing system, was the

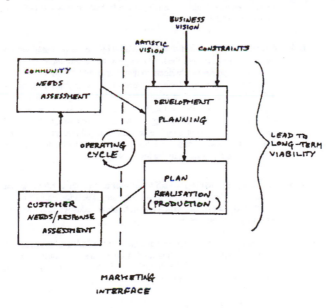

Figure 7.18 *The Dukes core business cycle*

MODEL CONSTRUCTION

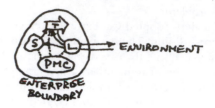

T — CORE PROCESSES [R.D.1]
L — LINKING PROCESSES [R.D.2]
S — SUPPORT PROCESSES [R.D.3, R.D.5, R.D.6]
PMC — PLANNING, MONITORING AND CONTROL [R.D.4]

ROOT DEFINITIONS

R.D.1——An Artistic Director and Production owned system, to mount a prescribed series of producing events and other provision within and external to the Dukes in such a way as to meet customer expectations while recognising the customer care policy and the financial targets to be achieved.

R.D.2——A system to develop and maintain an effective interface between the Dukes and its immediate and wider community so that a classified range of arts-oriented education and entertainment needs of an expanding and loyal customer base can be specified which are coherent and current while ensuring that the "offerings" of the Dukes are promoted to the community in a timely manner, utilising the promotional mechanisms of others as available but reacting to the Dukes advertising policy.

R.D.3——A system to ensure that the physical resources available to the Dukes, both internal and external, are used effectively in attracting customers and potential customers and in satisfying production needs while operating within financial constraints.

R.D.4——A chief executive owned system, operated by the senior management team in association with the board, to plan the development of the Dukes, its operating policy and budgets so that it is capable of continually matching its "offerings",(within acceptable business risk), in terms of coherent programmes of producing events and other provision to the needs of selected sectors of its community so that its resultant reputation leads to it becoming a "cultural flagship" within the community; also to ensure that the execution of the plans realise derived financial targets while reacting to alternative sources of provision and constrained by the total finance available and the policies of the fund giving bodies.

R.D.5——A system, operated by the staff of the Dukes, to ensure that the human resources available are capable of executing its developing role in such a way that balances organisation and individual needs while acting within personnel and union policies.

R.D.6——A system to match the finances available to the Dukes to the needs of its development plan by attracting funds from a variety of sources to supplement its income from all "offerings" while recognising the Dukes policy on operations in general.

Figure 7.19   *A CPTM relevant to 'The Dukes' theatre.*

realisation that the theatre was not actually run as a business. It had had financial problems and had recently received a grant from the National Lottery. We argued that this provided a breathing space, not a solution. Thus our concentration was not on marketing alone, but on the relationship between marketing and the business. Marketing was seen as an essential interface function and, unless that interface operated effectively, long-term viability would suffer.

Our concentration, therefore, was to derive recommendations to bring about this interface function within, what we termed, a basic business operating cycle. The cycle is illustrated in Figure 7.18.

The conceptual model representing the CPTM is given in Figure 7.19.

THE ARMY

At the other extreme to the small theatre referred to above is the British Army. This is a highly complex organisation. It is geographically dispersed, structurally complex, politically exposed and subject to considerable change. The particular change processes that gave rise to this project are those surrounding the use of information, developments in associated technology and the changes in doctrine related to joint and coalition operations. These changes are major and require a complete migration from the development of information systems based upon a 'stovepipe' philosophy, in which the resultant systems are independent, to a philosophy based upon 'interoperability', where the resultant systems are capable of integrated communication.

In order to explore the implications of the impact on information systems development, a project was established to produce a business process model relevant to the Army.

Again a CPTM was assembled using the Enterprise Model. It is not my intention to give the complete set of RDs that were used in the development of what was called 'The Single Army Activity Model', (the SAAM), but just to give an example to show the nature of the RDs used. One of these RDs, to represent the T is as follows:

A superior commander-owned system, operated by a commander and subordinates, to continually make decisions about the deployment, employment and sustainability of land forces, together with the execution of those decisions, in order to successfully achieve the superior commanders intent with respect to a specific mission, whilst learning from this process and recognising the changing operating (physical) environment and operational constraints.

The model that resulted from the assembly of the total set of RDs (six in all, of similar complexity to that for the T), is reproduced as Figure 7.20.

The model of Figure 7.20 is at the first resolution level. In order to be useful as a source of information requirements, further expansion was required. The model and its developments were captured using a software tool called 'MooD'. This is briefly described later and the total context in which the model was used is described in Appendix Three.

This chapter has concentrated on the Enterprise Model method of assembling a CPTM and a number of real examples have been included in order to give the flavour of what is involved and the scale of actual model building. It is the most powerful of the four methods described but, as some of the examples show, a particular situation may call for a combination of methods. Don't prejudge a situation. Let the most appropriate method emerge from the specific situation.

Figure 7.20 *The Single Army Activity Model*

Chapter Eight

Application to Training Strategy and HR

INTRODUCTION

In Chapter Seven an analysis of human resource management was discussed as part of the Met. Office BPI study, and this chapter is concerned with the 'human' aspects of organisational analysis as an area of particular interest. By this I do *not* mean analysis at the level of political, behavioural or cultural considerations, but the exploration of organisational issues surrounding training, career development, performance appraisal and the management of human resources in general. It is specifically the application of conceptual models to some of the above issues that will be described.

Whenever we insert 'Actors' into a RD, we are emphasising this 'human' role within the concept being developed. Logic suggests that if the overall concept is to be complete and capable of functioning, if it were to map onto reality, then the 'Actors' must be sufficient, competent and properly allocated. Thus the inclusion of this particular CATWOE element will demand a particular set of activities (or subsystems) for the resultant model to meet the criteria of its *minimum* and *necessary* activity specification. It could be argued that in any model for which 'Actors' are specified there will be a generic set of activities to consider. Previous examples will support the argument, though the choice of actual wording must depend upon the way 'Actors' are specified within a RD. A number of examples are contained in Chapter Two but consider the most general specification:

A system, operated by Actors A to - - - - -

This is modelled as Figure 8.1.

Each activity can be seen to address the issues mentioned above. Activity 8 ('Develop Actors') is concerned with training and career development. Activity 9 ('Monitor performance') represents the source of performance appraisal and the whole subsystem is concerned with human resource management. The constraints will be those aspects of E in CATWOE that are related to personnel management. Thus they may represent the manpower and/or personnel policy constraints.

If there is a policy of no recruitment then activity 6 ('Acquire Actors') would not be included. A policy of no redundancy would remove activity 7 ('Dispose of Actors') and an organisation structure constraint would remove activity 4 ('Allocate Actors to activities').

Activity 1 ('Determine the scope and range of expertise required to do all activities') links this subsystem to the remainder of the model of which this subsystem is a part; hence the broad arrow denoting an activity information input. It is this activity that defines the skills needed and the numbers of those skills required to enable the total system (defined by the complete RD) to

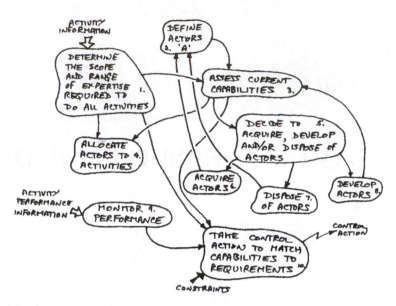

Figure 8.1 *'Actor' management subsystem*

work if it were to map onto reality. The system must be capable of working if the mapping process is to identify potential deficiencies in the real world.

A number of projects will be described in which this concept was used to define the structure of the analysis. The first two are concerned with training and it is argued that before any judgements can be made about the adequacy of training provision activity 1 (of Figure 8.1) must be undertaken which in turn defines a requirement for the remainder of the model. This is an application of the 'service system/system served' relationship since the provision of training is a service to whatever the Actors have to do (determined by the system served). As illustrations of this particular aspect of human resource management let us consider two projects with a concern for training. The first project is concerned with the development of a training strategy for the Royal Navy.

THE ROYAL NAVY

Introduction

The Naval Service contains the Royal Navy, the Fleet Air Arm (FONA) and the Royal Marines and as such is a highly complex organisation. There is a great variety of tasks to be undertaken in a modern naval service and hence the training requirements are equally varied. The variety is compounded by the particular personnel policy which requires personnel to be redrafted and re-appointed on a three-yearly cycle. Thus the current training organisation, which has developed over many years in response to changing demands, has also become extremely complex. The project to which this particular application refers was concerned with a strategic review of current training provision in order to develop potential strategies for the future provision of training which could lead to an organisation that was simpler to manage, more effective in terms of the training delivered and more efficient in terms of the training resources consumed.

The project team was under the management of a Captain. There were six other officers and I provided the intellectual structure of the project and the SSM–related analysis.

It was a requirement of the project team that an audit trail should exist in order that the recommendations derived could be traced back to the assumptions made. This implied that the whole of the analysis should be explicit. SSM was seen as the appropriate vehicle through which the audit trail could be provided.

Project Management

It had been decided that the PRINCE project management method was to be used and the organisational arrangements required by this approach had been established. In particular, there is a requirement for a high-level project board who oversee the project and 'sign off' deliverables at various stages of the project, together with the Project Assurance Team (PAT) who have the responsibility for the quality of the work done.

PRINCE was originally developed for the control of IT projects where something like SSADM (Structured Systems Analysis and Design Method) is being used as the design method. It requires (a) well-defined stages to be established within the project and (b) at each stage, the definition of a set of deliverables which are again described in detail (as product descriptions). The project initiation document (PID) is where all this detail is described and this is produced prior to any analysis of the situation. The role of the PAT is then to compare the actual deliverables against the product descriptions and to reach judgements about their quality. On the assumptions that this is the case decisions also need to be made as to what should be submitted to the project board and in what format.

There are difficulties associated with using PRINCE on non-IT projects and in particular when using SSM.

(a) The detail of the deliverables is not known prior to the start of a project.
(b) In order for the PAT to be an effective quality monitor they need to be familiar with the language in which the analysis is carried out.
(c) The PAT need to be involved in the project more than they have time to be. Because of (b), reporting to the PAT in a language which they do understand requires considerable effort which detracts from making progress on the project. Also because of (b) more reporting is needed than would otherwise be necessary.

However, the purpose of this description is not to discuss the unsuitability of PRINCE in relation to an SSM project, but to illustrate the application of a particular methodology and associated models to this highly complex situation.

Business Analysis—Why Model?

In order to make decisions about the strategic development of training for the Naval Service and to derive options for the delivery of that training it is necessary to make some basic assumptions. In addition, if those decisions and options are to be defensible, the assumptions made need to be explicit and communicated.

For example, it will be necessary to form a view as to what the size and shape of the Naval Service is taken to be in order to make judgements about the volume and scope of the training provision required. It is in forming that view that business modelling can make a contribution. Training is not an end in itself and it is taken as given that training is a support for the *business* of the Navy. If military capability is to be maintained (at whatever level) then it is essential that the personnel who deliver that capability, and who plan and manage the delivery, are adequately trained in the total range of skills and disciplines to run the business effectively.

What then is the business of the Navy?

This becomes a difficult question to answer when the political and military environment of the UK is in a state in which major single threats have been replaced by minor (but potentially significant) distributed threats. Nevertheless, a role needs to be defined and the management processes need to be in place in order that the Naval Service can derive and satisfy that role in an effective and efficient way. Thus it is not only the operations of the business that require appropriately trained personnel but also management processes which lead to the difficult decisions referred to above.

What is needed therefore is a CPTM to represent what we take the business of the Navy to be. Since we were not doing a strategic review of the Navy itself but required a model from which to derive skill requirements, all that was needed was a defensible starting point. The annual plan of the Navy contained a usable mission statement. This was then taken as the source of the business model.

This model can be taken to be an appropriate and relevant description of the Naval Service and hence each activity in it would need to be undertaken by naval or other suitable qualified personnel. The skills and competencies of the personnel required can therefore be defined on the basis of the respective activities.

The Business Model

As stated above, the business model is the source of training needs in terms of the range and scope of what has to be delivered. The design of the training provision in terms of volume, frequency, etc. will be determined by the decisions made about the size and shape of the Naval Service of the future, but the business model represents the necessary starting point.

If the business model is to be representative of the Naval Service a definition of the overall purpose must be chosen which, itself, is recognisable as a plausible statement of its mission. The RD chosen as the source of the derived version of the CPTM model, derived from the published mission statement, is as follows:

> A First Sea Lord-owned system, operated by suitably qualified (skilled) personnel in association with other agencies, to maintain and develop sufficient military capability and appropriate infrastructure to realise its role in the execution of the defence policy of the UK while making 'best' use of appropriate technological developments and recognising the impact of the changing political and military environment, but within the constraints imposed from financial considerations, government initiatives and the structure of TLBs.

> (Note: TLB—Top Level Budget holder.)

The model was produced through a number of hierarchical levels but essentially it represented a statement of the activities that the system must do to be the one described by the above definition. Once produced the model could be decomposed into a number of subsystems. The model produced is too large to display here, but a diagrammatic version was used as a means of communication within the Navy, and this is reproduced here, as Figure 8.2 in order to convey the model scope. This model is effectively in terms of its subsystems.

Subsystem Descriptions

Each subsystem consists of a number of activities interconnected so that they collectively seek to achieve a particular defined purpose. In addition to this group of operational activities there is a further group concerned with monitoring the performance of the operational activities and, on the

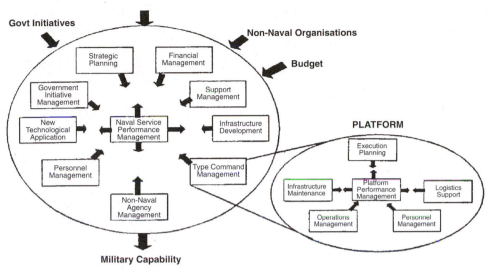

Figure 8.2   *The Navy model*

basis of the performance information so generated, taking control action, where necessary, to ensure that the particular purpose is achieved.

It is the logic of the model that if the individual subsystems achieve their particular purposes, the model as a whole will contain the minimum necessary set of activities to realise the overall definition of purpose previously presented. The subsystems described are:

- Strategic Planning
- Government Initiative Management
- Infrastructure Development
- Type Command Management
- New Technological Application
- Personnel Management
- Support Management
- Non-Naval Agency Management
- Financial Management
- Naval Service Performance Management

All the activities in the business model are on-going all the time and hence there is no starting point. Operations will be taking place at the same time as strategic planning. It would have no relevance to reality if this were not the case. Thus there is no defined order to the above list of subsystems but Strategic Planning is a reasonable place to start.

Strategic planning

It is taken as given that, whatever the future role of the Naval Service is, it is to contribute to the UK's defence policy. The achievement of the role will be financially constrained but the ultimate product of all the ensuing activities (or business processes) will be the delivery of military capability in whatever form is required.

This subsystem essentially consists of the 'exploration' and 'defining' activities that will lead to the articulation of the role of the Naval Service, the required roles of the various Type Commands and other support roles. A product of this subsystem is also Naval Policy.

Since all the activities will be 'on-going' activities and hence, the roles defined will be updated and relevant to whatever the current UK requirement is, given the changing political and military environment in which it is operating.

Government initiative management

As well as a continuous input of UK defence policy into the business, it is required that the model should respond to government initiatives which may well be *ad hoc* and totally unrelated. Nevertheless, the RD takes them to be a constraint and this subsystem handles the management of the *response* to those initiatives. The initiatives may impact upon the desired role, Naval Policy or specific tasks to be undertaken and it is the overall purpose of this subsystem to assess the impact and to ensure that the required action is implemented and managed.

It may be the case that some initiatives require the introduction of totally new activities, unrelated to running a Naval Service (e.g. Market Testing) and this subsystem ensures that these are recognised and actioned.

Infrastructure Development

The realisation of a particular role will require the defining, linking and support of organisationally and physically discrete functions. Infrastructure will be necessary to provide integration and facilitation of these functions. The activities in this subsystem describe this process and its management.

Type command management

Because of the constraint of the current command structure in the RD the organisational terminology of 'Type Command' has been used to represent the group of activities that realise the roles prescribed to them by the Strategic Planning subsystem. Each Type Command is taken to be similar in relation to these activities and this subsystem will be replicated by the number of Type Commands defined. In developing the model, separate definitions were derived to represent systems relevant to surface fleet and the marines. It was found that, if the most detailed level of description was related to the concept of a 'platform', the models were identical. A 'platform' is defined as any operating entity, i.e. a ship, helicopter, submarine, platoon of marines, etc.

Although this is the most detailed subsystem in the model its content can be described through further partitioning. Thus its subsystems are:

- Execution Planning—the product of this set of activities is a management plan which defined the 'operational capability requirements' and the 'readiness state requirements' of each platform within the command.
- Infrastructure Maintenance—is at the level of the Naval Service itself, each Type Command will need to maintain its own infrastructure if it is to operate as an integrated set of functions.
- Logistics Support—although this could be seen as part of infrastructure it has been separated logically, because the activities and their requirements are less stable and need different skills to organise supply, maintenance, etc. of operating platforms.
- Operations Management—this set of activities describe the tasks and their management undertaken by a Type Command in association, if appropriate, with non-naval agencies.
- Personnel Management—as with the infrastructure maintenance activities, this subsystem reflects the Personnel Management at the level of the Naval Service but in particular to those personnel allocated to a Type Command.

• Platform Performance Management—since the Executive Planning subsystem will have laid down performance expectations in the form of 'operational capability requirements' and 'readiness state requirement' this subsystem is concerned with monitoring the total effectiveness and efficiency of the Type Command as reflected in platform performance.

New technology application

The phrase, 'making best use of appropriate technological development' in the RD leads to a general set of activities concerned with scanning the developments underway, relating them to all areas of the business and to managing the application of those shown to benefit the business. Technology covers the range of developments specific to platforms, infrastructure (IT, etc.) through to intellectual development (design and analysis techniques, etc.).

Personnel Management

All resources available to the Naval Service need to be managed but personnel require specific activities since personnel have career, social and cultural expectations which need to be recognised and related to the organisational (business) needs. The subsystem includes recruitment, development (training), capability assessment and allocation (including disposal). The activities are subject to Naval Policy (personnel) and finance in particular, but within these constraints the activities seek to match total (allocated) personnel capability to business requirements while recognising personal needs.

Support management

The set of activities in this subsystem are concerned with achieving the support roles defined by the Strategic Planning subsystem. Performance measures are included as are the monitoring and control of all activities concerned with supporting the operations in total.

Non-Naval agency management

It is recognised that the role of the Naval Service and the execution of those activities to realise its role may require association with other services, civilian organisations or foreign agencies. The activities in this subsystem are concerned with assessing the impact, translating the impact into tasks to be undertaken by the Naval Service and then with managing the association so that the tasks are undertaken with the required performance.

Financial management

All activities within the model are constrained by the overall finances available and the way they are allocated. Each set of control activities within the model are subject to those constraints, but this subsystem, in particular, is concerned with making the allocation and monitoring and controlling the adherence of each subsystem to its allocation. It is the responsibility of each subsystem to manage its own finances within the constraints applied by this particular subsystem. Additional constraints (arising, for example, from the Naval Policy derived in the Strategic Planning subsystem) are also the responsibility of the Financial Management subsystem.

Naval Service performance management

Within the RD the First Sea Lord is given the overall ownership of the system. The implication of this within the model is that his expectations for performance, in total, must be identified and the whole service managed so that it achieves these expectations. Thus the set of activities define, at this level, performance measures (critical success factors), collect and process information relevant to those measures and take control action through all the other subsystem controllers to ensure the achievement of desired overall performance.

The Next Step

The model described briefly in the previous section is a logical construction of the set of activities that the system must do to be the one defined. It may now be used in two stages.

Mapping

The reality of the Naval Service is highly complex and has developed to its present state through time rather than through the logical process leading to the model described above. However, the model will lead to a coherent set of questions about the current state of the Naval Service. Thus for each activity in the model the following questions can be asked of the current situation:

(a) Does the activity exist?
(b) Where in the current organisation is it located?
(c) Could its current performance be improved by better training?
(d) If the activity does not exist, should it?
(e) What would the training implication be arising from its introduction if it should exist?

    The above questions need not be answered in any detail since the purpose of mapping is to determine the relevance of the model to reality. The answer 'Yes' to the majority of question (a) would be sufficient confirmation, particularly if supported by 'Yes' answers to question (d).

Training needs analysis

Assuming that the mapping leads to acceptance of the model as a definition of the business activities to be undertaken by the Naval Service, each activity can be analysed in terms of the skills, competencies and expertise required in the personnel allocated to carry them out. This then leads to a definition of the range and scope of the training that must be available as the output of any training organisation irrespective of how it is provided.

    As stated earlier, the model has only described activities to the level of a platform. It is assumed that the range and scope of skills and expertise required to operate a platform are well defined. Thus further expansion of the model is not required in this area as a means of defining more detailed requirements from the training system.

    The project so far had defined the business model and, as a result of a skills analysis, had defined a skills hierarchy for each of the subsystems. This is summarised in Table 8.1. It had been found in this analysis that a set of skills were replicated in each subsystem and these were extracted into a set headed 'General Management'. The 'platform'-derived skills were added to this hierarchy.

Table 8.1 *Skills hierarchy*

Platform skills	Non-platform (specialist) skills	General management skills
Platform handling	Infrastructure	Communication skills
Platform systems	Safety	Inter-personal skills
Platform maintenance	Logistics (supply, etc.)	Personal management
Personnel maintenance	IT/IS	Counselling
Warfare	Facilities	Presentation
Finance	Design/maintenance	Leadership
Law★	Finance management	Conceptual thinking
Safety/security	Personnel management	Change Management
Communications	Manpower planning, etc.	IT
Weapons handling	Planning	Budget management
Support logistics	Strategic	
Met & oceanography	Operational	
Training★	External agencies	
Professional	Procurement	
Personal attributes	Contract management	
Ceremonial	Technology management	
Public relations	Project management	
	Cost/benefit analysis	

★ Also specialist skills

Training Provision Assessment

The business modelling completed so far has enabled the range of expertise needs (and hence the required output of training provision) to be defined. An assessment could now be made of the actual training provision. Thus the following questions were addressed:

(1) Does the range of training provision match the requirements?
(2) In what areas is provision deficient?
(3) In what areas is overprovision made?

Training is currently provided through a number of discrete establishments both internal and external to the Naval Service hence considerable effort was needed to obtain reliable information in response to the above questions. This was minimised by producing a structured questionnaire in which a skill listing was produced and the various training establishments were required to identify those courses which were aimed at developing competence in each skill area.

Gaps in provision were immediately obvious but duplication was only potential. Further analysis of these areas was needed to determine the *level* of skill competence that the course was intended to develop.

This analysis identified the degree of match between range of skills required and range of skills provided. Before complete assessment of provision could be carried out forecasts of numbers requiring training had to be made. These would be dependent upon manpower planning assumptions and personnel policy assumptions. In order to assess the effects of these assumptions on the training requirements a *System Dynamics* model was developed and used to predict the capacity requirements in specific areas. The above assessment was used within the overall process of constructing a strategy for the future shape of naval training.

Training Provision Management

The above has described how a business model of the Naval Service was used to define skill requirements which in turn were used to assess the adequacy of the actual training provision.

This is still only part of the picture. The assessment was completed by undertaking an audit of the management process involved in transforming a total need for training into an effective and efficient organisation for satisfying that need as an on-going requirement.

This required the construction of another business model to use as the basis for comparison against the current training organisation. A view was taken of the overall purpose of training and a RD formed as follows:

> A training executive-owned system, operated by appropriately skilled personnel both within and external to the Naval Service to enhance the skill and expertise of those personnel requiring development in order to satisfy their prescribed role and career requirements within the time scale defined, but recognising naval policy constraints and those constraints arising from financial, establishment, facilities and cultural considerations.

The model resulting from this definition is given in Figure 8.3 along with its subsystem decomposition.

Objective assessment of the current training organisation required the establishment of the evaluation criteria which support the judgements made and which also support the options for the future.

Evaluation criteria

The approach to the derivation of these criteria was based on the terms in which each activity in this model could be assessed; related to both its existence and its performance. Thus, for each activity it was necessary to:

(a) identify one or more *outputs* which could confirm the existence of the activity within the current organisation

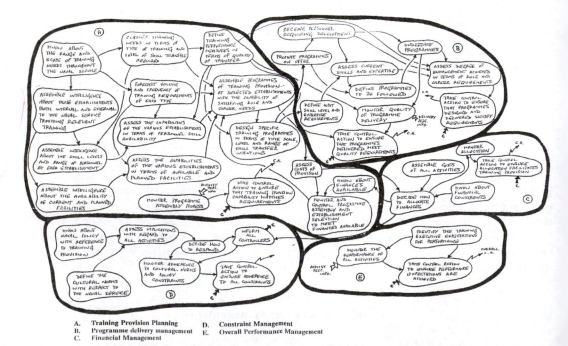

A. **Training Provision Planning**   D. **Constraint Management**
B. **Programme delivery management**   E. **Overall Performance Management**
C. **Financial Management**

Figure 8.3   *Training model*

(b) identify criteria by which to judge the *quality* of these outputs
(c) identify the *cost drivers* for the activity

The identification of outputs and quality criteria together defined the *efficacy* of the activity: the cost drivers assist in determining the *efficiency* with which it is carried out.

The application of the efficacy and efficiency criteria to the current training organisation in total led to the derivation of evaluation criteria for *Effectiveness*. This is assessed in relation to the complete system rather than its individual activities.

Again, because of the complexity of the organisation, structured questionnaires were used but in this case, because of the particular interpretation of the evaluation criteria, they were supplemented by workshops carried out at each training establishment.

Application

This section elaborates the criteria developed to assess each of the three Es—Efficacy, Efficiency and Effectiveness—and, for the first two, details how the current training organisation was measured against the criteria.

Measurement of efficacy

'*How well is the activity carried out?*' and, by implication, '*is the activity carried out at all?*'

Training establishments and HQ organisations with training interests were asked to confirm the activities carried out within their units. For each activity, outputs had been identified which, if identified within the organisation, confirmed that the activity was carried out within that organisation. Units were asked to indicate whether these outputs do exist, and/or propose other outputs which could equally confirm the existence of the activity.

Quality criteria were also proposed for each identified output, and units were asked to indicate how well they met these criteria. It was accepted that these individual judgements would, in many cases, be subjective, but it was considered that the data received from the expert practitioners responding to the criteria would be sufficient to provide a significant consensus view.

Finally, units were asked who (individual or group) carried out the activity within the organisation.

Measurement of efficiency

'*How much does the activity cost in relation to the required quality of its output?*'

The intention here was to identify the cost drivers for the various activities. In the questionnaire, units were asked to confirm or correct the suggested cost components, and also, in the case of personnel costs, to estimate the amount of time spent on the activity each year (in person–days or person–years as most appropriate).

Measurement of effectiveness

'*How well does the system satisfy the requirements of the owner?*'

The Training System activity model was derived from a RD formed from a statement of the training mission, which was accepted by the project board. It was argued that if each activity can be assessed in terms of its quality (efficacy) and consumption of resources (efficiency), sufficient measures of performance have been specified. The question that remained, however, was whether the overall process of training provision performed adequately.

The criteria which addressed this question are the measures of effectiveness and these refer to the performance of the overall system, related to the expectations of the training executive through reference to the operational requirement and environmental constraints.

Efficacy and efficiency are based upon the activities within the business model of the training system and hence can be defined explicitly. Effectiveness, as stated above, is dependent on the expectations of the training executive in terms of the overall provision of training. Thus effectiveness of the totality of the activities within the business model cannot be assessed until the structure of the training executive is defined. Information systems would need to be in place to do all these performance assessments and, since the expectations of the training executive may change, it is only the information systems that could be specified in relation to the overall effectiveness at this stage.

Findings

The total assessment led to the overall finding that both the specification of needs and the training provision were highly fragmented. There are a number of customers of training, each specifying their requirements in different ways. Since these requirements are not independent there is no clear picture of the overall demands placed upon the training organisation. Also there are a number of suppliers of training both inside and outside the Naval Service and again no overall picture of the capability of the training organisation existed. The situation found (at a broad level) is illustrated in Figure 8.4.

For confidentiality reasons the detailed findings cannot be disclosed but the illustration in Figure 8.4 is sufficient to defend the need for a training organisation which rectified this fragmentation.

The business model of Figure 8.3 was used to define an organisation structure and a set of roles which would provide an on-going integration of both the training needs specification and the training provision.

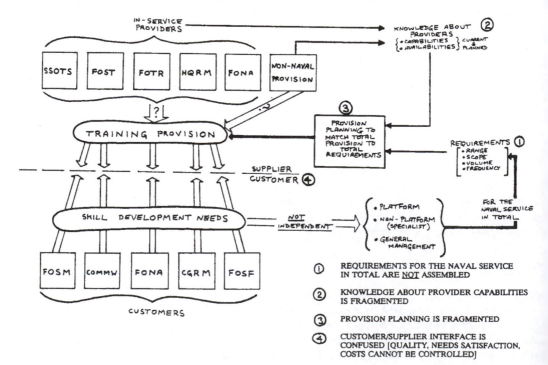

Figure 8.4 *Broad findings*

Organisation Mapping

A number of activities in the training model are concerned with the design and delivery of training and therefore in any organisation structure these activities would have to be replicated at each establishment providing training. Various mappings were undertaken:

(a) to identify replicated activities (establishment based)
(b) to identify the remainder (HQ based)
(c) to identify roles within both (a) and (b)

The relationship between (a) and (b) was taken to be a concern for training quality and hence the roles linking HQ with each establishment were those with a direct responsibility for quality. This represented the organisational philosophy used to select a particular structure from the many possible.

Figure 8.5 illustrates the set of roles and role structure derived at this stage of the study and which represented the source of the organisational options within the recommended strategy. The derivation of these roles required a number of assumptions.

Assumptions

The first assumption is that the design and delivery of training will be through a number of establishments, both internal and external to the Naval Service. Thus a number of activities on the training model may need to be replicated and be carried out at each establishment.

The second assumption is that the remaining activities can be undertaken within some central (training HQ) organisation and can be grouped according to a 'common interest' (or product).

The areas of authority of the various control systems within the model suggest a particular hierarchical relationship both in the central (HQ) organisation and within establishments. This hierarchy is represented by Figure 8.5 in terms of the role names chosen for the activity groupings. The relationship between the central (HQ) roles and those at each establishment is taken to be a concern for the quality of training provision and hence the link is from a 'training provision

Figure 8.5   *Overall training structure*

management' role (in which decisions are made on which establishments provide what training programmes, i.e. the customer/supplier interface) to the 'quality assurance role' at establishments. The management roles are defined in terms of the activities within each boundary but they may be described briefly as follows:

(a) **Training directorate role:** This role has overall responsibility for the performance of training provision. It has authority to take whatever action is needed (within specified constraints) to ensure that the skilled personnel available to undertake the business of the Naval Service are appropriate to that task. The role must also ensure that it fulfils that requirement with a performance that meets the training executive requirements.

(b) **Training provision planning role:** Ensures that the training that is available in total is responsive to changing needs and is at all times capable of satisfying those needs.

(c) **Training provision intelligence officer and requirements analyst role:** These are supporting roles to 'training provision planning'. The 'requirements analyst' is concerned with identifying training needs across the service and will require significant information support based upon a skill classification and projected personnel complements and personnel changes. The 'training provision intelligence officer' role is again heavily information-supported in terms of what training is currently available both internal and external to the Naval Service. These are support roles so that training requirements and sources of provision can be brought together within the planning function.

(d) **Finance manager role:** Is concerned with using the overall financial budget in the best way. It is this role that decides how to allocate funds in a way that facilitates training provision and will set sub-budgets for each establishment within the training organisation.

(e) **Training provision manager role:** Has an overall concern for the quality of training provided irrespective of whether the provision is internal to Naval Service or external to it. This role will have associated with it a quality assurance role at each establishment.

The remaining roles are replicated at each establishment within the control of the training organisation.

(f) **Admissions officer role:** This role has responsibility for the trainee reception process. It will handle applications to the stage of ensuring that the applicants will be embarking upon training programmes/courses that are appropriate to their entry qualifications and future career and role requirements.

(g) **Course/programme team role:** Course/programme design and delivery are the responsibility of this role. It includes not only the course/programme content but also the costing of modifications and design and the total delivery within specified budgets.

(h) **Quality assurance officer role:** Is the link between each establishment and the central (HQ) 'Training provision manager' role. It will also have responsibility for feedback monitoring in terms of quality of achievement of personal and role requirements.

Conclusions—Audit Trail

Soft Systems Methodology, as used in this project, effectively started 'below the line' with Systems Definitions (RDs) developed from taken-as given statements of the purpose of the Naval Service and of training extracted from current internal documents. These then led to the two business models of Figures 8.2 and 8.4. They were confirmed as relevant both on the basis of the service knowledge of the project team and also by the construction of a tabular 'confirmation' document based upon the existence of each activity.

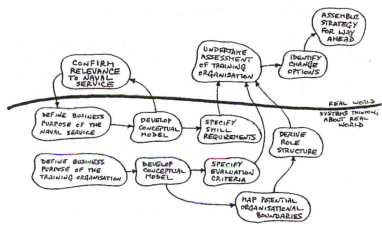

Figure 8.6 *Structure of SSM*

These models represented the basic assumptions of the business of the Naval Service (that requires skill support), together with the necessary business activities of the skill provider (i.e. The Training Organisation). They therefore provided the starting point for the audit trail. Assessment of the current training organisation was undertaken on the basis of the activities within the model providing an evaluation of both the structure and scope of training. Evaluation criteria were defined prior to the assessment and hence any judgements made that led to the formulation of desired changes and hence the strategy for the way ahead, were all based upon an explicit analysis.

Figure 8.6 illustrates the shape of SSM used within this project and Figure 8.7 provides a diagrammatic version of the audit trail.

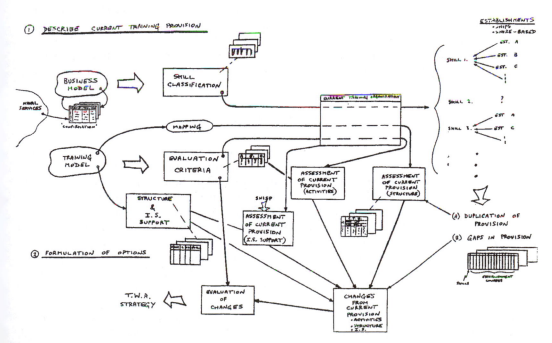

Figure 8.7 *The audit trail*

ASKAM CONSTRUCTION LTD

Askam is a small (about 30 employees) construction company based a few miles south of Lancaster. My offices were rented from Askam and so we had a fairly close relationship. Some of their senior managers shared an interest in the kind of work that I was involved in and it is probably because of this close relationship that the following project took place. It is unusual for a small construction company such as this to use consultants and it makes a useful contrast to the Navy project which has just been described. Askam were also interested in training. They had been involved in the 'Investors in People' initiative and as a result were concerned about the development of skills within their own personnel. One of their senior managers had been given the responsibility for in-house training and he discussed with me the possibility of developing a training strategy. As it was to be 'their' strategy he wanted guidance on what was to be done to establish this as an on-going process within the company.

The main differences between this and the Navy project are as follows:

(a) Size of organisation.
(b) In the Navy project a training strategy was produced which included a review of their training establishments. In Askam only guidance was produced on how to establish a training strategy as part of an on-going process.
(c) The Navy project took 40 days of my time, only 4 days were used in Askam.
(d) In the Navy a published mission statement was taken to be a defensible starting point. In Askam a consensus view of their objectives was obtained through interviews and discussions.
(e) The Navy had a complex bureaucracy, Askam was essentially informal. The only structure that existed was a management group consisting of four senior managers together with the necessary contracting management structure established for each construction site. Other roles were administrative, accounts, quantity surveying and design. The only relationship between these was contract based.

Because of the small and relatively informed nature of Askam it was felt important to emphasise some basic principles which might not have been necessary in a more sophisticated organisation with its own human resources management function.

From the point of view of completeness within the description of this project they are reiterated here. The reader may also find them useful.

Basic Principles

Training is a support for the activities undertaken by the business (Doing and Managing Activities), it is not an end in itself. From the individual's point of view, training may provide career opportunities beyond Askam and therefore be related solely to the individual's need and not the needs of the company. It may be highly motivating to the individual to have the opportunity for self-betterment at the expense of the company (if only in time) and this motivation could help in implementing the particular training that *is* company oriented. Prior to the implementation of any training strategy, therefore, some mechanism must exist for finding out, recording and *updating* the needs of the individual and their current capabilities. It is this recorded information that provides the first part of the answer to the question—who needs what training at what level for what purpose? The second part of the answer requires an analysis of the company in order to define purpose.

If training is going to be taken seriously it cannot be totally informal and *ad hoc*. Like other significant activities within the company, it needs to be planned, monitored and controlled and, irrespective of the content of the training, the procedures for doing this need to be given some thought. Thus the first part of establishing a training strategy is to introduce responsibility for it within the company and to ensure that procedures are in place for answering the following questions:

- Planning
    (1) What training is needed?
    (2) Who requires specific training?
    (3) When is it to be made available?
    (4) Who is going to provide the training?

- Monitoring
    (5) How is the training to be assessed?

- Control
    (6) What options are available to improve training?

Question No. 1 is on-going and some form of company analysis is needed in order to provide the starting point (or baseline) for the training strategy.

Company Analysis

As mentioned earlier, interviewing and discussion were used to obtain an agreed statement of company purpose. This was the starting point for the remainder of the analysis. This statement of purpose was converted into a RD though, in fact, two definitions were taken to produce the model; one representing the total company and the other representing an expansion of one of the activities to do with completing a project. The definitions are given below.

(1) A J.L.-owned system, operated by Askam and other contracted staff to provide and develop a civil engineering and building service to clients within a prescribed geographical area by creating and responding to those opportunities seen as beneficial to the company and by realising resultant contracts in such a way that satisfies client requirements for timeliness and quality, personnel career and job satisfaction needs and company financial requirements while recognising the constraints arising from legal (including heath and safety regulations), competitor and environmental considerations and the recognised working practices of the industry.

(2) A system to transform a contractual agreement into a completed project with a performance that balances customer satisfaction against overall final cost while accommodating the particular site conditions, temporary work requirements and the availability of personnel and equipment. (Note: J.L. is John Lowry, the owner of the company. It was later argued that the management group had an overall concern for performance and, therefore, should be 'The Owner'.)

The model resulting from the combination of these two definitions is given in Figure 8.8 as the total model.

This model was used as a description of what we were taking the company to do *now* (in terms of *what* it does, not *how* it does it). Each activity was examined in terms of the skills that an individual would require in order to be a competent practitioner in that activity. Hence taken as a totality, the model of Figure 8.8 leads to a statement of the skills needed by the total set of individuals within Askam. This set is represented by the skills hierarchy in Figure 8.9.

The mechanism referred to earlier for assessing individual needs is to decompose the model into its subsystems and to group the results of the assessment according to the subsystem requirements. Figure 8.9 represents this grouping.

The process of developing a training strategy is to identify skill shortfalls and to explore ways of rectifying them over a specific timescale. The method that was proposed was to, initially, construct two matrices. A simple matrix could be constructed as follows in Table 8.2.

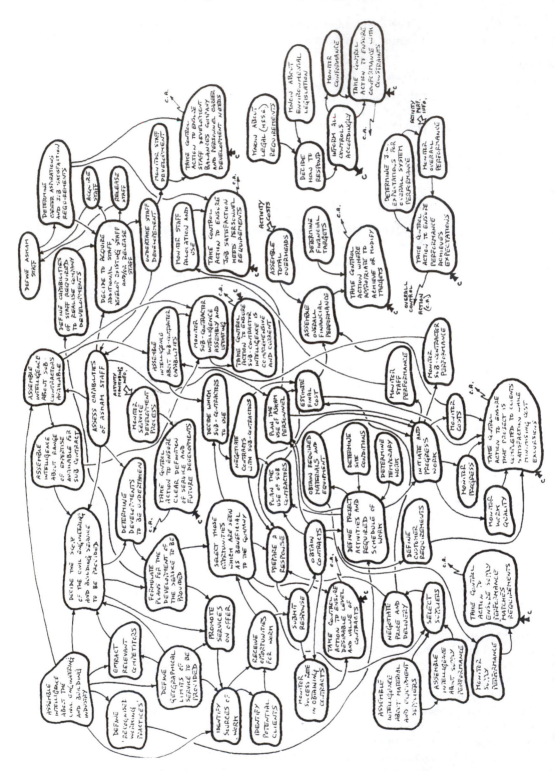

Figure 8.8 *CPTM relevant to Askam*

Table 8.2 *Current skills matrix*

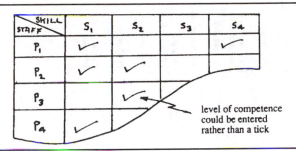

Once completed, the gaps could be related to the jobs of the particular individuals (and/or promotion prospects) and a second matrix assembled which recognises the company priorities in relation to filling the gaps (Table 8.3).

Training Strategy

It is useful to consider a training strategy in two parts. The first part refers to the short term. The main purpose behind this aspect is to ensure that current company personnel are 'up to speed' in whatever skills are needed to run the company now. It is in respect to this that a comparison of the model, of Figure 8.9, against current practices within Askam was used.

Table 8.4 represents an extract from the comparison. This includes those activities (and their priorities) which could be improved through training. This is the input to the second matrix below (Table 8.3), which was then used to derive the short-term strategy. Short-term was defined as the time to implement current skill deficiencies. It needs to be an on-going process as personnel and personnel roles change.

The long-term training strategy is related to where the company is going in terms of its development. The long-term training strategy can only be derived from a long-term business strategy. The important activities, in this respect, from the model of Figure 8.8 are:

'Formulate plans for the development of the service to be provided'
'Define capabilities of staff required to realise company developments'

The latter activity is dependent upon the former, hence the requirement specified above. A recent example had been the development of Askam Marine (concerned with underwater construction

Table 8.3 *Short-term priority matrix*

SKILL / STAFF	S_1	S_2	S_3	S_4
P_1		①	②	
P_2			①	②
P_3		No PRIORITY/REQUIREMENT		
P_4		③		
P_5	①			

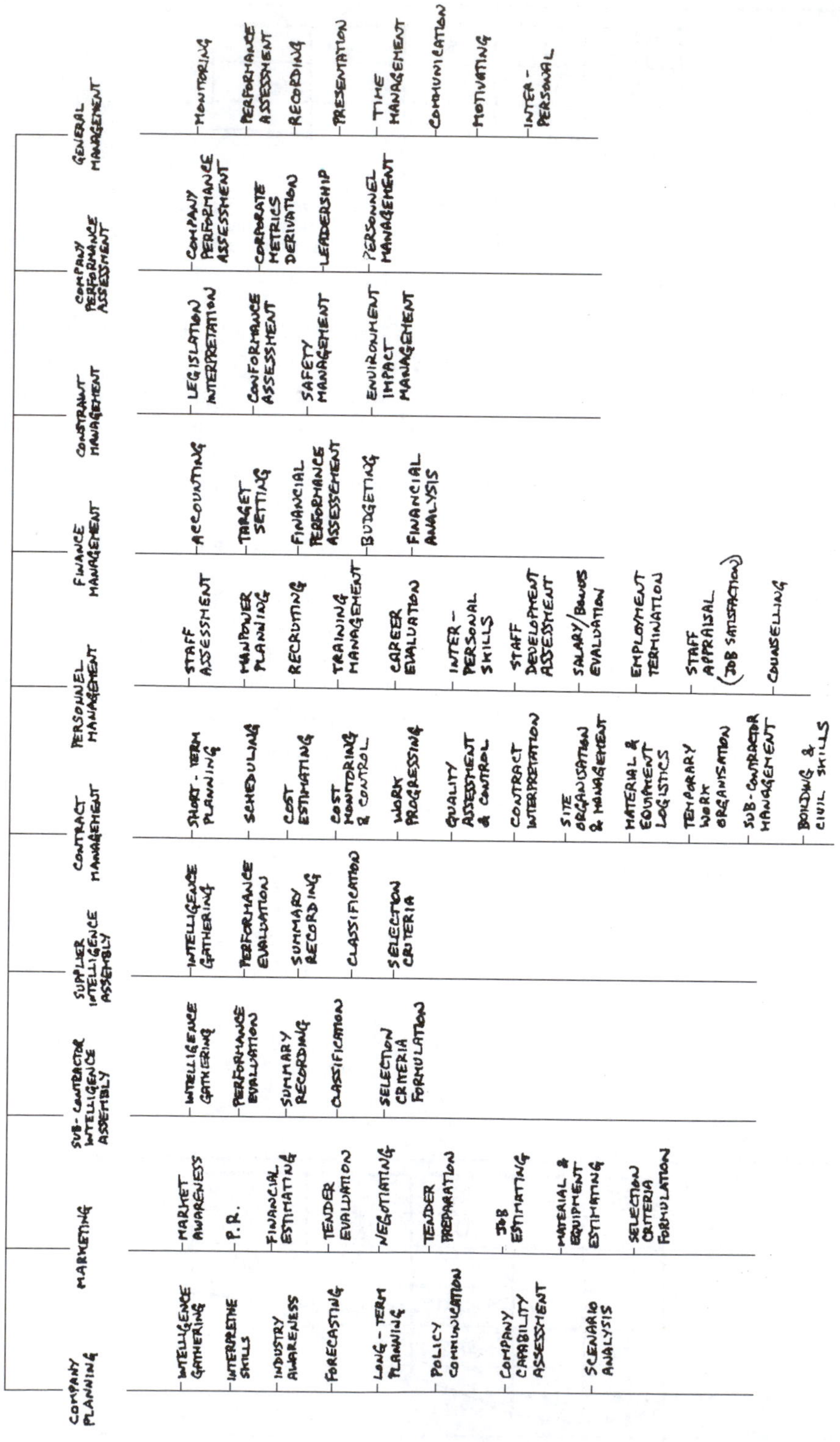

COMPANY PLANNING	MARKETING	SUB-CONTRACTOR INTELLIGENCE ASSEMBLY	SUPPLIER INTELLIGENCE ASSEMBLY	CONTRACT MANAGEMENT	PERSONNEL MANAGEMENT	FINANCE MANAGEMENT	CONSTRAINT MANAGEMENT	COMPANY PERFORMANCE ASSESSMENT	GENERAL MANAGEMENT
Intelligence Gathering	Market Awareness	Intelligence Gathering	Intelligence Gathering	Short-term Planning	Staff Assessment	Accounting	Legislation Interpretation	Company Performance Assessment	Monitoring
Interpretive Skills	P.R.	Performance Evaluation	Performance Evaluation	Scheduling	Manpower Planning	Target Setting	Conformance Assessment	Corporate Metrics Derivation	Performance Assessment
Industry Awareness	Financial Estimation	Summary Recording	Summary Recording	Cost Estimating	Recruiting	Financial Performance Assessment	Safety Management	Leadership	Recording
Forecasting	Tender Evaluation	Classification	Classification	Cost Monitoring & Control	Training Management	Budgeting	Environment Impact Management	Personnel Management	Presentation
Long-term Planning	Negotiating	Selection Criteria Formulation	Selection Criteria	Work Progressing	Career Evaluation	Financial Analysis			Time Management
Policy Communication	Tender Preparation			Quality Assessment & Control	Inter-Personal Skills				Communication
Company Capability Assessment	Job Estimating			Contract Interpretation	Staff Development Assessment				Motivating
Scenario Analysis	Material & Equipment Estimation			Site Organisation & Management	Salary/Bonus Evaluation				Inter-Personal
	Selection Criteria Formulation			Material & Equipment Logistics	Employment Termination				
				Temporary Work Organisation	Staff Appraisal (Job Satisfaction)				
				Sub-contractor Management	Counselling				
				Bonding & Civil Skills					

Figure 8.9 *Skills hierarchy relevant to Askam*

Table 8.4 *Comparison model of Askam*

Activity	Exist	Who	Judgement	Priority	Comments
Decide the scope of the civil engineering and building services	✓	JL	Requires additional attention	2	Requires internal feedback and external intelligence, margins and markets
Assess capabilities to Askam staff	✗		No formal systems exists	2	Information required to assess training needs to attain company and personal goals
Monitor success rate in obtaining contracts	✓	KJ	Previously established system no longer used	2	Measure effectiveness of marketing and pricing and provide intelligence on current markets and warnings for future trend.
Take Control Action (CA) to ensure desirable level and value of contracts	✓	JK/KS	Action currently taken but effectiveness of action not clear	1	Helps to ensure company achieves targets
Take Control Action to ensure subcontractor intelligence is comprehensive and current	✓	internal	Poor	1	Subcontractors carry out approx. 50% of work and their performance reflects greatly on the company
Assemble intelligence about material and equipment suppliers	✓	Respond internal	Poor	2	Coordinated database on subcontractors and material, equipment suppliers envisaged.
Define capabilities of staff required to realise company development	✗			1	Formal
Take Control Action to ensure staff development balances company development and personnel career development needs	✓	JK/KS	Institute training programme	1	Training required—tailored and general
Take Control Action to ensure overall system performance achieves expectation	✗			1	Monitor, measure, react
Take Control Action to ensure the project is completed to client satisfaction while minimising cost excursions	✓	JL/BH & MK	Poor	1A	Training felt to be lacking in this area hence the desire and need for staff training

and maintenance). It was necessary to establish what requirements were implied. Askam Marine had been an *ad hoc* development and was, in essence, a response to a personnel-driven opportunity rather than a necessary expansion based upon a business strategy. It has since been abandoned. The short-term strategy was derived and actioned but the formality of linking a long-term training strategy with explicit business planning has not been undertaken.

SKILL GROUP HEAD

Within another large company, which was seeking further formalisation of its training, a new role was introduced. The organisation was in the communications business and the new role was introduced within the IT function. This function required the development of a number of skills, from software design, computer systems development, testing and roll-out, to project management. In order to ensure that the necessary skill development took place a new role was created, that of skill group head.

Although the role was intended to be broad-based and with responsibility for a set of skills, no definition of the role existed and there was no job specification. It is not unusual for a role to be created as the result of a 'bright idea' and for various individuals then to be given the responsibility of realising it. In this instance a conceptual model was generated to represent a RD encapsulating the desired purpose to be fulfilled by the role. The model reproduced as Figure 8.10, specified *what* the role holder was required to do.

How to do it was left to the individual. Allowing this degree of freedom was seen to provide commitment to the role and also to accommodate the potential flexibility needed to relate to the specific skills being considered.

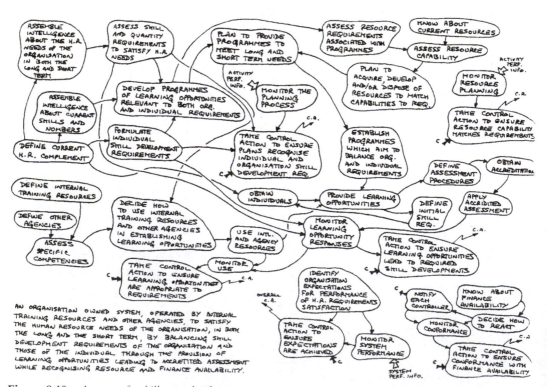

Figure 8.10   *A concept for skill group head*

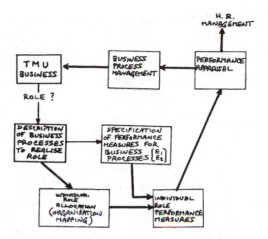

Figure 8.11   *A concept for performance assessment*

PERFORMANCE ASSESSMENT

Performance assessment (or appraisal) is an important feature of human resource management in most organisations. Management by Objectives (MBO) is a process commonly used in which, for a particular role, targets for the coming year (0.5 year or quarter) are agreed between the role holder and his or her superior. Performance is then evaluated against the degree of achievement of those targets. This process is essentially piecemeal and although targets are explicit they may be related to business processes that overlap (or significantly interact) with those of other role holders. It is not clear how such interactions are accounted for in the resulting evaluation.

The use of conceptual models to represent the role of a particular organisation unit ensures that any resultant evaluation of the performance of the various role holders within that organisation unit is coherent, explicit and defensible. These become extremely important criteria when the organisation concerned is using a performance-related pay scheme.

This was the case in a project undertaken for a consultancy company which was providing computer-based services. A particular part of the company had the responsibility for the delivery of a specific group of services and this was called the Technology Management Unit (TMU). The concept which was used to investigate performance is illustrated in Figure 8.11.

The business unit of concern is the TMU and as emphasised earlier the first question to be answered is 'what is the role of TMU?' This can be answered by developing a CPTM to map onto the organisation boundary of TMU. This becomes the description of the business processes to realise the role. Individual roles within TMU can be defined by mapping their responsibilities onto the CPTM (i.e. organisation mapping). The activities (business processes) within the CPTM lead to performance measures for each activity based upon the use of Efficacy (E_1) and Efficiency (E_2). Combining these with the results of the organisation mapping will identify the measures of performance appropriate to the particular role holders.

The evaluation of those measures provides the performance appraisal. The information so derived can be used to effect change in the business processes themselves as well as to provide the HR management function with the basis for the component of pay related to performance assessment (see Figure 8.11).

Within the particular company the role of TMU was represented by the RD and model in Figure 8.12.

One of the roles identified was the management of service delivery (subsystem 1). Other roles were combinations of the remaining subsystems. As an example consider the role represented by subsystem 1.

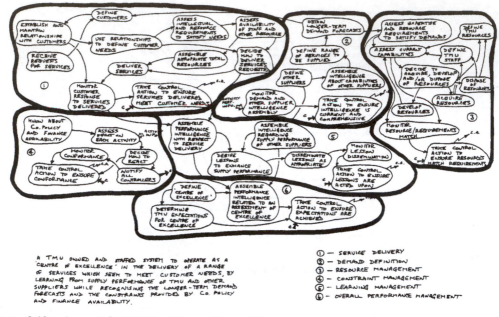

Figure 8.12   *A concept for TMU—subsystem decomposition*

The evaluation of Efficiency for this role is computed from the two components:

- Services actually delivered/service delivery capability (i.e. delivery resource utilisation).
- Percentage customer acceptance within the service level agreement (SLA).

Efficiency is assembled from a consideration of resource usage (manpower, time and IS/IT support). Thus:

- Actual HR usage as % of planned use
- Time to achieve customer acceptance/time specified in SLA
- Cost of IS/IT support

Thus Efficacy measures the existence and quality of the deliverable and Efficiency measures the resources consumed in achieving that deliverable. Similar measures of performance for each of the activities within the boundary of subsystem 1 will identify areas of change within the business processes that the particular manager can effect to improve performance.

CONCLUSION

This chapter has sought to illustrate the use of conceptual models to address the concerns of human resource management; in particular those of training, a specific role within HR development and the processes of performance assessment. It is the case that successful HR management is dependent upon many other factors including interpersonal relationships, values and culture development, attitudes, priorities, etc. but it is also the case that without defensible and coherent processes HR management will stand little chance of succeeding. The use of conceptual model building, as the basis for deciding what those processes need to be, is a good start.

A more detailed analysis of the processes of HR management, derived as a means of carrying out a strategic review of this function, is contained within the discussion of the Met. Office project in Chapter Seven.

Chapter Nine

Generic Model Building

INTRODUCTION

After the emphasis on uniqueness and the introduction of W as a necessary variable within SSM, it may seem totally inappropriate to discuss 'generic' models. However, there are situations within organisation-based analysis where they can be useful. Also, they have a place in the context of demonstration or illustration. In Chapter Two, Figures 2.6 to 2.11, a generic model was used to illustrate the nature of the logical processes used in the construction of a conceptual model. Again, in Chapter Three, Figure 3.7, a generic model of a problem-solving system was used to introduce the idea that the intellectual processes involved in problem solving could usefully be viewed as purposeful activity and modelled through the mechanism of a RD.

In both these examples, the use was solely illustration. The RDs to be used in specific situations must, of course, be made specific to those situations.

My concern in this chapter is to introduce a few examples where use was made of generic models to aid the investigation of a problem situation and which were argued to be useful in progressing the investigation. The first example was in a recent project within the National Health Service and here a generic model was used to scope the project itself.

THE MORECAMBE BAY ACUTE AND PRIMARY CARE TRUSTS

The Morecambe Bay area is the largest in the UK. It was formed from three former trusts in the area: The Royal Lancaster Infirmary; Furness Hospitals and Westmorland Hospital Trust. The merged organisation (The Morecambe Bay Hospitals NHS Trust; MBHT) serves the largest geographical area in England and brings together three organisations from two different counties with more than 45 miles between its two main hospital sites.

As well as a large geographically dispersed set of health-based resources, the organisation is also complex. The Morecambe Bay area has six health organisations providing healthcare to a population of 310 000. These are the Morecambe Bay Health Authority, the Morecambe Bay Acute Trust, the Bay Community Trust and three Primary Care Groups based in Barrow, the South Lakes and Lancaster and Morecambe. Recently there was a move away from a split between purchasers and providers to an approach based upon commissioning services aimed at improving the health of the population.

The project was within the government's initiative on 'information for health' and consisted of two parts. One part was to define the information requirements for commissioning with reference to one of the Primary Care Trusts (PCT) and the other was to define the information requirements to provide electronic patient records (EPR) with reference to one of the Acute Trusts.

The initial concern with both projects was to determine their scope. Since there was no definitive statement as to what commissioning was or any definition of how wide patient records might be, this was an important consideration.

The procedure that we adopted to define 'scope' was to develop a broad-based model of health-care provision, to follow this with a series of interviews with selected stakeholders, to derive individual primary-task models and to then map these onto the healthcare provision model in order to assess its legitimacy. Once we were satisfied that the model of healthcare provision was itself of adequate scope (which might have involved iteration), we could identify those activities within it that could be taken to represent 'commissioning' and also the set of activities that could be taken to use 'patient'-type information and also contribute to that information. Thus our defined 'project scope' represented an assumption, but it was an *explicit* assumption that had been derived in discussion with our client on the basis of a selection of activities from a model that had been 'validated' in terms of legitimacy and scope. The scope of the areas of concern for both projects were derived and agreed with the client by adopting this procedure.

The healthcare provision model was developed as a CPTM using the 'Enterprise Model' assembly method. The following seven RDs were used:

T   A system, operated by medical and other resources to execute discrete episodes for the treatment of specific patient conditions to the satisfaction of both the patient and the defined medical personnel within the time and resources determined by an explicit care pathway.

L1   A system to bring together patients requiring treatment and the required levels of medical resources at a time and place appropriate to the treatment required while recording and making available the medical history of that patient.

L2   A system to make healthcare advice and services available to the community in order to reduce susceptibility to a range of conditions requiring treatment while using the results of relevant research and generally available knowledge in this field.

L3   A system to assemble classified intelligence about the healthcare needs of the community as it changes in response to demographic and personal (birth/death) conditions, while storing and disseminating this intelligence as required.

S1   A system to match to its healthcare needs, the variety and scope of the total medically oriented resources, in such a way that allows flexibility in usage, responsiveness to national and local changes and allows effective and authorised exploitation of developments in relevant technology.

S2   A system to ensure that healthcare provision continually improves its performance by adapting its operations through the assembly, storage and dissemination of lessons arising from the total processes.

P,M,C   A health authority-owned system, operated by dedicated human and physical resources, to plan the development and structure of healthcare provision within the authority and to realise its implementation, while reacting to the geographical structure of the region, national arrangements, health legislation, local policy, national standards of provision and the total finances available.

The structure and resultant model are given in Figure 9.1. This was decomposed into 13 sub-systems as illustrated in Figure 9.2. This model was used to describe the activities and logic of the model to the client (he understood the status and language of the model), but it was the model of Figure 9.1 that was used to define project scope. Mappings are illustrated in Figures 9.3 and 9.4, which show the scopes of commissioning and patient records respectively.

The activities within each boundary were the source of information requirements and progressed according to the information version of SSM (Wilson 1990).

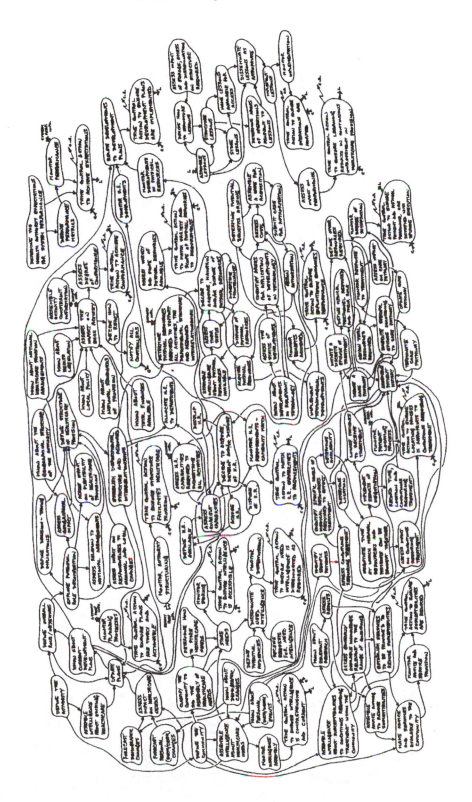

Structure of model and subsystem decomposition

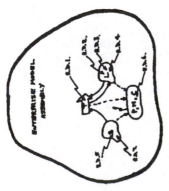

SUBSYSTEMS

(1)—Development planning for provision
(2)—Plan implementation management
(3)—Healthcare need assembly & dissemination
(4)—Authority structuring
(5)—Constraint management
(6)—H.R. management
(7)—Physical resource management
(8)—Technology exploitation
(9)—Ill-health avoidance service provision
(10)—Patient location management
(11)—Care/treatment episode execution
(12)—Overall performance control
(13)—Learning management

Figure 9.1 *A healthcare system (the original figure may be viewed on ftp://ftp.wiley.co.uk/pub/books/wilson/)*

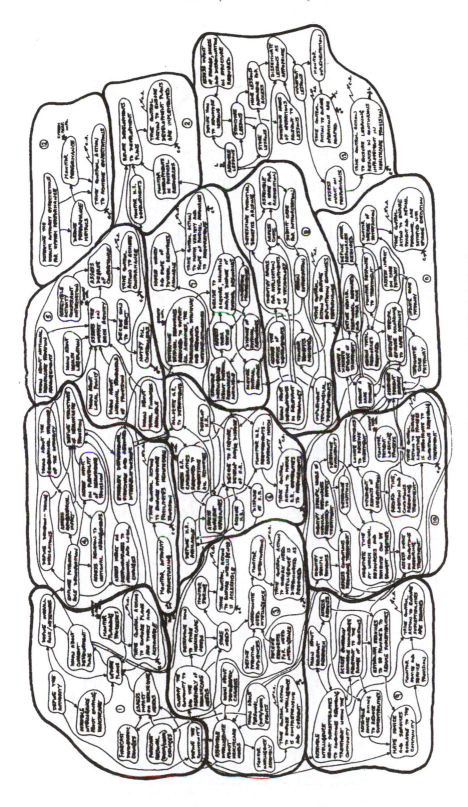

Figure 9.2 Subsystem decomposition (the original figure may be viewed on ftp://ftp.wiley.co.uk/pub/books/wilson/)

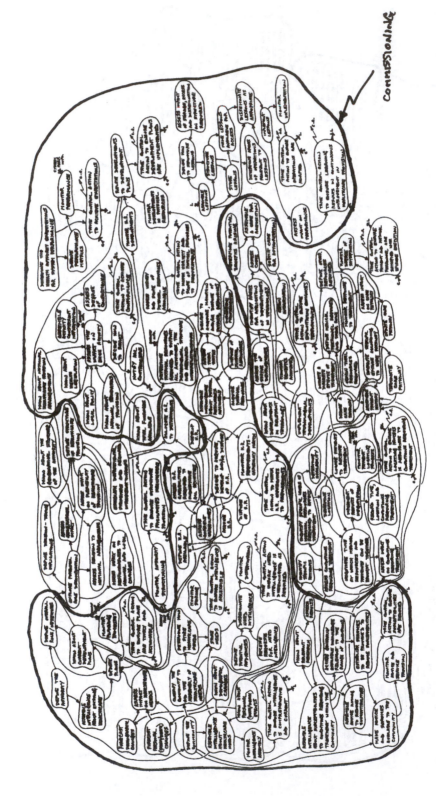

Figure 9.3   *The scope of 'commissioning' (the original figure may be viewed on ftp://ftp.wiley.co.uk/pub/books/wilson/)*

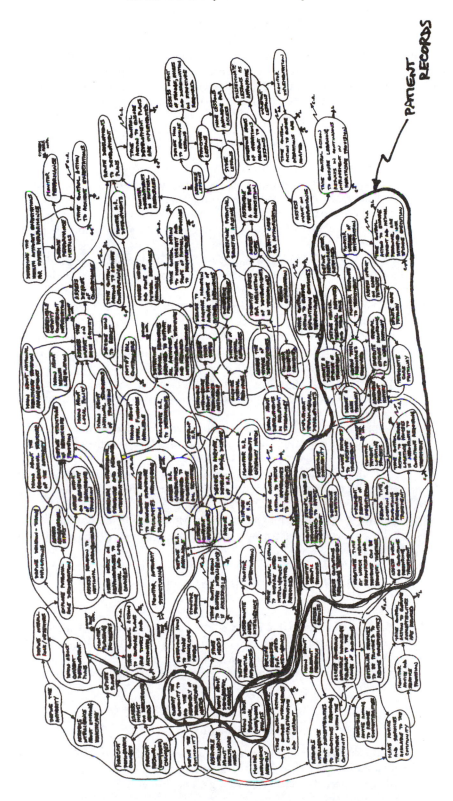

Figure 9.4 *The scope of 'patient records' (the original figure may be viewed on ftp://ftp.wiley.co.uk/pub/books/wilson/)*

THE MET. OFFICE

During the execution of the Met. Office project (discussed in Chapter Seven) it became apparent that a number of models were required that represented activities occurring across organisational boundaries. It was argued that in order to avoid undue emphasis arising from current interdepartmental issues the models would be more useful if derived as generic models.

Planning, Learning and Change Management

One set of processes that fell into the above category were those to do with planning, learning and change management. Although they were seen to be concerned, initially, with strategic level processes it was realised that they cascaded down through the total organisation. Thus a model that described them in generic terms could be used recursively throughout the organisation. A CPTM was constructed based on seven RDs for the 'Enterprise Model' assembly method.

T   A system to execute a defined planning process by accessing relevant learning and environmental intelligence in order to derive actionable change programmes while responding to internal and external pressures to change.

P,M,C   A Divisional Management Board (DMB)-owned system, to define the agreed planning process and its decomposition to be executed in order to realise the strategic vision of the Met. Office while accommodating the current divisional and branch structure together with their individual desired intent within the MOD DIA guidelines, legal and regulatory constraints.

L(1)   A system to disseminate the specified change programmes resulting from the planning process so that authorised projects may be formulated for implementation within the respective areas of the Met. Office.

L(2)   A system to ensure that authorised change projects are realised according to overall requirements while learning from the process and ensuring the achievement of expected business benefits.

L(3)   A system to assemble environmental intelligence to support the planning process in such a way that potential future scenarios can be formulated relevant to the Met. Office vision and the internal pressures to change arising from the processes of innovation.

S(1)   A system to ensure that learning is extracted from Met. Office operations in total and that it is structured, stored and made accessible in order to contribute to improvement in Met. Office performance.

S(2)   A system, operated by Met. Office planning personnel, to ensure that the capabilities are available to realise the various change programmes, in both the human resources and the technology available.

These RDs produced the CPTM illustrated in Figure 9.5 and the decomposed version in Figure 9.6.

So far the model has only been used at the highest organisational level, but as it gets used for more detailed comparison, the 'ownership' will have to be redefined, the vision will become Divisional rather than Met. Office and 'environmental' will be external to the Division rather than external to the Met. Office.

Communications

The planning, learning and change management processes described above are applicable to a range of organisational levels and can hence be re-used as the investigation becomes more detailed. This was the argument used to support the generation of a generic model.

A further argument was mounted, in support of a generic model, for a system that would have relevance irrespective of the organisational level. This was a system to define communication process requirements, i.e. those business processes that would result in the appropriate communications between all levels of staff. The model could be seen as those processes that could be used to derive the requirements for an Intranet, but this was not the purpose of deriving the model. It was used as a basis for questioning and improving current methods of communication.

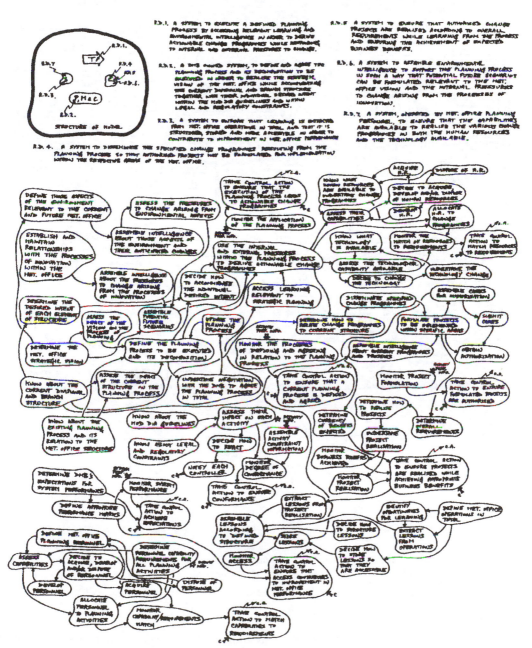

Figure 9.5 *A concept for learning and change management (the original figure may be viewed on ftp://ftp.wiley.co.uk/ pub/books/wilson/)*

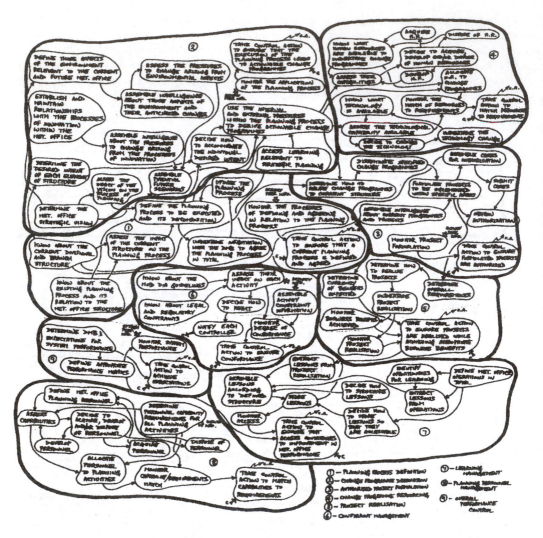

Figure 9.6   *Subsystem decomposition (the original figure may be viewed on ftp://ftp.wiley.co.uk/pub/books/wilson/)*

In this instance a single RD was derived and this, together with the resultant model, is given here in the hope that such a generic model might be useful to the reader. The RD used was:

A Company Secretary-owned system, operated by company personnel, to facilitate the timely and accurate exchange of information and opinion concerning the changing Company role and its activities, between all levels of staff, by ensuring that the format of messages aids understanding, that the channels available have required characteristics and that advantage is taken of developments in relevant technology, but recognising company policy on confidentiality and information retention, finance availability, the requirements of the Public Records Office and MOD security.

The model and its subsystem decomposition are illustrated in Figures 9.7 and 9.8 respectively. For application elsewhere the 'ownership' and 'environmental constraints' would need redefining.

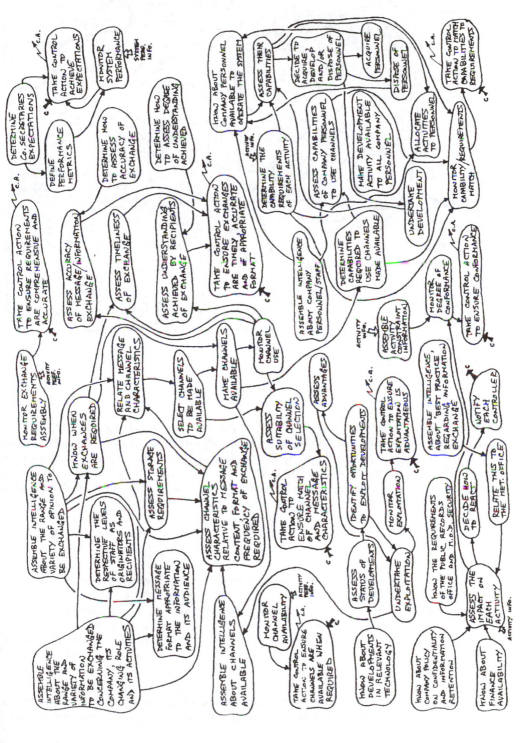

Figure 9.7 *A communication system*

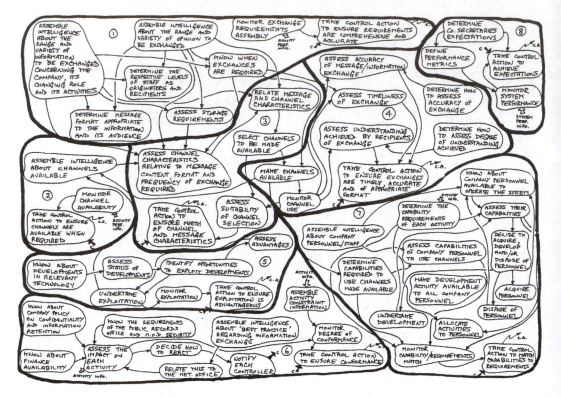

Figure 9.8 *Communication subsystems*

QUALITY MANAGEMENT—ISO 9001

A final example which arose within the Met. Office project but which has general applicability is a concern for quality management. In this instance the argument for the relevance of a generic model is that the resultant processes are due to the imposition of an external requirement or standard. Here the particular standard is ISO 9001. Thus, any organisation that wishes to obtain accreditation as a quality organisation must be seen to be adopting a predefined quality management structure. The Met. Office was interested in ensuring that all of its Divisions and Branches were properly organised in relation to this particular quality standard and, hence, the process improvement study had to address this aspect. The notion of a 'standard' implies commonality of 'measures of performance' in relation to the management of quality, but what are they 'measures' of? We can answer this question by defining the purpose of ISO 9001 and then by defining what activities must be in place to achieve the defined purpose, i.e. by producing an RD and associated CM.

Reference to the documentation describing this standard leads to the requirement to produce a CPTM since the description is too complex to capture 'purpose' in a single RD.

Five RDs were used to define the elements of the 'Enterprise Model' and these are given below:

T　　　　A system to satisfy customer requirements for a product by ensuring that the stages from concept formulation, through design to production are executed with minimum risk to achieve the specified quality standards within the required time and financial constraints.

L   A system to ensure that relationships with the customer are maintained and developed in order to ensure that the products delivered recognise and conform to the customer need.

S(1)   A system to ensure that the physical resources necessary to support and operate the defined quality processes are made available while responding to opportunities to explore new technology as a means of improving performance of those processes.

S(2)   A system to ensure that the skills and capabilities of the personnel, undertaking the quality processes in total, match requirements, while balancing individual and organisational needs but within the derived HR policy.

P,M,C A quality manager-owned system to derive the quality policy, standards, roles and related responsibility/authority requirements for the institution and operation of quality processes within and throughout an organisation, while ensuring that lessons arising from the operation of these processes are recorded and acted upon to lead to continuous performance improvement, while reporting as necessary but recognising legal constraints and the accepted standards of the industry.

The model resulting from these RDs, assembled into the CPTM, is reproduced as Figure 9.9. This model decomposes into eleven subsystems as illustrated by Figure 9.10. The model represents the set of activities that needs to be in place, in order to implement ISO 9001, irrespective of the business area to which it applies.

Another model must be generated, in association with it, that is specific to the business area to give a complete representation.

THE UNIVERSITY OF UTOPIA

An example of the application of a generic model arose within a project to derive an approach to IS/IT strategy development within a university. Since reference cannot be made to the particular university the discussion of the approach and the situation has been generalised. The university had never produced an IS/IT strategy. Piecemeal development of computer support had taken place over the years though some standardisation of the technology had happened. Prior to the introduction of the next generation of the technology (at that time, expected around the year 2003), the university decided to develop an IS/IT strategy to enable more effective application of the new technology.

A university is a complex organisation with three major areas of activity. There is the management of the institution itself, including the maintenance and development of buildings, the provision of support services such as library facilities, student accommodation, catering and the necessary infrastructure. There is also the wide variety of academic departments with their own administration associated with the development and operation of courses ranging from Diploma to Masters level. Third, there is the research area, including that of the academic staff, as well as the department-associated PhD programmes.

Given this degree of complexity within the one organisation it is not easy to see how a single IS/IT strategy can be evolved. However, we believed that this was possible, given some assumptions which could lead to variety reduction; in particular, through the use of a generic 'departmental' model. Such a model could ignore subject-based variety and assume that the information required related to the particular area of expertise would be the responsibility of the particular department.

All departments admit students who satisfy acceptance criteria. All departments develop and run courses for those students, which lead to qualifications awarded on the basis of assessment. All

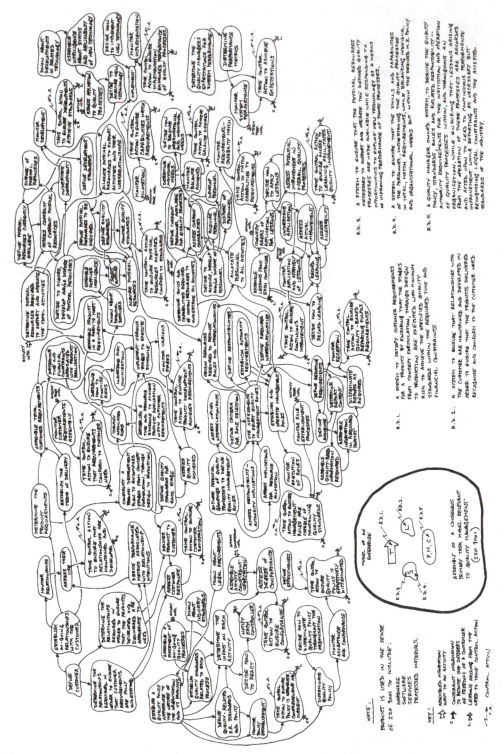

Figure 9.9   *A concept for ISO 9001 (the original figure may be viewed on ftp://[ftp.wiley.co.uk/pub/books/wilson/])*

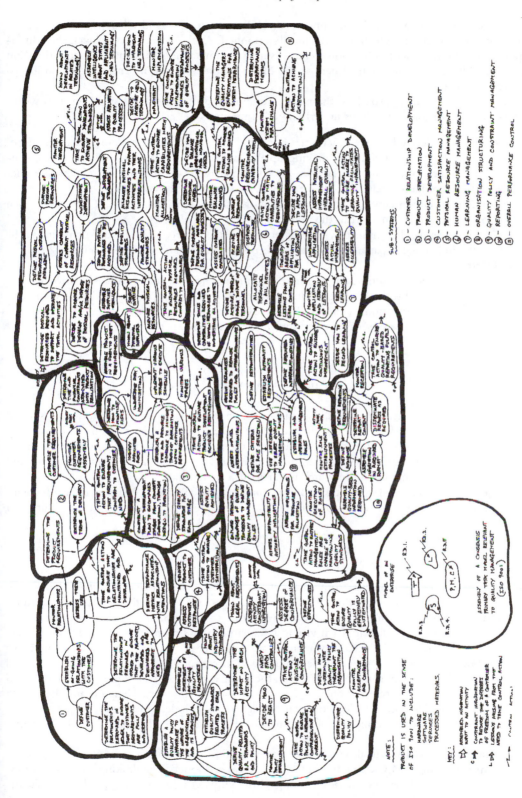

Figure 9.10 *Subsystems relevant to ISO 9001 (the original figure may be viewed on ftp://ftp.wiley.co.uk/pub/books/wilson/)*

departments maintain staff with the appropriate skill and expertise and all departments operate within an administration, which is hierarchically arranged. At the departmental level, the administration is concerned with admissions, course support, timetabling, meetings organisation and reporting. All departments are members of schools or faculties, which, in turn, are responsible to Council and Senate.

Before discussing the approach to the model building appropriate to this situation, it is worth emphasising the major assumptions underlying the approach:

(1) Information is derived from the activities requiring it. Thus the basis for information requirements is the total set of activities making up the 'taken to be' institution. Since we are considering the derivation of a strategy we are concerned with the institution in transition and, hence, the information related to the process of transition is also required.

(2) Information requirements lead to the assembly of information systems (IS). Then, only when the IS have been determined can the IT requirements be explored.

(3) Information needs, determined by a consideration of the subject area of a department, can be left to the individual departments. Thus, subject-based information will be excluded from the IS/IT strategy.

(4) Some idea of the environmental factors determining the potential future scenarios for the institution will need to be available. Thus it is assumed that a comprehensive business strategy will precede the derivation of the IS/IT strategy. If not, the approach will have to start by deriving a business strategy based upon future vision statements for the institution.

Approach Adopted

Assumption (4) above determines the actual start of the analysis but, as in all such studies, it is useful to express the situation. Thus a 'rich picture'(Chapter Three) has been derived on the basis of the generalised description given above, which illustrates the assumptions, in total, about the situation (see Figure 9.11). This highlights the institutional activities, processes and structural elements and emphasises the transitional situation, which is our focus of attention.

A major question is related to what we take the 'university 2003' to be. (We were concerned with a 5-year time horizon, but the work was done in 1998.) Thus the first stage must be the resolution of this question.

Stage 1

Obtain 'future vision' statements from a predetermined business strategy or derive them from interviews (or workshops) with relevant stakeholders. These may cover the variety of institution aims from 'teaching only' through 'selected subjects only' to 'research only'. These may be seen to be desirable as well as undesirable. Each vision statement can be structured into the form of a RD and corresponding models derived. Dependent upon the degree of variety in these vision statements they could be combined into a single model using the W-decomposition method. This model could then form the T in the Enterprise Model. Given the great variety, separate Enterprise Models will need to be constructed. A 'research only' vision would not contain course elements and this would have an impact on the kind of 'departmental' model to be included. However, for every other vision a generic departmental model could be part of the T within each vision-related 'Enterprise Model'.

An issue-based model(s) will also need to be constructed for the institution development process. This forms part of the P,M,C element within the 'Enterprise Model'. The 'linking' elements consist of environmental intelligence gathering to support the knowledge assembly regarding the factors

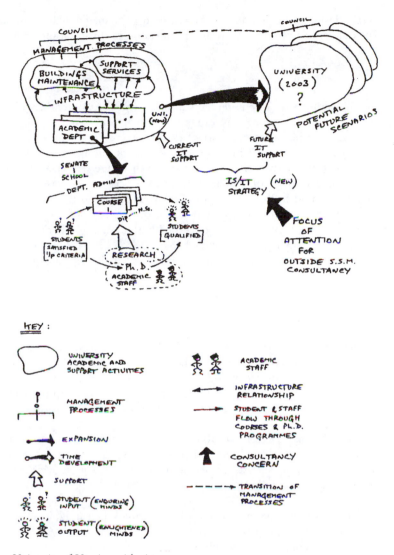

Figure 9.11 *University of Utopia—rich picture*

that govern the development of the institution, together with institution promotion, lobbying and negotiation to achieve desirable rather than undesirable potential futures. The 'support' processes are those required to develop and maintain institution facilities in total, including buildings, services and infrastructure.

The deliverables of stage 1 are the set of CPTMs which represent the adaptive systems describing each vision (or the combined vision, given low variety).

Stage 2

The total 'information category' requirements can be derived for each CPTM by constructing information tables for the subsystems obtained by decomposing the model(s) of stage 1.

Some subsystems will be common to all models and, hence, the information requirements can be divided into sets which represent 'vision-dependent' and 'vision-independent' requirements (i.e. irrespective of the vision, information will be required to manage facilities, finance, human resources, etc.). The deliverable of this stage is the specification of information requirements.

Stage 3

Some way of combining information requirements into information 'system' requirements needs to be explored. This may be determined by organisational or functional groupings. However, 'organisational mapping' will be an integral part of this stage as a means of defining 'user' roles. Whatever the basis that the particular institution chooses for defining information system require-ments, a deliverable is the future IS needs. Incorporated into this stage will be a comparison against current IS provision in order to identify opportunities for re-use as well as new requirements. A 'Maltese cross' may be found to be useful as a means of undertaking the required comparison. The identified changes to the current IS provision will form the basis of the IS strategy. The IS strategy *must* precede the IT strategy, since it is concerned with defining 'what' is required. The IT strategy determines 'how' the IS is to be provided. See Wilson (1990) for a description of the information-oriented version of SSM in which a more detailed description of the above three stages appears.

Stage 4

Technology options need to be explored. The options may be constrained by the costs of migrating from current technology, but the implications must be examined. The total deliverable, i.e. the IS/IT strategy, includes the decisions on technology, phasing of IS requirements on the basis of the issue-based information collection (defined in stage 2 to support the adaptive elements within the CPTM) and the organisational responsibilities for performance monitoring and control of the change processes.

Of the above stages, only stage 1 is relevant to the discussion of this chapter. It was argued that significant reduction in variety could be obtained by producing a generic model that could be expected to map onto an academic department. Again it was the 'Enterprise Model' approach that was adopted. The RDs used are as follows:

RD1   A school of studies-owned system, operated by suitably skilled and knowledgeable staff, to produce students with appropriate qualifications by exposing them to courses supported by research while acting upon the admission and assessment criteria relevant to those courses and operating within the financial constraints specified by higher management.

RD2   A system to ensure that the courses on offer, in both the long and the short term, are appropriate to the changing characteristics of the selected market and that the facilities available match the requirements of the courses provided, while recognising the courses offered by competing institutions and the conditions laid down by the relevant accredita-tion and award-giving bodies.

RD3   A system to assemble intelligence about the appropriate student and career market in order to support course development and student acquisition, while recognising the competitive element and the potential for external funding.

RD4   A system to allocate available facilities to the total activities related to course presentation, research and the defined administrative procedures associated with financial and depart-mental management together with reporting as required.

The model resulting from these RDs is reproduced as Figure 9.12. The subsystem decomposition is reproduced as Figure 9.13.

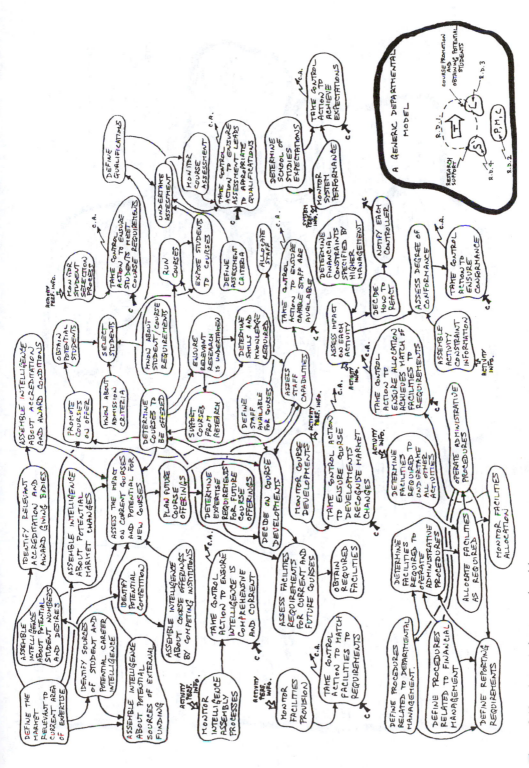

Figure 9.12 *A generic departmental model*

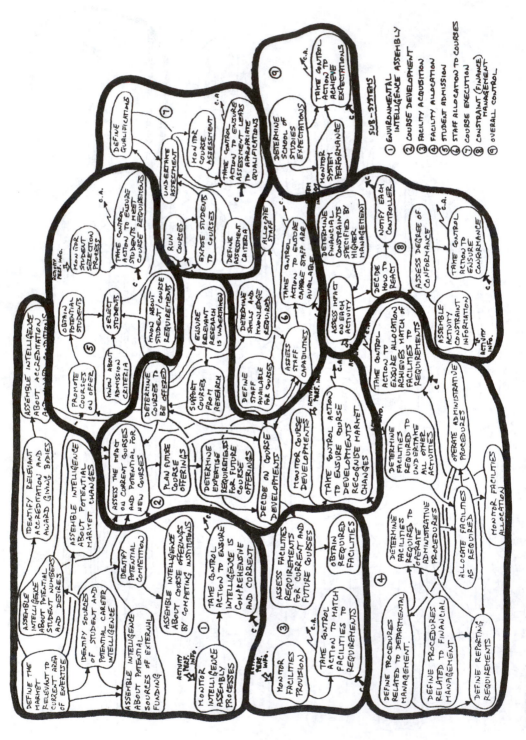

Figure 9.13 *Subsystems relevant to generic departmental model*

As the model structure illustrates, RD1 includes some elements of S and L as well as the T. It may frequently be the case that a RD centred around one of the enterprise model elements will contain some other elements. In the case of RD1, to expose students to courses one must obtain students, hence it made sense to include this aspect of 'Linking' within the RD.

Similarly, for the courses to be research supported one must undertake research. Thus there was an aspect of S also included in RD1.

The model of Figure 9.12 can now be used as the T element within an Enterprise Model for the institution as a whole. Of course, there is more than one department and the model of Figure 9.12 requires some elaboration to include those activities to assemble a set of such models. Since we have ignored subject dependence, these activities are merely associated with totalling resources and allocating finance. Within the remainder of the model, systems were developed as follows:

S	Buildings development and maintenance
	Services provision
	Facilities (e.g. library, catering, sports, etc.)
	Infrastructure development
L	University promotion
	Grant acquisition
	External representation
	Reporting
P,M,C	Management of the university, i.e.
	Strategic planning
	HR management
	Finance management
	Performance monitoring and control
	Change management

The CPTM describes the activities that represent 'what' we are taking the institution to be doing in the future and in the 'Transition' process. These activities are the source of information requirements needed to support the institution in this state of change and, on the basis of what the desired vision is taken to be, the final state. Thus, comparison against what information is currently provided leads to the definition of the changes required by the information strategy. The IS strategy represents the assembly of I-requirements into IS requirements which in turn (stage 4) leads to the production of the IT strategy. The information derivation is beyond the scope of this book but, as a brief illustration, consider the beginnings of an information table for a selection of activities from the generic model of Figure 9.12.

Table 9.1 is an example of the assembly of operational and performance information. The measure of performance (M of P) information categories are determined from:

E1—Efficacy (i.e. what you have to monitor to know (a) that the activity has been done and (b) that it has been done with adequate quality)

E2—Efficiency (i.e. what you have to monitor to know what resources have been consumed in achieving the above efficacy).

These two measures represent 'management' or performance-monitoring information for each activity. The 'targets' against which performance is assessed and against which the decision to take control action, or not, are defined in the control activities themselves. The set of tables, so derived, represent the deliverable from stage 2 in the approach described earlier.

Table 9.1 *Operation and performance information*

Activity	Promote courses on offer	Obtain potential students	Select students	Run courses	Undertake assessment
Input	• Course details • Locations of promotion • Costs • Available finance	• Student ID • Student CV • Course required • Promotion	• Admission criteria • Student ID • Student CV • Student requirements	• Course timetables • Staff availability • Facility availability • Student IDs (selected)	• Assessment criteria • Course module to be assessed • Form of assessment • Time of assessment
Output	• Promotion • Course required	• Student ID • Student CV	• Student IDs (selected)	• Course module to be assessed • Form of assessment • Time of assessment	• Student ID (selected) • Module ID • Assessment results
Measures of performance	• List of locations • Applications from each location • Cost	• Application list • Quality of applicants • Cost	• Selected list • Quality of selection • Cost	• Timetable achievement • Student/peer feedback • Cost	• Assessment results • Quality of assessment with respect to course taught • Accuracy of assessment • Consistency of assessment • Cost

CONCLUSIONS

The above examples of the use of generic models is intended to illustrate a number of reasons for ignoring the situation-specific features that make such situations unique. It was initially argued that it was the uniqueness of each situation that made organisational analysis so complex and was the underlying reason for the development of a modelling language that was rich enough to cater for the multiple perceptions of the actors in those situations. This is still the case and every study should start from that assumption. *Generic models should only be considered if a defensible argument can be mounted for their adoption.*

Chapter Ten

Conclusions

In the Preamble to this book the point was made that defensibility was the criterion to be used in organisation-based analysis if the situation under examination was to be regarded as 'soft' rather than 'hard'. If this was the case then 'optimisation' or the 'right' answer was unlikely to be achievable. It was further argued that the defensibility of any outcomes relies on making the analysis that leads to those outcomes explicit. Unless this is the case, then what emerges from the analysis is little more than opinion. What is called for is an *explicit audit trail*. This means that both the concepts being used within the thinking process and the thinking process itself need to be made explicit. In order to achieve this, an appropriate language must be available in which to express these two features. The emphasis of this book has been on demonstrating how to ensure that the way in which that language is constructed and used is also defensible.

The language that emerged from the action research programme at the University of Lancaster was based on the concept of a Human Activity System. For this to be a powerful and defensible analysis tool, confusion must be avoided between the human activity that takes place in actual organisations and the activity described in the concept. This turns out to be a difficult distinction to make and to maintain. It represents one of the major sources of confusion for students since it is our natural language that is being used both to construct the concept and to describe the real world to which it is being applied.

The distinction is not problematical if we are using differential equations, or some other branch of mathematics, to describe how we are thinking about some taken-to-be 'hard' aspect of reality, because it is obvious that mathematics is a modelling language. Human activity is altogether more complex and requires a more sophisticated and richer modelling language if we are to cope with the ill-defined and messy aspects of 'soft' situations. Our natural language has this capability.

However, we must remember that when we are developing a model, (in whatever language is appropriate), we are *not* describing reality but we are always describing *how we are thinking about reality*.

As long as we retain the thought that what we are describing, in relation to these two aspects, are two totally different things, i.e. in one case we are describing *what is in our head* and in the other case *what is outside it*, the confusion might be avoided.

It is actually the case that we are using two different languages even though we might be using the same words. At a particular level of resolution, the language of the concept is always in terms of 'what' whereas in the real world (at the same level of resolution) the language is in terms of 'how'. We cannot do a 'what' without deciding 'how' to do it. So that our observations of the real world (i.e. of people actually doing things) are of the decided 'hows'. Thus, if 'what' we want to do is 'take exercise' we might choose to 'ride a bicycle' or 'pump iron'. These alternatives represent choices *at the same level of resolution.*

If we wish to change the level of resolution then each of these 'hows' can become a 'what', i.e. if 'what' we want to do is 'pump iron' we can decide 'how' to do it. *The level of resolution is the key to avoiding confusion.*

Given that we wish to make the thinking process explicit, the RD/CM pair are the mechanism for its achievement. They represent the fundamental building block of SSM and so provide the basis for defensible analysis. The supporting tools which help to ensure the proper structure and formulation of these concepts (i.e. CATWOE and the FSM), are also necessary components of the intellectual process. They need to be declared in order to demonstrate the legitimacy of the constructs so derived. However, once sufficient practice has been accumulated, they tend to become internalised and thought about as the RD/CM are being developed. Within this book, it is assumed that by the time that an analyst is producing a CPTM, sufficient expertise will have been acquired to omit reference to CATWOE and the FSM. They are still relevant and should be available if needed. *This is all that should be internalised.* The RD/CM pair (or sets of pairs) should never be internalised but should always be available, even to the analyst who is developing them, so that it is known that legitimate concepts are being used. Once the basic concepts themselves are allowed to be internalised we are back to making assertions or merely offering opinion.

Frequently, I have been asked the question 'what computer tools are available to support SSM?' There are, in fact, very few. Within the information-oriented version of SSM (Wilson 1990), computer-based representation of the 'Maltese cross' is sometimes used, but I personally find that it adds little of value to the process. A software program that is used extensively is called MooD (Salamander 2000). The example, given in Appendix Three, uses MooD. All the MOD applications and Met. Office work, using SSM, record the conceptual models in this language. I don't find it a helpful application at the conceptual model development stage, since it is essential, I find, to have the entire developing model on display; particularly if it is a CPTM that is being produced. A sheet of A0 paper is the most practical aid during model development. However, once completed, MooD provides a useful medium for storing and transmitting a large model.

As a simple example to illustrate this discussion, let us take a project concerned with a strategic review of the consulting company, Hi-Q Systems. This study was to be followed by an analysis of information requirements and both aspects required the development of a CPTM to cover the scope of the whole company. As an illustration consider the element of the Enterprise Model associated with the T. Figures 10.1 and 10.2 illustrate the two formats of the models representing my version and the MooD version respectively. The subsystem decomposition in MooD can be demonstrated through the use of colour and that was the case here (hence the greyness in some of the activities).

Explicit boundaries can also be represented in MooD and as a second example consider one from the Met. Office project. Within the HR management analysis, a detailed model was developed relevant to a part of the organisation known as 'The Job Advice Centre'. This represented an expansion of one of the activities within the total 'HR management' model. Sufficient detail could be produced by using a single RD. Figure 10.3 presents the RD/CM pair (without decomposition into subsystems). The equivalent model (with decomposition), described in the language of MooD, is given in Figure 10.4.

A number of 'drawing' packages exist which could be used to record already-developed models, but the significant advantage that MOOD offers is that it can reproduce hierarchical model decompositions while retaining the logical dependencies.

Although a computer-based tool exists, which seems to be well received and used, it is worth remembering that *the model is never the deliverable.* It is an intellectual construct to be used in some organisation-based analysis and it is what the model leads to (either as the source of a service system or as a standard to compare against reality) that is the useful outcome. Given this role, the model need not be communicated, except to others within the problem-solving team.

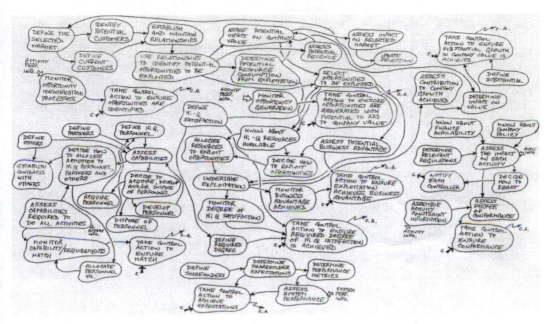

Figure 10.1 *The 'Hi-Q' model for T (the original figure may be viewed on ftp://ftp.wiley.co.uk/pub/books/wilson/)*

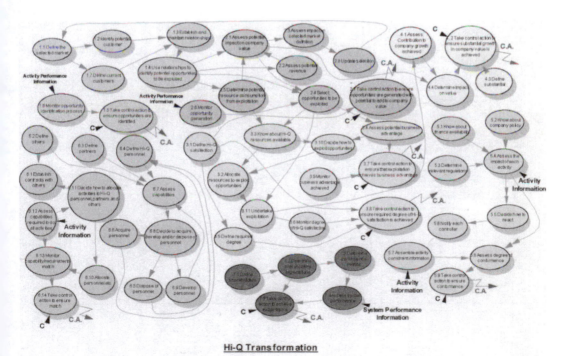

Figure 10.2 *The MooD version of Figure 10.1 (the original figure may be viewed on ftp://ftp.wiley.co.uk/pub/books/wilson/)*

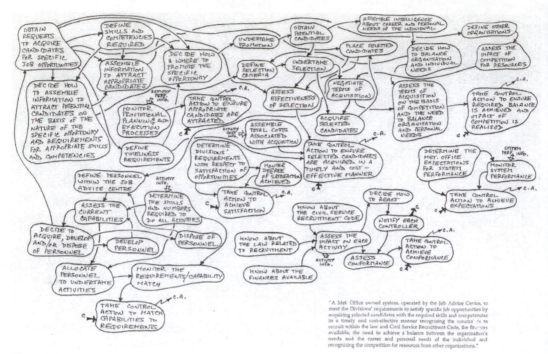

Figure 10.3   *CM corresponding to the Job Advice Centre (the original figure may be viewed on ftp://ftp.wiley.co.uk/pub/books/wilson/)*

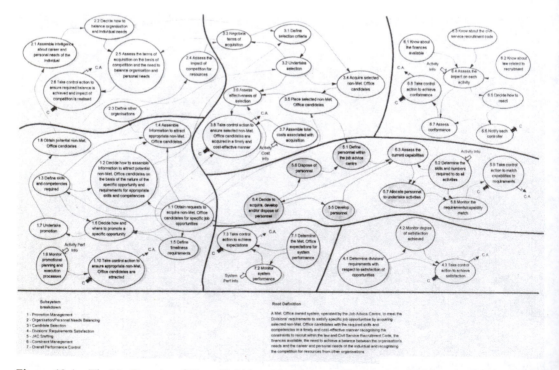

Figure 10.4   *The MooD version of Figure 10.3 (the original figure may be viewed on ftp://ftp.wiley.co.uk/pub/books/wilson/)*

The previous chapters have attempted to reinforce the logic stream of analysis within the total range of intellectual processes that make up SSM. They have also illustrated the developments that have taken place over the last few years related to the class of analyses needing a definition and description of an intellectual construct, which maps onto an organisation boundary. This is the CPTM.

It is worth emphasising that the 'consensus' referred to in the title of this concept is the consensus of the problem-solving team and *not* of everyone within the particular organisation. Thus it represents an explicit answer to the question, 'what are *we* taking the organisation unit to be doing?' This concept then becomes 'the basis' on which the rational analysis of the set of organisation-oriented problems, illustrated by Figure 1, can be progressed.

It is unfortunate that some of the academic publications that appear argue for the removal of rationality in relation to the analysis of real-world problem situations. Action research, the original source of SSM, has always tried to be useful and learn from application and I have not yet seen any evidence that argues for its removal on the grounds of improving utility. Action research is not scientific research, which can argue for repeatability in its findings; that is not achievable in human-dominated situations. Neither can it lead to public knowledge about the interpretation of events. What we can expect from action research is a set of transferable ideas that have application across a wide variety of situations. Some of these ideas rely on the application of logic; not groundless logic, but that which is informed by the general act of living on this planet. Some would-be practitioners may find this application difficult and argue for the abandonment of it. I would wish to argue for the retention of as much logic and rationality within the intellectual processes as is possible. This book was written to offer help in this endeavour.

Appendix One

The Albion Group

(1) The information contained in the following pages describes a situation in a company in which you, as a consultant, have been asked by the Managing Director of the group to carry out an investigation.

(2) The main purpose of this exercise is to give practice in analysing a problem situation.

(3) Information is available in the form of:
   (a) set of internal letters about a particular problem in the company
   (b) some additional notes prepared recently for other consultants
   (c) other information relating to certain areas of activity in the group.

(4) The description of the process technology of the group is intended to provide a plausible sequence of events leading from raw material to finished product that is adequate for the purpose of the exercise.

(5) It does not purport to be a detailed description of actual processes in any industry. Similarly, the market forecasts and sales figures do not apply to any specific product.

(6) Assume the year to be 1984.

(L1)

Albion Group

Albion House, St James's Square, Kingston-upon-Hull

Clark Kent
SSM Consultants
135 Wandsworth Road
London SW8 2LY

Dear Mr. Kent,

<u>System Study</u>

I am enclosing a letter in which our Stockist Manager is applying for £642,000 for warehouse expansion. Clearly, there is some case for increasing our finished stocks, but since they have managed reasonably well for the last few years with the present stock policy, I wonder whether the application is unnecessarily large. Bearing in mind the low profitability of the Division, I am unwilling to inject capital into our Stockist without more understanding of the situation.

I am enclosing copies of letters which I think you should see. Let me know if you require any further information.

I would like to have advice on what action to take over this request for expansion and stock increase. Please investigate this and let me know what course of action you recommend and the approach you have used in arriving at it.

Yours sincerely,

H.C. Symonds

Managing Director, the Albion Group

Albion Group Case Study

(L2)

Surface Stockists

Treated Hardboard Surface Specialists, Ealing, London W5

The Director of Finance,
Albion House,
St. James's Square
Kingston-upon-Hull.

Dear Mr. Turner,

You will remember that we discussed the possibilities of extension of our present premises when I last visited you. I would now like to make a formal application for £642,000 for extensions to our warehouse facilities.

There are two reasons for this extension. Firstly, we need to increase our overall stock level by 30% to assure our customers of a better delivery. Secondly, we anticipate an increased demand for finished board, especially in the heavy gauges.

I enclose the T11 expenditure application form.

Yours sincerely,

J.R.B. Small

T11	

Expenditure Sought
 	
    £642,000
 	
Reason for expenditure
 	
    To extend warehouse 3
    to increase volume
    storage by 30%
	Applicant
	
	    J.R.B. Small, Manager
	    Surface Stockists
	Details
	
	    Purchase 5 acres £500,000
	    Building adjacent to
	    warehouse no. 3 £42,000
	    Handling equipment £100,000
	                         -------- 	
	                         £642,000
	                         -------- 	

Albion Group Case Study

(L3)

Tower Construction Co
97 Conduit Street
London EC 5

J. R. B. Small,
Stockist Manager
Surface Stockists (Albion Group Ltd.)
Ealing
London, W5

Dear Sir,

We have surveyed the land adjacent to your No. 3 Warehouse and have studied your requirements.

We estimate that the costs will be:

Building extension 125 ft. x 75 ft. x 35 ft.	£42,000
Handling equipment & storage racks	£100,000
	£142,000

We await your further instructions.

Yours faithfully

pp. R. T. Thomas
Estimates Manager

Albion Group Case Study

Tower Construction Co

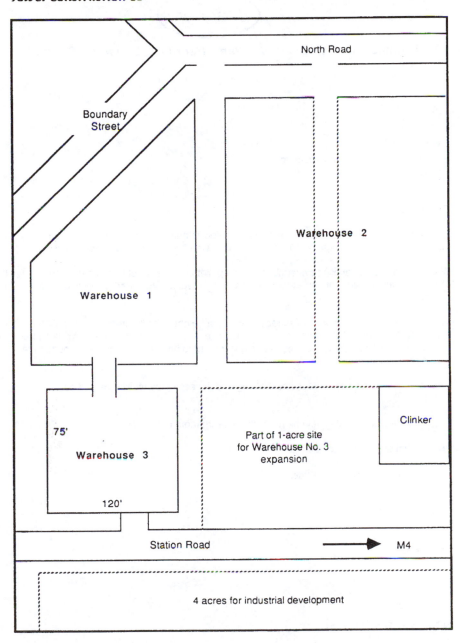

Warehouse Extension Plan

Albion Group Case Study

(L4)

Thomas Mander Limited, Plant Handling Division, Sheffield, 4

J.R.B. Small,
Surface Stockists (Albion Group Ltd.),
Ealing.

Dear Mr. Small,

Our engineer has inspected your premises and reports that we should be able to increase your effective warehouse volume by 40% without increasing floor area used, or roof height.

We have devised a handling system based on a pallet unit (the pallet size can be modified by you). This has been installed with great success in G.K.L., Mudlow Steel, Farles Bearings and many other companies.

We would increase your present storage matrix to a height of 28 ft. (from the original 20 ft.). This would involve substantial strengthening of certain key frames and floor covers. A fork lift truck based on a Warwick Climax design is used in our system and to handle the throughput you require, six trucks would be necessary.

The total cost of increasing your stockholding and accessing capabilities would be:

Increasing racking volume (including strengthening of structure)	£175,000
Palletisation of containers	£67,000
Six "Highlift" Mander trucks	£84,000

	£326,000

Yours sincerely,

N.T. Cross (Thos. Mander)

Albion Group Case Study

(L5)

<u>Albion Group Ltd</u>

<u>MEMO</u>

From: Chief Accountant   To: Finance Director

I have looked into the question of the alternative investments –
new buildings, or improvements to existing ones - at Surface
Stockists.

I am afraid I will not be able to let you know my
recommendations before mid-January.

It seems as if an investments analysis of some sort should be
made - but the pressure of work near the end of our Financial
Year makes it impossible for me to give you an immediate reply.

The purchase of land in that part of London is always a good
investment, and the purchase price of £500,000 for 5 acres is
not excessive for the area. It is unfortunate that Real Estate
Holdings are unwilling to sell the 1-acre site on the north side
of Station Road by itself. However, I believe that as we have
the ability to purchase at such a good price we should accept,
and develop the excess 4 acres through our own financial
expertise. The rate of return on investment should easily exceed
that on our current operations.

I enclose some information about land prices and rents in this
area. Also, depreciation rates for our plant and buildings. I
feel that from these we should be able to evaluate the worth of
the alternative investments to us in the future.

M.R. Thompson

Albion Group Case Study

(L6)

<u>Albion Group Ltd</u>

<u>MEMO</u>

From: Chief Accountant   To: Finance Director

I enclose a letter from the Ealing Borough Surveyor, showing
what an attractive proposition the 5-acre site is. The
opportunity of receiving a high return is extremely attractive.

Here is some other information I promised you:

    Building Depreciation

        Offices (NBV £1,600,000)   10% straight line
        Factory (NBV £1,250,000)   14% straight line

    Plant Depreciation (NBV £3,870,000) 20% straight line

Our present activities are producing profits of 6% after tax on
turnover, and this percentage has decreased from 9%, 7.5%, 7%
over the past three years.

M.R. Thompson

(L7)

London Borough of Ealing

Borough Surveyor's Department
Hermitage Road
London, W5

Our Ref: EB/71/G03

The Chief Accountant,
The Albion Group Limited,
Albion House,
Hull

Dear Sir,

With reference to your request for a survey of the 5-acre plot on both sides of Station Road, we have completed the inspection and find:

(i)   that the land is well supplied with drainage, sewerage and other utility systems

(ii)   that the density of packing clinker on the N.W. corner is sufficient for supporting heavy structures

(iii)   that no road development scheme is planned to cross the land

Officially, you must realise that we cannot comment on the value of the land, but similar plots have sold at up to £120,000 per acre in Ealing, and Station Road, with its easy access, is an attractive site. Land prices have increased by 17%, 20% and 22% over the past three years and rents for buildings in the centre of Ealing have increased by 18% per year over the past five years.

We will send a detailed survey to you soon, and invoice you then.

Yours faithfully,

T. Cockraine
(Chief Surveyor)

Albion Group Case Study

(NA 3)

From Sales Manager, Albion Mills

SALES PRICES

Gauge	9	8	6
Thickness	1"	.75"	.50"
Wood cost (£ per 10^3 lb. board)	100	100	100
Resin cost (£ per 10^3 lb. board)	21.2	19.6	18.0
Overheads per 103 lb. of board (recoverable on same basis as direct material cost is incurred)	11.2	11.2	11.2

Cost to us	132.4	130.8	129.2
Sells at	139.6	140.8	145.6
Percentage profit	5.5	7.7	12.7
No. of boards produced (x 000)	55	60	85

Clearly, our bread and butter line is the light gauge board, with a profit margin of nearly 13%. The margin on the heavier gauge is much less, and we are losing out at this end of the market. We suspect that several competitors are selling heavy board at a loss in order to maintain their sales of lighter board. Our own light board is selling very competitively, on both price and quality.

Albion Group Case Study

(NB 10)

Albion Works Production Process

1   Albion Works have for the past twenty years produced a high quality Mill
     Board with excellent waterproofing and fire resistant qualities. It uses
     long fibre softwood imported from Scandinavia and shipped into Hull,
     together with special resins.

Production Details

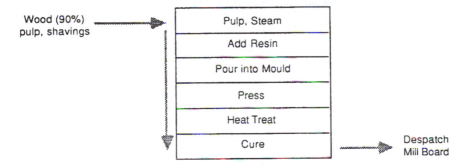

2   Our pulping and steam injection equipment is capable of handling 10^8 lb.
     per year on 2 x 8-hour shift working, 5-day week.

3   Resin added varies with thickness of sheet to be produced.

4   The moulds are standard area, 8' x 20', and of three thicknesses. Each
     mould is slid on to a frame which holds 10.

5   There are five ovens and three frames per oven. One frame for loading, one
     for firing (55 mins. in the oven) and one for cooling and unloading and
     curing. Ovens are worked on 2 x 8-hour shifts. Recently we have been
     considering increasing our oven capacity and buying a new oven specially
     for the lighter gauges.

6   Curing is the final drying and resin bonding period of three days.

7   Our board is near enough the same density as the wood we start from - 30
     lb./cu.ft.

Albion Group Case Study

(NB 10a)

Albion Works Conversion Factors

	9	8	6
Gauge	9	8	6
Thickness	1″	0.75″	0.50″
Cu. ft. per board	13.33	10.00	6.67
Wt. (lb.) per board	400	300	300
Area (sq. ft.)	160	160	160

Albion Group Case Study

(NB 31)

BETTERFINISH FABRICATIONS

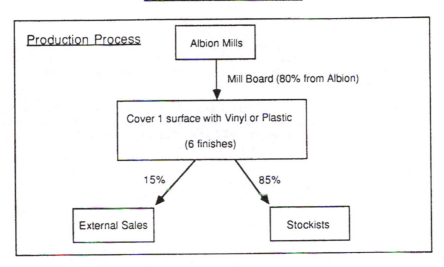

1   Nearly all our lighter gauge board comes from Albion. Most of our
    bought-out board is the heavy gauge board:

Thickness	1"	.75"	.50"		
Gauge	9	8	6		
From Albion	15	60	85	)	x 000
From outside	35	–	5	)	Boards

2   We use five covering machines, multipurpose "Challands Applicators".
    with a machine throughput rate of 350 ft. per hour. We work two 8-hour
    shifts per day, 5 days a week, 50 weeks per annum.

3   There are six different finishes, one of which is rolled continuously
    on one machine. Other machines are scheduled with a sequence of
    different finishes.

4   The boards are coated with Bestick 'Permabond' and then fed through the
    8' wide rolls together with the coating sheet (vinyl or plastic)

5   Machine throughput rate is governed by the machine design (limited by
    dryers at the back of the machine). Machine changeover times are 35
    minutes for gauge change and 15 minutes for a finish change. Roll
    alignment is critical; over pressure causes the surface to spring and
    under pressure creates no adhesion at all. We feel quite happy that the
    machines are the best on the market for quality and throughput.

Works Manager. B.

Appendix One

Albion Group Case Study

(NB 32)

BETTERFINISH SALES

85% of our production goes straight to our stockists. We have a couple of large contracts for direct supply of heavy gauge, negotiated recently, but our profitability on these is not large. In general, we are keen to stay off the heavy gauge.

Although we know we could sell more heavy gauge, we are having difficulty in producing sufficient to meet our existing orders. As the contribution* on each heavy board is relatively low (£13.24 on 9g., £13.76 on 8g., £14.28 on 6g.), there is no incentive, given our present output problems, to manufacture more heavy gauge. We buy much of the heavy gauge board from Laver Bros., since they charge £1.12 less per board than Albion, but supplies are limited and we have a long lead time on delivery. We are trying to negotiate with Albion for a reduction in price since their delivery is better. They may reduce their prices marginally, but fear that their profit margin might suffer.

Our stockist is tending to place a lot of small orders, and we are trying to come to some arrangement over increasing order size. We are told that until the stockist's holding capacity is increased, orders will remain small.

Sales Manager. B.

* Contribution is the difference between the selling price and the material costs (board + surface)

Albion Group Case Study

(NB 35)

From Production Scheduler, Betterfinish

I work from the list of order which I receive from Surface, and
also from the few direct orders from outside the group.

I know there have been complaints about our delivery performance
on heavy gauge. It's hardly my fault - I'm under pressure from
the Factory Manager to limit the amount of 9g. we process. I try
to rush through all the lighter gauges as quickly as possible to
help Surface.

Albion Group Case Study

(NB 43)

From Works Manager, Betterfinish

The production manager at Albion House has emphasised the need for autonomy
so much that I feel under obligation to no-one to manufacture surfaced
board if it is not profitable to us to do so. I'm afraid that recently
(because it would reduce our machine utilisation, is always a good excuse),
we have been delaying production of heavy gauge. My production scheduler
has my full authority to do this, especially on these small orders of heavy
gauge, so that we can recover our overheads and reach the profit targets I
am setting.

The case is quite clear. We obtain a contribution per board of £13.24 on
9g. £13.76 on 8g. and £14.28 on 6g. If we have to buy 9g. from Albion (and
we have to take 15,000 of these to from them in order to meet demand), we
have an even lower contribution of £12.11 per board. We must negotiate with
Albion for better terms, and if we cannot manage this, we will try to
negotiate for bulk rates with Laver Brothers. For a given gauge, all six
finishes bring in the same contributions.

Appendix One

Albion Group Case Study

(NB 44)

BETTERFINISH   Week 17

Specimen Production Schedule (Partially Complete)
for Machines 1 and 5

Machine 1			Machine 2			Machine 3			Machine 4			Machine 5		
Gauge	Finish	Ft	Gauge	Finish	Ft	Gauge	Finish	Ft	Gauge	Finish	Ft	Gauge	Finish	Ft
9	5	600										9	2	280
8	6	720										9	2	320
6	4	240										6	2	160
9	1	80										9	2	1120
6	1	920										6	2	960
6	3	160										8	2	340
6	6	840										8	2	280
8	3	140										6	2	40
6	1	540										6	2	180
8	1	140										6	2	80
6	3	60										8	2	40
												6	2	960
												9	2	640

(NG 1)

Albion Group

Albion House, St James's Square, Kingston-upon-Hull

MBO Consultants
Market Towers
London SW8 5QU

Dear Sirs,

<u>Management by Objectives Study</u>

I have recently been appointed managing director of the Albion Group by J. F. Tyzacks, Merchant Bankers, who have recently acquired a majority shareholding.

My terms of reference have not been detailed yet; hence a start by this Management by Objectives exercise.

Clearly I have to increase the profitability of the group as a whole. There is a seemingly healthy spirit of competition inside the group, which I feel must be essential for good overall profitability.

Albion Mills is the oldest part of the group and I feel that I should look more closely into their management methods, as there is, without doubt, a lot of management of the 'old school'. Betterfinish and Surfaces I think present less of a problem, and I am quite happy, initially, to let them manage themselves until I have a better feel for the group situation.

We have a lot of experience in the preparation of prefabricated building sections and surface boards. It is this experience which Tyzacks wish to use to best effect in the improving market situation which is foreseen during the next few years. My success in directing the group must be measured in terms of overall group profits, and our ability to grow to meet the market demands.

Yours faithfully,

H.C. Symonds

Managing Director, the Albion Group

Albion Group Case Study

(NG 10)

Albion Group

Albion House, St James's Square, Kingston-upon-Hull

Clark Kent
SSM Consultants
135 Wandsworth Road
London SW8 2LY

Dear Mr. Kent,

Information about the Albion Group

I am afraid that it will be impossible for you to meet the senior members
of the Group due to their previous commitments and to the tight time scale
on this project.

Therefore, in order to give you some background into our activities, I am
enclosing notes made about the Group*, which were prepared recently as a
preliminary exercise for a Management by Objectives study.

I have not had time to look at these myself, and would be interested to
hear if you find them useful as a basis for assessing the Group, with
particular reference to improving our overall profitability.

It will be most helpful to me to receive fairly specific suggestions,
rather than general comments like the desirability of improving
communications within the Group.

Yours sincerely,

H.C. Symonds

Managing Director, the Albion Group

*	NG10	NG1			
	NS11	NS34	NS25		
	NB31	NB32	NB43	NB44	NB35
	NA10				

THE ALBION GROUP LTD. (HULL)

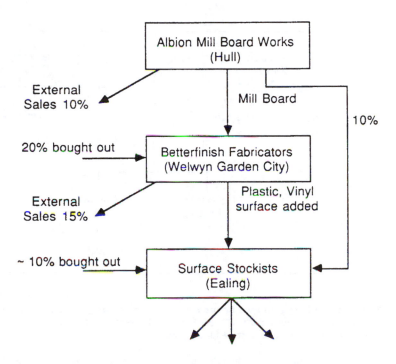

Albion Group Case Study

(NG 33)

Albion Group Organisation Chart

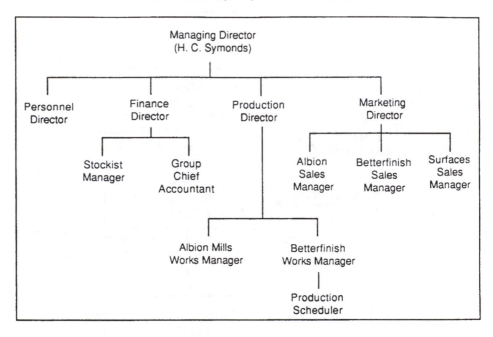

1   There has always been encouragement for strong autonomy of Albion Mills,
    Betterfinish and Surface Stockists. Internal competition is good for
    use, keeps us efficient and on our toes.

2   The works managers at Albion and Betterfinish, and the Stockist Manager
    at Surface Stockist, are responsible for the profitability of their
    companies

3   The Board meets monthly to discuss technical, personnel and expenditure
    plans. Prior to this there is a Management Meeting, at which the senior
    management report to their functional Directors.

4   There is a quarterly report on revenue and expenditure, that is, on
    Sales and Firm Orders, and on material and production costs.

(NG 34)

MARKET RESEARCH INC.

SURVEY OF THE ENVIRONMENT SURROUNDING THE ALBION GROUP
carried out for J. F. Tyzacks, Merchant Bankers

These are the key points taken from our main report, which will be published in January 1985.

1   Our Market Survey, already in the hands of the Albion Group, shows a healthy increase in demand for heavy gauge board.

2   The market is shared by seven companies; the Albion Group is in the top three of these for turnover and assets.

3   Each company has a stable nucleus of customers (who take approximately 70% of output). The users of board are fairly conservative, and will only change their suppliers if there is a good reason to do so (e.g. consistently poor delivery performance).

4   It is hard to assess price competitiveness as contracts are on a highly personalised basis. However, each company appears to maintain the same price to each of its customers.

5   The customers, who are in the prefabricated kitchen and bathroom furniture and wall section trades, appear to request a range of delivery times. The majority of orders require delivery in under three weeks, and it is uncompetitive not to meet this delivery service requirement.

6   Surfaces has contact with some of the largest users - 'English Lily', 'Elizabethan' and 'Ramply'. Prefabricated Bathroom Units are also fairly large users. In the main, customers are fairly small.

7   The technology in the board producing industry is fairly static, and no developments are anticipated in future (apart from instrumentation improvements in the control of the pulping process). However, it is known that in the application of surfaces to boards, 'Starboard', a subsidiary of Laver Bros., is developing a new process. In this process the board is given a surface by spreading liquid plastic over the board in a controlled manner.

Albion Group Case Study

(NS 11)

SURFACE STOCKISTS

From Stockist Manager

We hold finished board from Betterfinish, and some untreated board from
the Albion Mill. We have facilities for trimming and specialist packing,
but our main task is one of supplying our customers with a reliable
delivery.

30% of our throughput goes to three major customers - 'English Lily',
'Elizabethan' and 'Ramply' - for kitchen furniture construction.
Prefabricated Bathroom Units are taking 15% and a further 15% is exported.

Why we want to expand

We are keen to explore possibilities of expansion, even if this means
stocking non-Albion Group board. An independent market survey, arranged by
us, showed a large increase in demand for the heavier gauge products, and
enquiries to us from customers support this finding. However, at present,
we are unwilling to quote a delivery date on heavy gauge products for new
customers, because delivery from Betterfinish is particularly poor. From
our point of view, it is profitable to sell, but we must be known as a
reliable deliverer. We would be uncompetitive if we offered delivery in
excess of three weeks, yet with heavy gauge it has often taken over three
weeks on average to fulfil an order, and so rather than risking being
unable to supply from stock, we are placing specific orders on
Betterfinish and requesting immediate delivery to help ensure that
specific customer needs are met. We are especially keen to do this for our
major customers.

How we aim to expand

An A.I.C. consultant looked into this last March and found that the mean
lead time* for our orders from Betterfinish is 16 working days. Thus, we
are aiming to increase our stock to the 20 working days level, which will
entail increasing our stockholding volume by 30%. When we have this larger
safety stock, we will be able to offer for delivery from stock and can
then start to place larger, more economic orders with Betterfinish. The
Warehouse Foreman, who is in charge of a lot of the re-ordering, storage
and despatch, will, I hope, take charge of the re-organisation of stock
when the expansion is complete, as I regard him as a key figure in our
ability to maintain reliable delivery.

* i.e. the time from placing an order with Betterfinish to receiving the
board from them.

Albion Group Case Study

(NS 25)

<u>SURFACE STOCKISTS - Sales of Board</u>

<u>Information available for sales over the period 1978 - 1983</u>

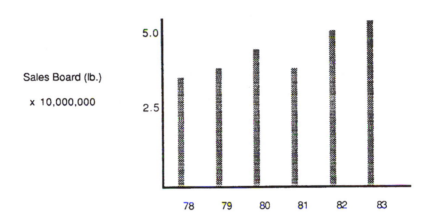

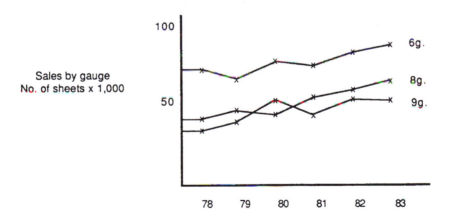

In 1983 we sold 95,000 6g., 65,000 8g., and 50,000 9g.

Albion Group Case Study

(NS 32)

Independent Market Forecast for Finished Board

(Market Research Inc.)

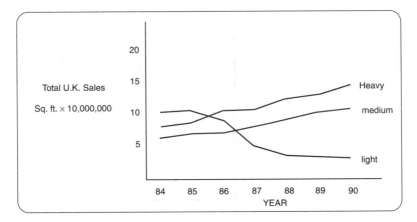

1   The main increase in heavy gauge is due to the increase in fitted kitchens and bathrooms, and prefabricated wall sections. Light gauge is decreasing because of the increasing use of plastic surfaces.

2   80% of the market is in the London Area, and Surface Stockists have good contacts with a large number of outlets in this area. From a distribution point of view they are ideally situated.

Albion Group Case Study

(NS 33)

SURFACE STOCKIST

Contribution from Finished Board

The contributions from finished board are:

9 gauge	8 gauge	6 gauge
£0.992	£0.90	£1.168 per cu. ft.

Contribution here is the difference between selling price and buying price.

Albion Group Case Study

(NS 34)

SURFACE STOCKISTS

From Warehouse Foreman

Although we are not completely full at present, I understand what the manager means when he says we must expand our stocks, and agree that the only way to ensure a reliable delivery is to have a good safety level. Besides, I'm keen to take on more modern machinery, more warehousing and more responsibility. As far as my job is concerned, it's my duty to trigger off a re-order for a fresh delivery from Betterfinish. We've got a system here whereby I order three weeks' worth board and re-order another three weeks' worth when it arrives, as the delivery from Betterfinish takes about three weeks. I think it is a fairly good system because it is easy to operate. Even my leading chargehand can operate it, and he often has to if I'm away.

Appendix Two

Exercises

The following examples represent illustrations of organisational problem-situations. Use whatever concepts and approaches you feel are appropriate to tackle the stated concerns. However, each situation is 'soft' and therefore lends itself to the ideas discussed within this book.

(1) A small publishing company wishes to launch a new technical journal as a diversification from its present concentration on book and manual publication. The editor sees the introduction of the journal as an opportunity for making use of new technology for the recording, storage, manipulation and accessing of all information related to circulation, trade advertising, production and finance. During the launch, decisions will have to be made about frequency of issues, size of production runs, number of articles and pages, etc. But since these decisions, will have to be reviewed continually on the basis of performance information once the journal is up and running, he sees no difference between the information required for the launch and that required on a continuous basis. Thus he wishes the technology to be available and in place as soon as possible. However, he wants to make best use of the opportunities provided by the technology, and hence would like you to undertake a fundamental and unconstrained analysis, to identify what information he needs to have available to manage the publishing of the journal in a way that makes it both effective and efficient.

(2) Gotham County Police Department are about to conduct a strategic review of their total operations with a view to improving both their effectiveness as a crime control service to the community and their use of resources in providing that service. As part of this review they are carrying out an audit of their current IT systems.

We are members of a consultancy company who have been asked to tender (bid) for either or both of the pieces of work mentioned above. It is our belief that the two areas cannot be separated since the information support needed (via the IT systems) is itself dependent upon the findings of the strategic review. We will therefore tender for the whole study.

I would like you to contribute to the tender by writing the section which describes our approach. Please illustrate the various stages with examples of models, etc. relevant to their business. We have already discussed various aspects of SSM with them so feel free to use systems language.

It is important that we recognise the various facets of police activity such as traffic control, security of property, community education, etc., as well as crime prevention and control. Clearly a police department is a multi-role organisation and both a strategic review and an information requirements analysis must recognise this. The organisation must also contain non–police-specific activities, e.g. human resource management, strategic planning, maintaining an awareness of the developments in relevant technology, etc. Deciding how to define this role must be an integral part of our approach.

The police department has already invested in significant IT support and has an ageing mainframe which contains all the processing and storage associated with criminal records, crime statistics, finance and personnel details. Although at the tender stage we cannot be expected to know the current status of the IT support, our approach must show how we would take it into account.

(3) Comminc (UK) Ltd are the UK subsidiary of an American Cable Telecommunications company. They are a relatively young organisation; having been operating for only seven years. They compete with companies like BT for the supply of a range of cable products, (such as TV and telephones) and other services to both business and residential customers.

They have a corporate headquarters near London but all the sales activity is carried out through eight geographically distributed franchises.

Being a new organisation, they have been given growth sales targets by their American parent, which they are not achieving. Part of the problem, they believe, is the lack of adequate customer/sales information on which marketing initiatives (campaigns) can be based and evaluated. These campaigns can be nation-wide and driven by the corporate marketing department at headquarters, or they can be based upon local initiatives, driven by a particular franchise. Either way, corporate marketing need to be able to assess the response to these campaigns as part of their desire to assemble customer intelligence which they can then use alongside competitor intelligence to help them decide how to attack the market and so improve their overall business performance.

Corporate marketing have decided that they need a 'data warehouse' and have asked the IT Department to provide it. There is no common understanding of what a data warehouse is or how it should be used though a budget of some £1.5 million has been authorised.

The IT project manager, (our client), knows about SSM and believes that it is worth investing in some SSM-based consultancy *in order to define what the role of marketing should be taken to be and hence, what information they need to provide the necessary support.*

We have been asked to provide a short tender (bid) document, which illustrates how we would go about this part of the project. We must give examples of the various stages that we propose in order to demonstrate the power of using SSM and its relevance to their situation. Please provide me with a draft document covering the above requirement so that I can convert it into a tender document format, add CVs, etc.

(4) A recently established group of consultants who operate as general business and management consultants are considering employing you as part of their BPR and IT section. They already have technical IT skills within the section but they have found difficulty in linking these skills to the more generally oriented business skills. They see you and your skills providing the required link and consider using you as a liaison individual within projects utilising both business and IT skills.

To help them reach a decision they require you to illustrate your approach by taking a management consultancy group as the client organisation and show, with relevant examples, how you would define its information requirements and relate these to the IT systems that it already operates.

Note: Make whatever assumptions you feel are necessary

(5) The Utopia Grand Hotel adjacent to the university campus is under pressure from the owner, Great Eastern, to improve the utilisation of its facilities and so enhance profit generation. The hotel has a multi-role and provides the usual facilities for its guests in the form of a range of room standards, bar and restaurant facilities, gymnasium and a swimming pool. The latter are also available for non-residents. It operates the usual room services and employs sufficient staff to ensure a four-star standard of provision. The hotel also operates a conference and teaching

facility available both to university and external organisations. This obviously interacts with the normal hotel function since the conference and teaching activity frequently requires hotel accommodation provision.

As part of this performance review the hotel manager is proposing to undertake an audit of current IT support. At present they operate a PC-based reservation system covering the hotel accommodation which is integrated with the Great Eastern nation-wide reservation IT system. Conference bookings are handled via a separate IT system (also PC-based). There is further IT support for the total accounting processes but activity to do with maintaining room amenities (including bedding, laundry, minibar, washing, commodities and tea making) are all manual.

Clearly an audit of IT support would have to start with an identification of information requirements related to the total hotel operation and management.

You are asked to contribute to the audit:

(a) by suggesting a suitable approach to the audit and
(b) by illustrating the various stages in this approach through the derivation of models etc, related to the hotel business.

(6) A small Kendal-based insurance company operates through a central headquarters and field sales representatives (reps). It provides a range of insurance products from straightforward whole-life policies, which pay a lump sum on the death of the policyholder, to endowment schemes, which pay a lump sum to the policyholder on a maturity date.

The headquarters processes the various policies, keeps records of sums due and paid out, together with all the records of the policyholders. The administrative staff, who deal with these records, are paid a fixed salary but the sales representatives are paid a basic salary plus a performance-related component (bonus).

The salaries office, which administers the pay-related activities, including the company policy on pay, has recently raised the issue of how the performance-related component is derived.

The sales reps are each allocated a geographical area within Cumbria, part of north Lancashire and north Yorkshire. They have both a marketing and a sales role so they each have the freedom to launch promotional schemes in their area, in order to attract potential customers, as well as undertaking visits to individuals at home or in the workplace.

The company pay the cost of these schemes plus all expenses. The sales reps are required to maintain records related to actual and potential customers, promotional schemes and their outcomes and all financial data. This is meant to provide opportunities for learning about ways of improving both the marketing and selling activity so that the lessons can be shared with other sales reps.

Some reps are good at maintaining records but others are not, as they currently receive no recognition for it.

Previously the sales reps received a bonus based upon the value of the policies that they attracted but recently it has been argued, by the salaries office, that some of the costs incurred in schemes for attracting new policyholders has been excessive and the schemes have not been all that successful. Performance, they argue, should be assessed on the basis of the 'whole job' not just the policy value.

This has given rise to a debate about what the 'whole job' means.

How would you use systems ideas:

(a) to explore this situation?
(b) to arrive at a definition of the 'whole job'?
(c) to determine what records should be maintained?
(d) to derive a rational basis for the performance-related pay component?

Appendix Three

The Development of the United Kingdom's Single Army Activity Model and Associated Information Needs and Its Relationship to Command and Control

Lt Col Geoffrey H Hunt
Maj Kevin E Galvin
Directorate General Development and Doctrine (DGD&D)
Ministry of Defence
Room 1314/1316, Main Building, Whitehall, London, SW1A 2HB
United Kingdom
Telephone Number 0171 2180993
E-mail kgalvin.bas@gtnet.gov.uk

Mr Stephen Strefford
The Smith Group
Surrey Research Park
Guildford, Surrey, GU2 5YP
United Kingdom
Telephone Number 01483 442218
E-mail srstrefford@smithgroup.co.uk

Mr Charles M Lane
Hi-Q Systems
The Barn
Micheldever Station, Winchester, Hants, SO21 3AR
United Kingdom
Telephone Number 01962 794200
E-mail clane@hi-q.co.uk

Abstract

In January 1996 work began on the development of the United Kingdom's Army Operational Architecture (AOA). Three models of the Army; High Intensity Conflict (HIC), Peace Support Operations (PSO) and a Business View covering the delivery of Military Capability were developed. Whilst this work was being undertaken, separate but related modelling and analysis was being carried out to produce a formal Statement of User Needs (SUN) to support the development of a future Formation Battle Management

System (FBMS). This work included the examination and modelling of the processes associated with Command and Control (C^2) on the battlefield including Intelligence Preparation of the Battlefield (IPB) and Intelligence, Surveillance, Target Acquisition and Reconnaisance (ISTAR) and the linkages to Combat Service Support (CSS) and Targeting. In January 1999 work began to develop a model, which covered activities that had not been in the previous models and also to consolidate the separate models into a Single Army Activity Model (SAAM), set within the context of Defence/Joint activity. This paper sets out how the model was built, its associated information taxonomy, how information was captured for each activity, the lessons learnt and how the work is planned to be exploited to analyse real world issues in order to develop future C^2 systems and support Information Management.

1. Introduction

In May 1998 the UK's AOA Version 1.0 was released on CD-ROM. Its aim was threefold; to explain what was meant by an Operational Architecture from a UK perspective, to provide access to the models which had been built using the Soft Systems Methodology (SSM) and captured using the MooD case-tool and to illustrate how an Operational Architecture could be used for a variety of analysis. It was planned that Version 1.0 would be followed by subsequent models, which covered those areas that had not been developed and that all the models would be merged to form the SAAM (in SSM this is referred to as a Consensus Primary Task Model (CPTM)). It was proposed that the SAAM, when complete, would consist of:

- A pictorial depiction of those activities which the Army should undertake to be the organisation, which is defined by capstone documents. These documents include; the Army Plan, Defence Missions and Military Tasks (as defined by the Strategic Defence Review (SDR) and subsequently the Strategic Plan), and high level Defence and Army doctrinal publications. This pictorial depiction includes activities to provide the land components of capability, generate the land component of a specific force and the employment of the land component of this specific force. The SAAM is termed 'conceptual' because it is derived from a logical decomposition of the definitions of the Army and is independent of current organisations and equipment. It defines **what** an Army must do to be the organisation defined in the capstone documents, not **what it does now** nor **how** it does it. Implicit in the pictorial depiction is the logical dependencies between activities.
- An information architecture, which defines, for each activity within the model, three categories of information: that required for the activity to take place; that produced as an output of the activity; that required as a measure of performance of the activity. From this the sources and sinks of information can be identified.
- The mapping of one or more Command and Staff Functional Areas (CSFA)[1] to each activity.

1.1 *Initial Plan*

The initial plan had seen this work beginning in June 1998 but resources were required to support the SUN modelling effort. This modelling was looking in more detail at C^2, IPB, ISTAR, Targeting and CSS, and was considered more important at that stage because it was intended to inform potential contractors for the British Army's FBMS about the relationship between these key areas. This is illustrated in Figure A3.1.

In addition, the staff within the AOA Team was tasked to look at what activities were associated with 'Force Preparation'.[2] This was a new term and it was through conducting a detailed analysis of the Business View (to be retitled Force Preparation) that the team were able to develop a paper that allowed a definition of 'Force Preparation' to evolve and identified key activities. Although this was important work and illustrated how an Operational Architecture could be exploited, it had delayed the development of the SAAM until January 1999.

---

[1] Command and Staff Functional Area are also referred to as Key Business Function's in other related areas of work; they describe generic types of 'real-world' functional processes undertaken within Defence.

[2] The term 'Force Preparation' is used within this paper to describe all military activities that take place prior to the operational deployment of a force and subsequent to its recovery or redeployment, and which must also be maintained during conflict. These activities are largely conducted in-barracks, but are all focused in support of operational effectiveness. Force Preparation as been defined as 'All activities necessary to define, resource and deliver British Army capability, within graduated readiness criteria, for operational employment in the Land Component of a joint/combined force'.

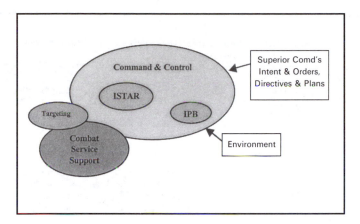

Figure A3.1. SUN Modelling Context Diagram

1.2 *The Challenge*

The challenge that faced the team was how this model was to be built and how could the existing work within the AOA and SUN be used and show clearly the linkage from the AOA into the SUN. The SUN models were effectively a subset of activities within the AOA that had been described in the language of the 'real world' and were then modelled to a higher resolution. Figure A3.2 illustrates the situation.

In addition:

- An information taxonomy was required so that the information captured by the modelling could be linked to the work ongoing in the UK's Defence Command and Army Data Model (DCADM) and existing Information Products (for example AdatP3 messages). The latter because information products, although providing the wrapper for information were being used by research staff within the Defence Evaluation and Research Agency (DERA) to describe the Information Exchange Requirements (IER) between organisations in the Joint Information Flow Model (JIFM).
- A mapping of one or more generic CSFAs to each of the lowest level of activity associated with each of the sub-models developed, which could then support the mapping of organisations, where lead responsibilities for key activities are likely to lie.

1.2 *Selection of Modelling Methodology*

The models developed as part of the AOA Version 1.0 had been developed using SSM, which had been adapted to support the AOA approach to modelling. A brief explanation of SSM is at Appendix A. This methodology had now become more widely accepted within the Ministry of Defence (MoD) and two of the Army's Commands were using both the methodology and the MooD case-tool to support the work in defining their own business processes and the Royal Navy had adopted a similar approach. It was therefore decided to continue with SSM however the team had an open mind on whether to continue to use MooD to support SSM or utilise other case-tools.

1.3 *Selection of a Case-tool*

The AOA Version 1.0 had used MooD Version 3.32 as a case-tool to support the modelling process. Using MooD the team had been able to develop Aggregate Models[3] for each of the sub-systems developed. A major

---

[3] In order to ensure coherence and compatibility of approach when building complex models, the AOA models were developed by decompositing activities into component sets of sub-activities which themselves were further decomposed to higher levels of resolution. The Aggregate Model represents the complete set of activities at the highest level of resolution together with the logical dependencies between these activities. Aggregate models at lesser levels of decomposition were also built to support specific analyses.

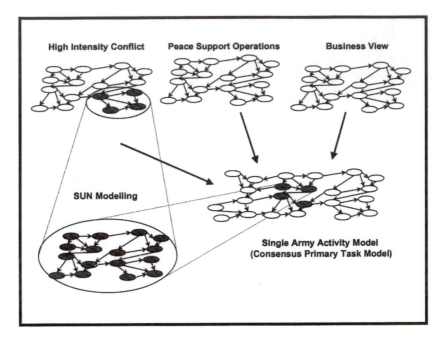

Figure A3.2. The problem in developing a Single Army Activity Model

problem however was to bring all the models together to form an overall aggregate model in order to conduct the analysis, and as the average number of activities for each of the three views modelled exceeded 600, MooD did not provide a practical solution to the problem. A member of the team came across an application called Power Designer, which contained a suite of tools, one of which was Process Analyst Version 6.1. Utilising this tool the team were able to produce models which included all the activities at Level 3 (i.e. the third level of decomposition of activities) on a single A0 sheet of paper. There were a number of drawbacks; activities were limited to 80 characters and a direct link to MooD could not be established due to the proprietary nature of the database in Process Analyst. As a result a number of potential case-tools were reviewed by the team prior to January 1999 to see if one tool could support both SSM and allow aggregate models to be developed. Ultimately it was decided that both MooD and Process Analyst would be used and the penalty of having to rebuild the models in Process Analyst would be accepted.

2. Developing the SAAM

2.1 *Initial thoughts in developing the SAAM*

Initial thoughts centred on the relationship between Military Capability and Military Operations and earlier work had indicated that there was a relationship between the generation of specific capability to meet a specific operation. Each of the three views modelled to support the AOA Version 1.0 had included a generic sub-model which, although given three separate names because the MooD Case-tool did not allow duplication of processes or activities, were all the same. These were 'Generate the Force', 'Generate Military Capability' and 'Generate Military Capability required'. In addition a comparison of the two operational views had provided a clear insight of those activities, which were either the same in each view or were similar. With this as a starting point a series of Root Definitions were developed and two high level models built. An early context diagram for the Military Operations model showing this relationship is at Figure A.3.

Work on the Force Preparation paper indicated that the relationship was however more complex, and that other areas, which had not been specifically addressed in either the modelling contained in AOA Version 1.0 or the SUN, had also to be considered. An example was Resource Accounting and Budgeting (RAB), which was a new process for managing MoD resources. This complexity is illustrated in Figure A3.4.

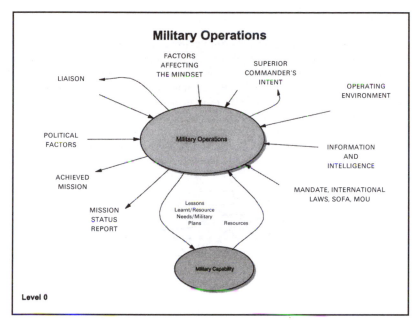

Figure A3.3. Initial Context Diagram showing relationship between Military Operations and Military Capability

The shaded area, in 'Green', is about the employment of Military Capability for specific Military Operations. What was clearly indicated by the analysis was that future battlefield systems would need to be supported by what had hitherto been described as Non-Operational Systems, particularly in the Deployment and Recovery phases of an operation.

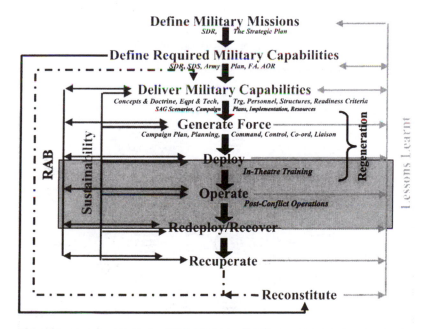

Figure A3.4. Force Preparation Diagram showing the more complex relationship between Military Capability and Military Operations

2.2 *Building the SAAM*

In December 1998 a contract was awarded to The Smith Group and Hi-Q Systems for support to the military AOA staff, forming a multi-disciplinary team responsible for building the SAAM. One of the key objectives was to reuse, where logically sound to do so, the existing work within the AOA Version 1.0 and SUN Models Version 4.1. To facilitate this process a member of the military staff mapped SUN activities against those in the AOA HIC and PSO models. At the same time the team began a top-down process of determining a series of Root Definitions that described the purpose of the British Army against the laid down Defence Missions and Military Tasks that had been agreed in the SDR. With the support of Dr Brian Wilson, a Level 1 CPTM was developed. This was based on the concept of an Enterprise Model. This is shown diagrammatically at Figure A3.5.

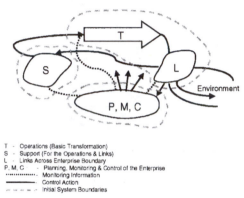

```
T     -  Operations (Basic Transformation)
S     -  Support (For the Operations & Links)
L     -  Links Across Enterprise Boundary
P, M, C   -  Planning, Monitoring & Control of the Enterprise
·············· -  Monitoring Information
              Control Action
- - - - - -  Initial System Boundaries
```

Figure A3.5. Model of any enterprise with initial SAAM system boundaries

Further refinement of the Root Definitions and the need to take in the relationship with the Defence and Joint environments lead to the development of the Context Diagram at Figure A3.6, which then allowed the development of four sub-models, which were colour coded and numbered as follows:

- Overall management and control of the Army (Grey—4).
- Provide and maintain the Land Component of military capability (Yellow—1).

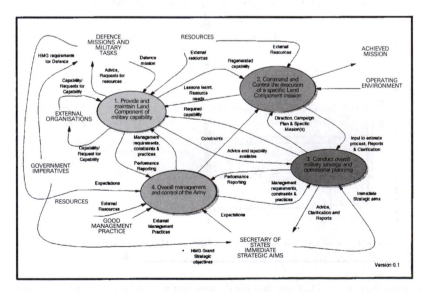

Figure A3.6. Context Diagram for SAAM

- Conduct overall military strategy and operational planning (Purple—3).
- Command and Control the execution of a specific Land Component mission (Green—2).

2.2.1 *The 'Scope' of the SAAM*

The links between the Army and the Defence, Joint and Combined areas were not well developed in previous work in both the AOA and the SUN which had addressed mainly single Service activity. In developing the SAAM it was essential to move from a single Service ('Sector') view to an Environmental view in which the Army operated as the Land Component of a joint/combined force. In this view, certain Army activities support purely single Service objectives whilst others take place in the wider environment; mainly that of the Land Component, but there are complex overlaps between the single Services (RN, Army, RAF) and Environments (Sea, Land, Air) views. The potential complexity of the 'extended' boundary of Army interest is shown in the diagrams in Figure A3.7 below which also show the boundary for the SAAM:

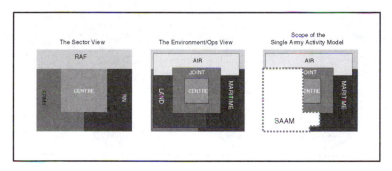

Figure A3.7. Sector, Environmental/Ops view and scope of the SAAM

The concept for broadening the scope of the SAAM is implicit in the definitions of the four major sub-models in Paragraph 2.2 above. Fixing this scope for the SAAM should then provide the 'hooks' for other OAs into the SAAM's environment and vice versa. Thus, if the boundary of Army interest were drawn on the context diagram for the SAAM at Figure A3.6, it would pass through some of the activities. An example is the sub-model for 'Conduct overall military strategy and operational planning' (Figure A3.8); this example also well illustrates the value and robustness of models developed using SSM.

The activities within the large central square represent those, which, logically, must take place to support the main activity of conducting overall military strategy and operational planning. This conceptual model may be 'instantiated' to look at the 'real world' by identifying which real-world organisation performs each activity. In this particular model with this particular set of activities, some are performed in the real world by the Joint staffs, some within MoD HQ, and some by Army organisations. Boundaries (or goose eggs) may therefore be drawn around activities to shown the boundary between the Army and outside organisations; the activities outwith the Army boundary then represent the overlaps or 'hooks' into the other environments within which these organisations exist. The activities within the model are independent of current organisations because they represent a logical view of what must take place, not how it takes place. Therefore the model would be just as valid a view in, say, 1990 as 1999 as 2009. However, between 1989 and 1999 the real-world boundaries would have changed with, for example, the increasing emphasis of Joint operations and the formation of the UK's Permanent Joint Headquarters (PJHQ) as a key player.

2.2.2 *Root Definitions and CATWOE*

The Root Definition 'attempts to capture the essence of the system being described and hence it is more than a mere statement of the objectives of the system. It incorporates the point of view that makes the activities and performance of the system meaningful' (Wilson, 1992). The Root Definition can be tested to see how well it is formulated. This test is performed against the following elements, often remembered by the mnemonic CATWOE:

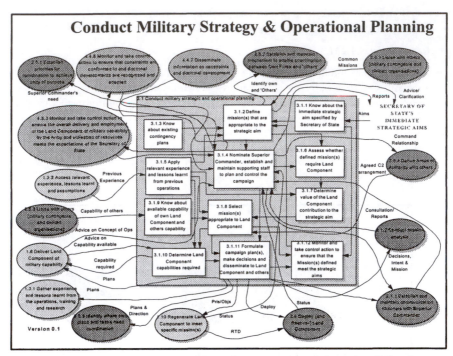

Figure A3.8. SAAM – Sub Model Conduct Strategic and Operational Planning

Customer
Actors
Transformation
Weltanschauung
Owner
Environment

The system exists so that a certain **Transformation Process** may be performed by **Actors** within the system for the benefit (or otherwise) of **Customers**. The system is controlled and resourced by an (external to the system) **Owner** and the system must operate within constraints imposed by the wider **Environment**. The Root Definition will have been written in consideration of some particular framework of perceptions or outlook (**Weltanschauung**) which make this particular Root Definition a meaningful one.

The root definition provides the basis from which a conceptual model can be built. The model is derived by writing down the activities, which **must** take place for the system to be that defined in the root definition; arrows, which show some type of logical dependency, link these activities. Models may be taken to higher levels of resolution by deriving root definitions for activities in the top-level model and then deriving the lower level model in a similar manner to the first. Opinions differ as to the number of activities in an ideal model; either few if any level of decomposition (i.e. a large 'flat' model) or several levels of resolution with relatively few activities against each root definition (i.e. a collection of linked 'deep' models). In practice, and because of the need to use a supporting tool, the latter approach, which had been adopted for the AOA, was retained for the SAAM.

The supporting Root Definitions and CATWOE for the SAAM are as follows:

• Overall management and control of the Army.

Root Definition: A Secretary of State-owned system to contribute to the Defence Missions and the immediate strategic aim, as laid down by the Secretary of State, by utilising appropriately organised Army personnel in conjunction with other forces and non-military personnel as appropriate to execute the total range of functions, represented by that organisation through the application of good management practice and the application of those constraints that are relevant to the achievement of Defence Missions and the immediate strategic aim.

C	Secretary of State.
A	Not specified.
T	Application of good management practice and the utilisation of appropriately organised Army personnel, other forces and non-military personnel to the achievement of the immediate strategic aim and provision of the capability required to meet the Defence Mission and Military Tasks.
W	The application of good management practice and appropriately organised Army personnel will contribute to the achievement of the immediate strategic aim and the generation of the capability required to meet the Defence Mission and Military Tasks.
O	Secretary of State.
E	Good management practice, constraints relevant, Defence Missions and immediate strategic aims.

• Provide and maintain the Land Component of military capability.

Root Definition: A system to advise on, provide and maintain the Land Component of military capability required, augmented by 'others' as appropriate, to respond to a series of Defence Missions and Military Tasks ranging from High Intensity Conflict against a sophisticated, complex and adaptive enemy in uncertain circumstances to the creation and maintenance of a benign operating environment (PSO) and others, as laid down by the Secretary of State, and within an agreed readiness criteria, whilst recognising previous experience, potential international relationships, technical and doctrinal developments and within financial and other appropriate constraints.

C	Secretary of State.
A	Not specified.
T	To advise, provide and maintain the Land Component of military capability required to respond to a series of Defence Missions and Military Tasks laid down by Secretary of State.
W	By knowing what range of missions and tasks are to be met, you can maintain the appropriate Land Component of military capability.
O	Not specified.
E	Need to take account of previous experience, potential international relationships, doctrinal and technical developments, and financial and other appropriate constraints.

• Conduct overall military strategy and operational planning.

Root Definition. A system owned by a Superior Commander and operated (by the Army) in conjunction with other forces, allied and neutral personnel, where appropriate, to provide advice both on the capability potentially available and utilisation of the Land Component during the conduct of the Strategic estimate and development of a specific Campaign plan, taking account of existing contingency plans and previous experience where appropriate, in order to contribute to the achievement of the immediate strategic aim as specified by the Secretary of State and within economic, political, legal and cultural constraints.

C	Not specified.
A	Other forces, allied and neutral personnel, where appropriate.
T	To provide advice both on the capability potentially available and utilisation of the Land Component during the conduct of the Strategic estimate and development of a specific Campaign plan.
W	Defining specific Campaign plan by taking into account previous experience and existing contingency plans where appropriate is the way to achieving an immediate strategic aim which will be specified by the Secretary of State.
O	Superior Commander.
E	Available capability, economic, political, legal and cultural constraints.

• Command and Control the execution of a specific Land Component mission.

Root Definition: A Superior Commander-owned system, operated by a commander and subordinates, continually to make decisions about the deployment (and recovery), employment and sustainability of Land Component of a military force together with the execution of these decisions, in order successfully to achieve the Superior Commanders intent with respect to a specific mission whilst learning from this process to bring about improvements in operational effectiveness and recognising the changing operating (physical) environment, operating constraints and coordinating action with other forces and nonmilitary organisations as appropriate to the mission.

C	Land Component of a military force.
A	A commander and subordinates.
T	To make and execute decisions successfully to achieve the superior commander's intent with respect to a specific mission.
W	Mission will be achieved by continually making decisions about the deployment (and recovery), employment and sustainability of Land Component of a military force together with the execution of those decisions. Learning from the process will enable improvement. The force may operate in conjunction with other forces and non-military organisations and therefore there will be a requirement for co-ordination.
O	A Superior Commander.
E	A changing operating (physical) environment and operational constraints.

2.3 *The Relationship to Command and Control*

The End State for Future Army C^2 for the British Army, achieved through Digitisation of the Battlespace (Land) (DBL), is defined as:

'A highly effective command and control capability that exploits information for force preparation, force generation and the conduct and sustainability of operations around the spectrum of conflict, that is optimised for joint combat within an alliance/coalition context, with the object of delivering tactical success, contributing towards operational impact and strategic significance.'[4]

Work in support of the SUN had focused predominantly on C^2, IPB, ISTAR, Targeting and CSS and it was important to ensure that the SAAM maintained this link, which although implicit in the AOA Version 1.0, needed to be explicit within the SAAM. Figure A3.1 showed the relationship between those processes that had been supported in the SUN Models Version 4.1. The Level 1 C^2 model is in Figure A3.9.

The SUN C^2 model was built to reflect the OODA loop (Orientation, Observation, Decision and Action). This was retained in developing the SAAM. The relationship of the SUN C^2 model to the SAAM is shown at Figure A3.10.

The key differences are that although the SAAM as incorporated the C^2 model based on the OODA loop and the underlying activities, they are now linked to the wider environment. In addition by following the SSM a clear audit trail now exists from the top-level context diagrams in the SAAM to the SUN models. The three MooD processes; 'Mission Analysis', 'Evaluation of Factors' and 'Consideration of Courses of Action (COA)' shown in the rectangle box marked 'Orientation' in Figure A3.9 have been incorporated into one MooD process 'Interpret Superior Commander's intent and determine potential COAs' in the SAAM and expanded at the next level.

2.4 *Level of Decomposition*

In the AOA Version 1.0 the models were taken to three levels, with the exception of a number of monitoring and control activities, in the SUN the level of decomposition was taken to four levels, the 4th level only for key activities. In the SAAM it was not possible to model to a specific level across the model. Each sub-model was therefore modelled to a level of resolution that was considered useful. This is illustrated in the diagram in Figure A3.11.

---

[4] Draft Paper 'Operational Parameters for Digitization of The Battlespace' (Land) (ADC/P(99)1 dated 12 Mar 99).

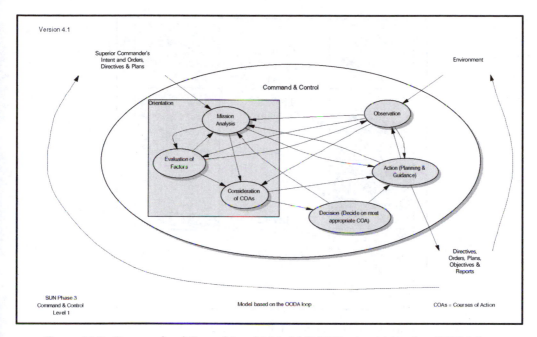

Figure A3.9. Command and Control Level 1 Model SUN Version 4.1 based on OODA Loop

It was only after the models were built that work could begin on capturing the information associated with each activity as either an input to the activity or an output from the activity, mapping CSFAs and identifying MoP for each activity. This was captured in MooD using an Object Association Model. It was at this point that work could also begin on developing an aggregate model. Aggregate models provide not only an ideal tool for conducting system or organisational mapping but also assist in the integrity checking of the complete model. The diagram in Figure A3.10 illustrates an aggregate model developed to support the AOA version 1.0 Business View. The mapping shown in Figure A3.12 is the system boundaries for each of the five sub-models developed.

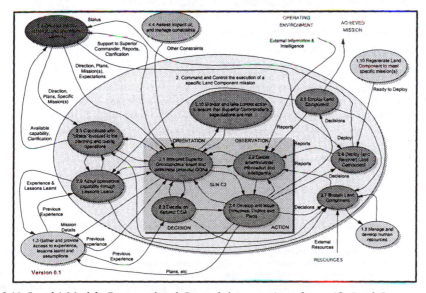

Figure A3.10. Level 1 Model–Command and Control the execution of a specific Land Component Mission

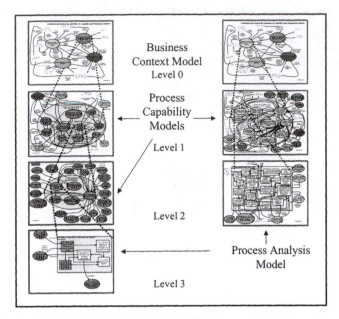

Figure A3.11. Decomposition Process using MooD Case-tool

3. **Information Taxonomy and Information Architecture**

3.1 *Background*

The SAAM has been built with the information requirements of an activity in mind from the outset. This has required a common understanding of 'information' in order to identify inputs and outputs to activities as well as the relationship of information to the measure of performance of activities. Consequently staff from both the AOA and the Army Data Services were engaged in discussions in the early stages of the development of the SAAM. This generated information relational terms (taxonomy) and a method for producing descriptions of data and information to support both the SAAM and DCADM respectively.

3.2 *Information Taxonomy and Information Architecture Development*

The method for developing the SAAM information architecture was as follows:

- Define information taxonomy, and information categories (input, output, MoP) to be captured in the SAAM.
- Create an information category catalogue from the AOA and SUN information categories, and reference to information products where applicable. The information products were derived from AOA/SUN, JIFM, DERA User Requirements Database (URDb)/Information Architecture/Battlefield Information System Tool (BIST) descriptions and STANAGS (ADatP-3).
- Map information categories from the catalogue to SAAM using MooD;
- Develop the SAAM information categories further as the activities are populated. Use the information in MooD to populate the top half of the Maltese cross.[5] An example of a Maltese cross is shown in Figure A3.13.

The successive stages in this development are described in the remainder of this section of the paper.

---

[5] In essence the Maltese cross is a four-part matrix. The upper half or north axis contains the activities taken from the activity model, the east and west axes are identical and contain information categories deemed essential for the support of those activities (The west axis (represents inputs) is the mirror image of the east axis (represents outputs)). The south axis is a listing of information processing procedures (automated and manual) that exist prior to any review. In a greenfield site the lower half of the cross will be blank.

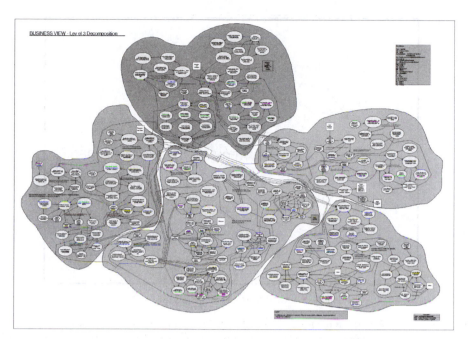

Figure A3.12. Aggregate Model of the Business View in AOA Version 1.0 marked with Subsystem Boundaries

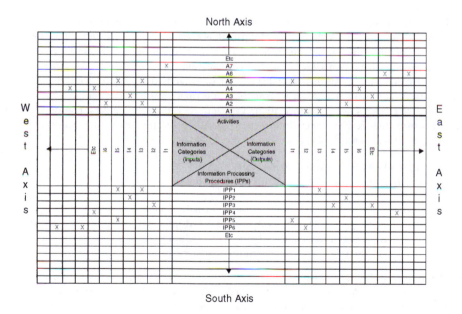

Figure A3.13. An example of a Maltese cross

3.3 *Information Taxonomy*

3.3.1 *General*

The relationship between information and data, described here as the information value chain, is illustrated in Figure A3.14. Information is used, through the learning process, to create knowledge that is acquired through

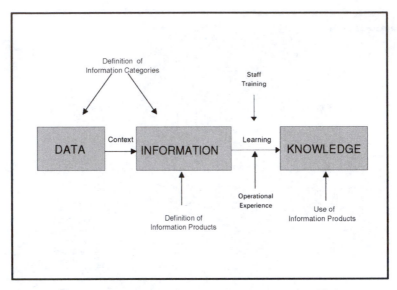

Figure A3.14. SAAM Information Taxonomy Value Chain

training (in such establishments as the Joint Services Staff College) and experience (such as Operations). Data is a series of observations or measurements. Data with context can be regarded as information. Data processing is the sequence of operations performed on data by a computer and only becomes information when read in context by a human.

Information categories are the set of information classes necessary to describe the nature of information that is required, or produced, by SAAM activities. Information products can be thought of as the *container* for carrying one or more information categories. In order for operators to use products, they have to populate templates by applying their knowledge through a combination of experience and the current operational circumstances. Taxonomy is a classification scheme, that is, a standard means of identifying and describing things, in this case meta-information. Meta-information is information about information', that is, information used to describe the properties of real information. The same concept exists for data. Figure A3.15 represents taxonomy of information relation (meta-information), detailing the framework for producing the SAAM information architecture. The taxonomy was required to facilitate:

- The creation of a SAAM Information Architecture;
- The structural definition of the SAAM Information Repository.

The SAAM Information Architecture comprises the information inputs to and outputs[6] from activities, expressed as information categories. The structure of the SAAM information repository is based upon inputs and outputs recorded as a series of hierarchical objects within MooD.

Figure A3.15 illustrates the relationships between the following:

- **Information Categories.** The information categories, in this instance derived from the names and description in the SUN and AOA catalogues, are contained within a hierarchy. The hierarchy is not unique, for example the information category 'enemy mission' could be under the heading 'enemy' but just as easily fall within a category 'mission' which has another child information category called 'own force mission'. The hierarchy is simply a tool to aid navigation through the information categories. The information categories captured in the SAAM as activity inputs and outputs are defined down to the level that is meaningful for the activities.
- **Information Products.** The individual elements of existing information products are used to derive and refine the lower level information categories. Once in place these categories can be utilised to define new

---

[6] Including MoP information.

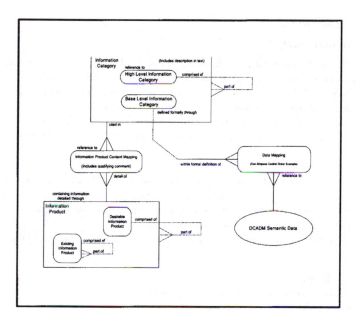

Figure A3.15. Taxonomy of SAAM Information Architecture

information products. An element of any given information product may map onto a number of information categories both within the same hierarchy and/or within separate categories as indicated in Figure 16.
- **DCADM Semantic Data.** It is anticipated that a convergence will occur between the lowest level information categories and the highest level semantic data defined within the DCADM. The degree of convergence should increase, as the information categories are refined. Any disparity that remains between low-
level categories and semantic data will identify areas requiring more detailed activity modelling. Ultimately
the completeness of convergence can only be established through cooperative evaluation between the
SAAM and DCADM projects.

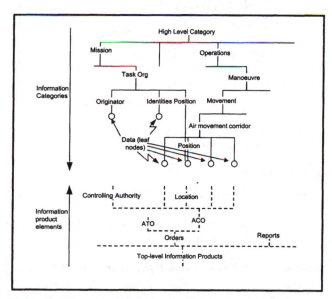

Figure A3.16. Convergence of Information Categories and Information Products

3.4 *Information Analysis Method*

3.4.1 *Stages of Information Analysis*

The method for producing the information architecture has evolved throughout the SAAM project. The first stage was to agree an information classification scheme, as described in paragraph 3.3 so that all analysts and subsequent users of the SAAM shared a common view of data and information. Subsequently a mechanism was needed to create a single information catalogue of information category names and descriptions. This was achieved firstly by logically rationalising the AOA and SUN information catalogues and then refining this by relating the content of existing information products with the information categories from the AOA or SUN catalogues.

An understanding of the utility of the information contained in the catalogues, when related to the real world was obtained which lead to the production of the initial SAAM catalogue. The SAAM catalogue, known as the SAAM information repository has been refined throughout the project. Once in possession of the SAAM catalogue and the MooD SAAM activities the mapping of information categories as activity inputs and outputs was completed to form the SAAM information architecture.

Figure A3.17 below illustrates the information analysis method adopted. There are four key stages to the method:

- Definition of the Information Taxonomy.
- Associating information product elements with information categories.
- Development of the SAAM Information Repository.
- Development of the SAAM Information Architecture.

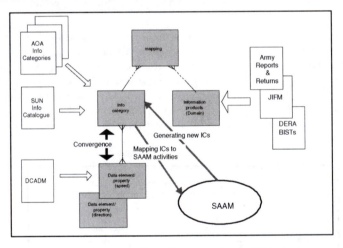

Figure A3.17. The Information Analysis Method

Appendix B describes how by using Airspace Control as an example, information categories were rationalised from the existing AOA and SUN work and enhanced where appropriate.

3.4.2 *Defining the Information Taxonomy*

The taxonomy details the framework for producing the SAAM information architecture. Its completion was essential to ensure that a consistent method was adopted in the development and refinement of the information catalogue. An illustration of the taxonomy produced together with an explanation of the relationships between its comprising elements has been provided in paragraph 3.2.

3.4.3 *Associating Information Product Elements with Information Categories*

The existing information product elements help identify information categories by both name and description. It was felt that an analysis of the operational products would enhance the descriptions of AOA categories and provide an in-depth understanding of how to develop and use the catalogue during the information analysis. A list of information products/information categories were obtained from the following sources:

- JIFM.
- DERA BIST descriptions.
- Army reports and returns.
- SUN Information Catalogue.
- AOA Version 1.0.

The information products were examined to establish which of the existing information categories, contained within either the AOA or SUN catalogues, most closely corresponded to each of the information product elements. Depending on the degree of correlation one of the following actions was taken:

- Where a direct correlation was found between the category description and information product element an association was created to the appropriate AOA or SUN category and no further action taken. These associations can be used in engineering new information products envisaged in follow on work.
- Where an appropriate AOA or SUN category was present, but deemed to require clarification, then the information product element names together with any qualifying comments were included with the category association. These details will allow the relevant category descriptions to be refined at a later stage.
- Where no appropriate AOA or SUN sub-category existed, information product elements were associated with the most closely related high level category. Clarifying information was included with the association so as to allow the creation of new sub-categories at the appropriate time.

An example of the results of the association of the selected JIFM product elements to AOA/SUN categories is in Appendix C.

3.4.4 *Development of the SAAM Information Repository*

Having associated various information product elements with the appropriate categories found either within the AOA or SUN activity models, the category hierarchies defined within each model were compared. Categories from the two separate models were combined with, or subsumed by, categories defined within the other to create the initial SAAM Information Repository.

3.4.5 *Development of the SAAM Information Architecture*

The initial SAAM Information Catalogue was imported into MooD as an Object Hierarchy. Once within this tool it was utilised to categorise the Information Inputs and Information Outputs for the modelled activities thus creating the SAAM Information Architecture. This information was recorded using MooD Object Association Models (see Figure A3.18). The SSM equivalent terminology is shown in brackets. The Object Association Models were then automatically interrogated and the results presented as the Activity Information Category Inputs and Outputs on the North half of a Maltese cross.

The process of categorising information flows identified a number of refinements to category names that were later applied to the catalogue.

Capturing inputs and outputs in MooD is achieved by assigning a service to an Object. For each activity an Information Category object was either *consumed* or *created*, or in the case of MoP, *measured by* and CSFAs *performed by*. It was by this method that the northern half of the Maltese cross could be generated and a separate Information Architecture Database populated. Within MooD the Object Association Model is presented as shown in Figure A3.19. The actual links and object diagrams are hidden.

4. **Validation, Evaluation and Exploitation of the SAAM**

Version 1.0 of the AOA was subject to rigorous validation, in order to ensure that the models represented a legitimate and coherent set of activities representing the purpose required of the organisation which the Army was defined to be in top-level planning and doctrinal documents. The activities within the model were also subject to evaluation to identify those, which might offer the most cost-effective areas for investment in

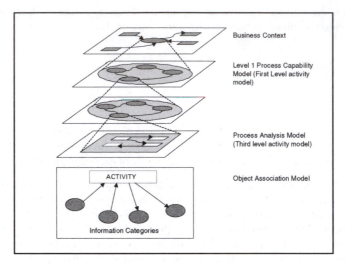

Figure A3.18. Activity Information Capture using MooD

1.1.1 Assume a mission related to conflict	
Input Strategic -Defence Missions Strategic -Current affairs Lessons learned -Previous Operations	**Output** Strategic -Defence Missions-Conflict related
CSFA/KBF CSFA -Management-Planning CSFA -Force Development CSFA -Operations CSFA -Intelligence/Mapping Provision	**Measures of Performance** MoP-Currency

Version 0.1

Figure A3.19. How Inputs, Outputs, MoP and CSFAs are presented in MooD

information systems to support, for instance, improved tempo of operations. Subject matter experts from all areas of the Army carried out both validation and evaluation. The SAAM was built by reusing as much of AOA V1.0 as possible, and the 'green sticker' principle can probably be applied with reasonable confidence to these areas of the model. Nevertheless, it is intended that the SAAM will be subject to similar rigorous validation and evaluation where necessary.

The 'ideal' and logical view provided by the SAAM of what activities the Army/Land Component should do and what information is required or produced by these activities, can inform a whole series of analyses by owners of Lines of Development[7] and those responsible for information management, organisational design

---

[7] Lines of Development identify the key areas and functions, which will drive the move to the Future Army. In the US Army this is the equivalent of DTLOMS.

and the provision of coherent information systems to support the effective operation. In general, this is achieved by mapping the model against actual (i.e. 'real world') organisations, information requirements, systems and SOPs.

The SAAM then provides a coherent and consistent over-arching Army-wide environment (or context) within which, lower level analyses can take place; a simple analogy is to that of the picture on the box of the jigsaw. The SAAM provides a coherent and consistent view of the wider environment into which the individual pieces of the jigsaw, be this related to operations, an information system, organisation or indeed doctrinal or force development issue, should fit. Examples of these analyses include:

- Support to production of Statements of User Needs (the actual SUN consisting also of textual descriptions—i.e. Concepts of Use).
- Doctrinal development.
- Capability gap/overlap analysis.
- Force development.
- Information management.
- Information system applications design.
- Information services design.
- Organisational structure design.
- Process improvement.
- Performance (efficacy, efficiency, effectiveness) monitoring of activities.

In general, analyses will be conducted by 'instantiating' the conceptual model into the real world. Given that the models are designed to be robust and have longevity, it is desirable that real world, and hence rapidly changing, data is not recorded in the actual model since this would then become monolithic and difficult to maintain. Ideally, real-world information should be linked to the model through one of the properties associated with the conceptual activity in the model. For example, in the diagram below, the real-world organisations of the G2 Intelligence Cell at say Division or the G2/G3 cell at Brigade can be linked to a generic activity within the model of 'Collating Sources of Information'. The link is via the real-world function of G2 Int, which we can map to a generic function (the CSFA), Intelligence, which is one of the properties associated with activities in the model. If, in the real world, staff functions are reorganised, and say G2 Int became X21, then all that we need change is the association (i.e. the link from the real to the conceptual world) between the CSFA of Intelligence and G2 Int to X21, and not every single instance of where G2 Int occurs in the real-world instantiation of the model.

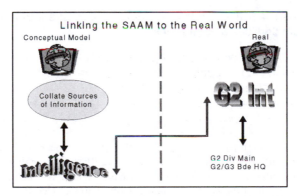

Figure A3.20. Linking the SAAM to the Real World

The diagrams at Figures A3.21 and A3.22 overleaf illustrate the principles in more detail.

A key enabler to the Federation of Systems for Joint Battlespace Digitization is an understanding of anticipated information needs and information flows across the battlespace. It is recognised by the Central Staff responsible for determining these needs in Joint CIS projects that the understanding had to be traceably derived from military processes in developing Operational Architectures for the Joint and Single Service

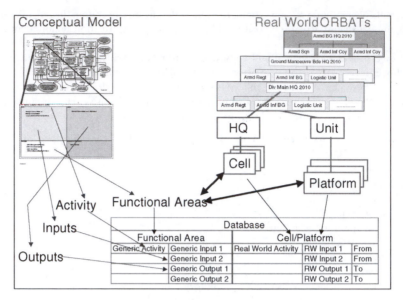

Figure A3.21. Potential Exploitation of the SAAM by mapping the Real World to the Conceptual Model

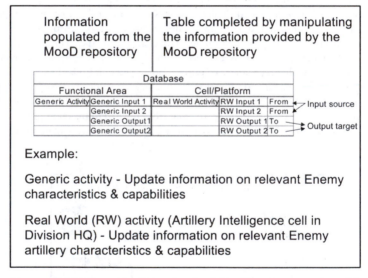

Figure A3.22. Example of Mapping Real World to Conceptual Model

environments. Figure A3.23 illustrates how the work from the relevant Operational Architectures is related to the work in developing the JIFM. Currently the linkage to the JIFM is through a common description of business function areas and information categories, which have been linked to information products. The SAAM work has already identified the need for a number of additional Key Business Functions (KBFs) in the JIFM (CFSAs in the SAAM) to adequately describe the Army's business. Further work is needed in the JIFM to provide the linkage to Operational Architectures.

4.1 *Future Work*

It is proposed that as well as exploiting the SAAM in its current format that the SAAM will be migrated to MooD Version 4.0, which the AOA staff, are currently evaluating prior to release. MooD 4.0 will offer

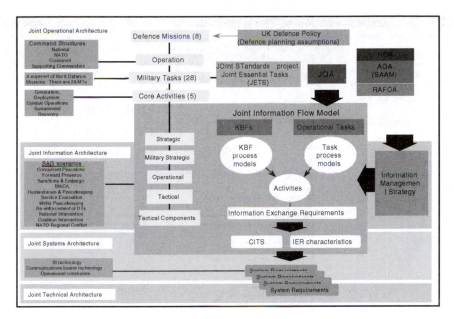

Figure A3.23. Relationship of Operational Architectures to JIFM

significant advantages in developing the information flows at all levels unlike MooD 3.32, which only allowed objects to be associated at the Process Activity Model level. This is illustrated in Figure A3.24, which highlights a selected activity at the Process, Capability Model level, the information required on the logical links and the associated information categories and the changed state of an object. In addition scenarios can be developed in MooD 4.0.

5. Lessons Learnt

A number of lessons have been learnt in the process of building the SAAM and its Information Architecture.

- The need to have a multi-disciplinary team involved in the process at the outset, with the customer maintaining control of the project. This creates a greater risk on the part of the customer but ensures that the work remains focused. This was particularly important in developing the conceptual models, as it was too easy to begin to focus on the real world of *how* things are done not *what* should be done.
- All members of the team needed to be familiar with SSM and how to use the MooD Case-tool at the outset given that the project had only 3 months in which to complete the initial work.
- An understanding of doctrine and awareness of future concepts.
- Maintaining links with the other Sectors and staff in the Defence/Joint environment so that they are aware of the work being undertaken.

6. Acknowledgements

- Dr Brian Wilson for his initial support in developing the Root Definitions and Level 1 CPTM and kind permission to reproduce the Overview of SSM at Appendix A.
- Dr Dick Whittington and staff at the Salamander Organisation Limited for their advice and support in the use of MooD.
- Maj H Duncan for the work involved in developing the SUN Models Version 4.1 and his pioneering of the methods too fully exploit the MooD Case-tool.
- Maj Mark Old for his support in building the SAAM and Information Architecture.

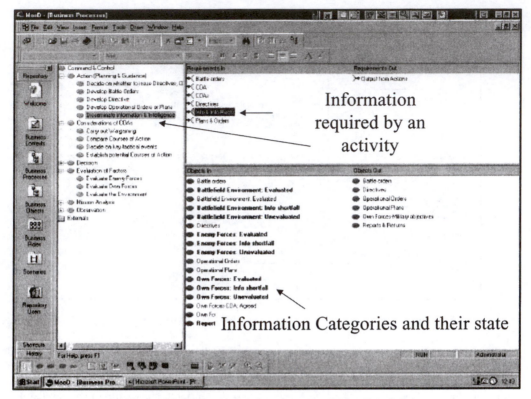

Figure A3.24. Screenshot from MooD 4.0 (Beta 2 Release)

- Maj Mark Thurlow and staff at the Army Data Services for their active participation in developing the Information Taxonomy.
- Mr R Dines from DERA for his support in developing the CSFAs in the SAAM, which were derived in part from his involvement in JIFM.
- Staff from the Smith Group and Hi-Q Systems who supported the team in delivering the end product in a short timeframe.

7. Appendices

A. An Overview of Soft Systems Methodology
B. Example of Applying Information Analysis Method to Airspace Control
C. Example of Product Mapping to Information Categories

8. References

[Wilson, 1992] Dr. Brian Wilson *Systems: Concepts, Methodologies and Applications*. Second Edition, John Wiley & Sons (ISBN 0-471-92716-3).

Appendix Four

An Overview of Soft Systems Methodology
(A method for the analysis and definition of information requirements)

1. Introduction

Soft Systems Methodology (SSM) is, in reality, a set of methodologies. Each methodology is represented by a set of ideas (concepts) structured in such a way that their use is appropriate to the situation being analysed. The use of SSM as a powerful problem-solving tool requires this flexibility. Each situation is unique and hence the methodology must be tailored to fit the situation and also the style of the analyst using it. Application of this kind is a sophisticated use of SSM and the analysts need to develop the ability to be so flexible as a result of considerable experience in a variety of situations. However, a few standard methodologies have been developed as a result of the experience of practitioners such as Peter Checkland and Brian Wilson and these have general applicability for particular types of situation, such as Information Requirements Analysis, Role Exploration, Issue Resolution and Re-organisation. An overview of the Checkland Methodology is shown in the diagram at Figure A4.1.

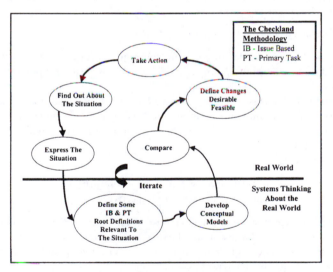

Figure A4.1. The Checkland Methodology

An overview of the information-oriented version is shown at Figure A4.2.

2. Why is the Soft Systems Methodology useful?

Approaches to systems development often fail to satisfy users' problems and requirements. Both the problems are not understood, or not identified, and therefore the information requirements which are supposed to address these problems are inappropriate, or at worst, not known. The secret to successful systems development is in understanding the users' situation, the problems associated with it and correctly identifying the informa-

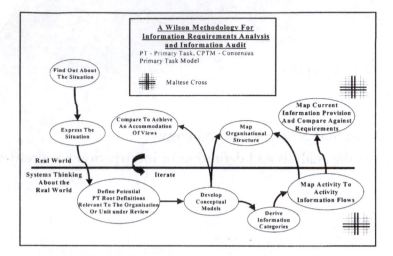

Figure A4.2. The Wilson Methodology

tion requirements. Often the problem is knowing what the problem is, and resolving conflicting views of problems and requirements between users. SSM addresses all these issues in the analysis and definition of information requirements.

Specifying information requirements relating to a business area is complicated. Information was confused with data and what are commonly referred to, as information systems are really data processing systems. If we take the definition of information to be:

'Data together with the meaning ascribed to the data'

Then we can develop a process of defining information requirements. This is based upon an analysis of how the data is used in supporting business processes. The SSM essentially supports the process of analysis of information requirements.

When we describe a set of business processes necessary for the achievement of a business objective further complications will arise; different individuals will interpret the objective in different ways. If, for example, we are developing information support for a prison, the set of business processes will vary depending on what we take the purpose of a prison to be.

We could take its purpose to be:

• To control the interactions of offenders and the community (a security perspective) or alternatively:
• To instill society's norms and values (a rehabilitation perspective)

Clearly the set of business processes required (and therefore the information support) would be vastly different in the two cases. In reality a prison is not any of these but is a mixture of these and other perspectives. However, different individuals will subscribe to different mixtures. This example, although extreme, represents the situation in all businesses though the differences may be subtler.

3. What does the Soft Systems Methodology provide?

• An explicit, organised and defensible way of reconciling different and/or conflicting perspectives.
• The means to build a model of business processes appropriate to the users within the area of concern.

4. The Use of the Methodology

The methodology starts with the construction of a 'rich picture' of the situation in which some concern has been expressed or in which some kind of information system is desirable. This identifies those organisational entities relevant to the investigation. It illustrates the interrelationships of material, information and other resources, in addition to the features of the situation, which give rise to the concern or request. Features of the social situation such as interpersonal conflict, views of the situation, etc. may have a significant impact on the conduct and outcome of the study and should be considered.

After this initial study the next stage in the method is to use the knowledge gained by the construction of the picture to derive a model representing the business processes which accommodate the many perspectives and issues.

It is assumed that whatever the business is about individuals within it will play a meaningful role. Their roles and purposes may well be different because of the many perspectives described above but they will not be acting randomly or without purpose. Their function is therefore significant and relevant to the development of the system.

Carefully structured definitions known as Root Definitions are built which state the purpose of the system, for each of the different user perceptions identified. Purposeful activity models (known as conceptual models) are developed next to represent this set of perspectives. These are built to form logical descriptions of what must be done to achieve the objective contained in each of the Root Definitions. These models then are not models of the situation but are modelling the perceptions of the situation.

A number of techniques are used within the methodology to assist in the analysis and definition of information requirements. The building of a rich picture, the organisational mapping (defining responsibilities for activities) and the Maltese Cross (which allows comparison between the information systems required and those already in existence) are all valuable techniques.

5. How are the products of SSM used?

The models may be used in several ways:

- To compare against reality in order to make recommendations for procedural change which can be argued to be beneficial.
- To form a single model, reconciling the many perspectives, representing a taken-to-be' description of a business area.
- To compare this model against reality in order to re-define roles and organisational structures.
- To use this model as a source of information requirements to support the business area.

This last approach is particularly useful when developing an information strategy within an organisation or carrying out an audit of current information support for a business area. It is also recommended to be used as an initial analysis for systems development projects using structured methods such as SSADM (Structured Systems Analysis and Design Methodology).

The rich picture provides the context of the situation in which such a development is taking place. The analysis identifies the organisational change, which is necessary effectively to incorporate the development. It also confirms, or otherwise, whether the proposed development is feasible, appropriate and if it should approved.

The SSM is a powerful, rigorous and prescriptive approach providing a sound foundation for proposed information systems development, with clearly defined.

Appendix Five

Example of Applying Information Analysis Method to Airspace Control Function

1. Introduction

The focus for the example has been taken from the Airspace Control function, due to its 'Joint' flavour and the availability of a Short Range Air Defence (SHORAD) activity model. Several of the main activities in this function, of relevance to this example, are shown below underlined:

<u>Control of AD Fire</u> (High–Medium Altitude AD (HIMAD), <u>SHORAD</u>, AD Fighters):
<u>Weapon Control State (WCS)</u>;
Arcs of fire;
Co-ordination with Joint Force (JF) AD, Operational Commander;
Use of Mobility Corridors for friendly forces Fixed Wing/Rotary Wing (FW/RW);
Control of Indirect Fire, BATES (Battlefield Artillery Target Engagement System) Messages:
SPRT GEOM (Support Geometry);
SPRT ACA (Support Airspace Control Authority);
Friendly Force Operations:
Manoeuvre;
All Arms AD (AAAD).

The following example of the SAAM information analysis is described using the four stages described in paragraph 3.4 in the main paper.

2. Definition of the Information Taxonomy

The informational relational terms expounded in paragraph 3.2 in the main paper are followed.

3. Associating Information Product Elements with Information Categories

3.1 *Identifying Information Products*

The following Information Products from the JIFM were identified as being relevant to this example:
Orders operations

- ACO (Airspace Control Order)
- ATM (Air Tasking Message)
- ATO (Air Tasking Order) Multinational
- ATO National
- Operation Order

- Call for fire message
- Movement Orders

The example relates to Control of Airspace in the context of SHORAD, WCS and Mobility Corridors for friendly RW/FW. The ACO product is identified as being most relevant and is selected for further analysis.

In addition to identifying the ACO information products within JIFM, the use of the ACO in the Air Defence Control BIST was also considered.

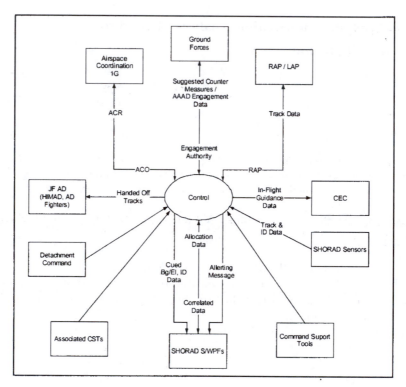

Figure A5.1. Air Defence Control BIST

Having identified the relevant Information Products it is necessary to examine the individual Information Product Elements. Examining the JIFM identified the following elements of the ACO Information Product:

- ACO Identifier
- Controlling Authority
- Area
- Period
- ACM
- Type
- Dimensions

The Air Defence Control BIST Definition and data flow diagrams were also examined in limited detail. This cursory inspection did not identify any additional elements to the ACO Information Product.

4. Identifying relevant AOA or SUN Information Categories

The method advocates inspection of the AOA and SUN catalogues to identify categories for information product elements. In its simplest form this requires a syntactical comparison using key words such as 'Air movement' or 'Airspace'. This procedure identified the categories shown in Table A5.1.

AOA	SUN
Operations	Control measures
Manoeuvre	*Airspace control measures*
Movement	
Air movement corridors:	
Locations	
Threats	
Hazards	
Cover	
Possible Diversions	

Table A5.1. Comparison of AOA and SUN Information Categories

Applying domain knowledge, together with a familiarity with Information Category names, it was possible to identify additional categories that although without syntactical similarity, were the most appropriate to the Information Product Elements in question. This process allowed the following associations to be established between Information Product Elements and Information Categories and is highlighted in Table A5.2.

Information Product Element (JIFM)	Description (JIFM)	Identified Category AOA/SUN	Type of association
Controlling Authority	Controlling Authority	TASKORG-Formation-Superior HQ	Closest available Category but requires the inclusion of a sub-category.
Area	Applicable Area Area of Interest	Operations-Named	Appropriate Category that requires refinement to category description.
Period	Effective Duration	Mission-Coord instrs	Appropriate Category that requires refinement to category description.
Airspace Control Measure (ACM) Type	ACM Type	Operations-Movement-Air Corridors	Appropriate Category no action required.
ACM Dimension	ACM Dimension	Operations-Movement-Air Corridors	Appropriate Category no action required.

Table A5.2. Initial information product to category association

5. Development of the SAAM Information Repository (Catalogue)

The method rationalised the AOA and SUN categories and formed the SAAM Catalogue. This was developed, in the context of the ACO example, using the results from the 'Type of Association' shown in Table A5.2 and produced the SAAM Information Categories shown in Table A5.3.

6. Development of the SAAM Information Architecture

A number of activities exist within the SAAM relating to Airspace control. The particular activity selected for further analysis was the SAAM/SHORAD Activity 'Derive Potential Courses of Action (COAs)'. There are a number of techniques that could be used to associate information categories with activities. In this instance the 'Use Case' technique from the Booch Object Oriented Design method was chosen. Potential 'airspace control' information categories are italicised.

Identified Category (AOA / SUN)	SAAM Category / Description
TASKORG-Formation-Superior HQ	Own Forces – Mission – Task Organisation – Originator
Operations–Named Area of Interest	Own Forces Ops Named Area of Interest; description now includes '(e.g. applicable area for Airspace control)'
Mission–Coord Instrs	Own Forces Mission Coord Instrs; description now includes ' (e.g. effective duration for Airspace control)'
Operations–Movement–Air Corridors	Own Forces - Operations-Movement-Air Corridors
Operations–Movement–Air Corridors	Own Forces - Operations-Movement-Air Corridors

Table A5.3. SAAM Catalogue Information Categories

Use Case 4.3: <u>Derive Potential Courses of Action</u> to achieve mission and provide required protection
Actor: Commander AD, AD Regt CO, AD Battery Commander
Pre–Condition: Extracted Orders. **(2.3)**
Description: Assess the current tactical situation (Land, Sea & Air).
Perform SHORAD Intelligence Preparation of the Battlefield (IPB) Process (3.2)
For each task:
Assess the AD assets system capabilities (13.2).
Assess the deployment posture: defence, attrition or ambush.
Assess current Emission Control (EMCON) State and its effect.
Assess current ***Airspace / (WCS)*** and its effect.
Assess logistic support, missiles, re-supply and maintenance support for each asset.
Assess communications connectivity.
Assess the need for additional AD assets from Superior Comd.
Determine the optimum mix of allocated AD assets (13.4).
Derive potential Degree of Protection achievable for task(s) under each deployment option.
Assess contribution to ***Counter Air Campaign*** for each deployment option.
Assemble candidate deployment options.
Post-condition: Candidate deployment options.

The Use Case consists of a textual description of all the processes/tasks involved in a given information flow. The nouns identified in such a description equate to the Objects (and attributes) required in an Object Oriented Design, but for the purposes of the SAAM Catalogue can be seen to identify the required Categories. Here the categories would be information inputs to the activity 'derive potential course of action'.

Appendix Six

Examples of Product to Information Category Mapping

Product	Category	Comments
Generic Product: Analysis		
General		
Specific Product: Assessment	Enemy-Capabilities	
	Enemy-Intentions	INTSUM (103)
	Management/control—	
	Performance Categories	
	Measurement of Fighting Power	
	Operational Planning	
	Structure/strength	
Generic Product: Analysis		
Operations		
Specific Product: Cabinet document	Civilians	Deployment of . .
	Deployability—Concurrent ops—Duration	6 month
	Deployability-Force generation assets	Recommend force level changes
	Deployability-Reserve activation plan	Review NTM for Reinforcements
	Environment-NBC	NBC Policy
	Geo-political	Ministerial Briefings
	Geo-political-Inter-service/allied	Cooperation
	Geo-political-Local culture/religious	Cooperation with Host Nation
	Geo-political-Political-Constraints on missions	HMG's Political Objectives and Strategic end state
	Image/ethos-Public empathy-PR	P Info
	Incidents	Briefings on breaches of agreements
	Legal	International law
	Legal—Govt Imperative	Impact on mission
	Legal—Negotiations Impact on ops	
	Management/control	Financial accounting
	Media—Current policy	
	Mission—Comd's intent	'Strategic Direction by CDS'
	Mission—Military objectives	
	Mission—Priority tasks	Intelligence, Mil Deception, PsyOps
	Mission—Priority tasks-EW	
	Mission—Priority tasks-Fire Support	Targeting
	Mission—Task organisation	'Assigned Forces', 'Command Relationships'

	Operational Planning	Commitments, Constraints,
	Operational Planning-Planning	Contingency planning
	Operations—Coalition-ROE	
	Operations—Named Area of	Deployment outside TAOR to
	Interest—Theatre	be cleared of ops
	Own Forces—Capabilities—	
	PsyOps	
	Own Forces—Pers—Burials	Repatriation of the dead
	Own Forces—Pers—PoW	
	Perceptions	
	Protection—Military	Deception
	Protection—OPSEC	
	Protection—Physical	Destruction
	Sustainability—Medical Services	Casualty Policy
Specific Product: OA Lessons	Doctrine—Lessons learned	
Generic Product: Orders		
Operations		
Specific Product: ACO	Mission—Cord instrs	Effective Duration
	Operations-Movement-Air	ACM Type, Dimensions
	Corridors	
	Operations—Named Area of	Applicable area
	Interest	
	TASKORG—Formation—	Controlling Authority
	Superior HQ	
Specific Product: ATM	Equipment—Aircraft—Fixed Wing	Type of aircraft
	Equipment—Weapons	Armament
	Mission–Priority tasks	Tactical air task details
	Own Forces—Locations	
	Target–Engagement–Method	TOT/ASAP/NLT, control, in-flight report
	TASKORG–Formation—Level	Sqn/Wing
	TASKORG–Formation—Type	Number of aircraft
Specific Product: ATO Multinational	Mission—Priority tasks	Offensive Air and SH sorties
	Operations	Air situation (superiority/parity)
	Operations—Coalition	
Specific Product: ATO National	Mission—Priority tasks	Offensive Air and SH sorties
	Operations	Air situation (superiority/parity)
Specific Product: FRAGOs	Enemy	
	Management of Information—Information—Sinks	'Distribution of FRAGO to subordinates'
	Mission	
	Mission—Concept of ops	
	Mission—Cord instrs	
	Mission—Priority tasks	Own force tasks
	Operations	Op overlay
	Operations—Command support	Command and Signals
	Operations—CSS	Service Support
	Own Forces	Including 'neighbouring formations'
	TASKORG	
Specific Product: Op Order	Deployability—Concurrent ops—Op locs	'HQ Locs'
	Deployability—Priority and objectives	'HQ Movement details'

Enemy	'Air activity'
Enemy—Capabilities	'Strengths'
Enemy—Capabilities—Fighting	
Enemy—Capabilities—Mobility/C Mob	
Enemy—Dispositions	
Enemy—Intentions	
Enemy—Locs	
Enemy—ORBAT	'Identities' 'composition'
Management of Information—Information—Sinks	'Distribution of Op O to subordinates', 'Signature'
Management of Information—Information—Sources	'Place of issue', 'Copy#',
Mission	'File #', 'Refs'
Mission—Concept of ops	Includes 'scheme of manoeuvre' and 'Main effort'
Mission—Constraints	'Critical support plans'
Mission—Cord instrs	'General, def ops, off ops, transitional phase, timing'
Mission—Priority tasks	'Manoeuvre force task's', 'air tasks'
Mission—Priority tasks—DF	'Avn'
Mission—Priority tasks—EW	
Mission—Priority tasks—Fire Support	'Arty comd rels', 'arty tac tasking' 'fire plan'
Mission—Priority tasks—IW	
Mission—Priority tasks—Protection	'AD', 'Engr'
Operations	Op overlay includes Map Refs
Operations—Command support	Command and Signals
Operations—CSS	Service Support
Operations—CSS—Critical shortages	'Critical supplies'
Operations—Movement—Capability	'Movement table', 'by-passing policy'
Operations—ROE	'Recognition and Identification instructions'
Operations—Security reqts	'Protective Marking', 'Ack', 'Authentication'
Own Forces	Including 'neighbouring formations', 'air situation'
Own Forces—Capabilities—Construction	'Defence stores'
Own Forces—Capabilities—Liaison	'Liaison channels'
Own Forces—Capabilities—Surveillance	'Counter Surveillance Measures'
Own Forces—Leaders	'Alternative Commander'
Own Forces—Use of EM spectrum	'CEI', 'Codewords', 'Nicknames'
Own Forces—Use of EM spectrum—EMCON measures	
TASKORG	Including 'Time zone', 'related OPO number'

References

Checkland, P.B. (1981), *Systems Thinking, Systems Practice*, John Wiley, Chichester

Checkland, P.B. and Scholes, J. (1990), *Soft Systems Methodology in Action*, John Wiley, Chichester

Checkland, P.B. and Tsouvalis, C. (1996), Reflecting on SSM: The link between root definitions and conceptual models, University of Humberside, Working Paper No. 5

Checkland, P.B. and Davies, L. (1986), The use of the term Weltanschauung in soft systems methodology, *Journal of Applied Systems Analysis*, 13, 109–115

Davies, L. (1989), *The Cultural Aspects of Intervention with Soft Systems Methodology*, PhD dissertation, University of Lancaster

ISO/DIS 9001 (2000), *Quality Management Systems—Requirements*, Draft BS EN ISO 9001: 2000

Salamander (2000), *MooD Business Transformation*, The Salamander Organisation Ltd

Smyth, D.S. and Checkland, P.B. (1976), Using a systems approach: the structure of root definitions, *Journal of Applied Systems Analysis*, 5 (1)

Wilson, B. (1984, 1990), *Systems: Concepts, Methodologies and Applications*, John Wiley, Chichester

Index